SWEDISH STUDIES IN EUROPEAN LAW

The Swedish Network for European Legal Studies is happy to announce the second volume in this new series of annual publications which acts as a forum for the publication of studies on European law by Swedish scholars. The annual contains peer-reviewed articles aimed at spreading Swedish legal research on European law to a wide international audience. The editors of the yearbook are Professor Per Cramér and Associate Professor Thomas Bull. The articles in the volume are concerned with European law, its development, impact and reform; furthermore they are original, analytical contributions to doctrinal debates and questions, by legal researchers mainly, but not exclusively, connected with the Swedish universities.

Swedish Studies in European Law

Volume 2, 2007

Edited by
Per Cramér and Thomas Bull

·HART·
PUBLISHING

OXFORD AND PORTLAND, OREGON
2008

Published in North America (US and Canada) by
Hart Publishing
c/o International Specialized Book Services
920 NE 58th Avenue, Suite 300
Portland, OR 97213-3786
USA
Tel: +1 503 287 3093 or toll-free: (1) 800 944 6190
Fax: +1 503 280 8832
Email: orders@isbs.com
Website: www.isbs.com

Hart Publishing, 16C Worcester Place, Oxford, OX1 2JW
Telephone: +44 (0)1865 517530 Fax: +44 (0)1865 510710
Email: mail@hartpub.co.uk
Website: http//:www.hartpub.co.uk

British Library Cataloguing in Publication Data
Data Available

ISBN: 978-1-84113-656-1

Typeset by Compuscript Ltd, Shannon, Ireland
Printed and bound in Great Britain by
TJ International Ltd, Padstow, Cornwall

Preface

The Swedish Network for European Legal studies is proud to present the second volume of the series *Swedish Studies in European Law*. The objective of the series is to act as a vehicle for the publication of studies on European Law by Swedish legal scholars in the English language. It is our hope that the publication will contribute to the dissemination of Swedish legal research on European law to a wide international audience and facilitate international academic communication. The peer-reviewed contributions presented in this volume are all concerned with current issues of European law, its development, impact and possible future reform. They reflect central issues of the present doctrinal debates in Sweden on European legal matters that have general implications beyond the national jurisdictional borders. The authors are primarily drawn from Swedish Universities but also include representatives from legal practice and the civil service.
This volume can be cited as 2 (2007) SSEL.

Per Cramér | Thomas Bull

Contents

Abbreviations

CA	Company Act
CBD	Convention on Biological Diversity
CCD	UN Convention to Combat Desertification
CEAS	Common European Asylum System
CECA	Coal and Steel Communities
CESR	Committee of European Securities Regulators
CILFIT	a case before the ECJ, Judgement of 06/10//1982, CILFIT/ Ministero della Sanitá
EC/ECT	Treaty of the European Communities
ECHR	European Convention on Human Rights
ECJ	European Court of Justice
ECR	European Court Reports
ECtHR	European Court of Human Rights
EEC	European Economic Community
EFTA	European Free Trade Agreement
EKU	instrument for ecologically suitable procurement
EP	European Parliament
ERT	Europarättslig tidskrift
ESC	European Securities Committee
EU	European Union
FDI	Foreign Direct Investment
FRONTEX	European Agency for Management of Operational Cooperation at the External Borders
GATS	General Agreement on Trade in Services
GPA	Agreement on Government Procurement
ICJ	international Court of justice
IG	Instrument of Government
IPP	The Commission's Communication on an Integrated Product Policy
MiFID	Markets in Financial Instruments Directive
MOJ	Ministry of Justice
NJA	Nytt Juridiskt Arkiv (Supreme Court Reports, Sweden)
NOU	National Board for Public Procurement
NUTEK	Swedish Agency for Economic and regional Growth
OECD	Organisation for Economic Cooperation and Development
OHIM	Office of Harmonization for the Internal Market
OJ	Official Journal

RÅ	Regeringsrättens årsbok (Supreme Administrative Court Reports, Sweden)
SCRO	Swedish Companies registration Office
SEMC	Swedish Environmental Management Council
SIEPS	Swedish Institute for European Policy Studies
SLIM	Simpler Legislation for the Internal Market
TEU/EUT	Treaty on European Union
UNCLOS	UN Convention on Law of the Seas
UNECE	UN Economic Commission for Europe
UNFCCC	UN Framework Convention on Climate Change
VAT	Value Added Tax
WTO	World Trade Organization

Table of Cases

European Court of First Instance

European Court of Justice

European Court of Human Rights

EFTA Court

International Court of Justice

Germany

Constitutional Court

Sweden

Supreme Court

Table of Legislation

European Union

Treaties

Directives

Regulations

Decisions

Germany

International Treaties

Sweden

Constitution

Statutory legislation

1

The Asylum System, Migrant Networks and the Informal Labour Market

GREGOR NOLL* **

1. INTRODUCTION

2004 WAS A landmark year for migrant agricultural workers in Spain. Previously, many workers lacked residence permits which placed them at the margins of the community. Now, the Spanish government had made a controversial decision:[1] the status of a large fraction would be 'regularised',[2] or, as media had it, they would receive residence permits as the result of an 'amnesty'. The government had come to understand that these workers were needed, and that it was not possible to return them to their home countries. By granting the permits, the state gave migrant

* Gregor Noll is a Professor of International Law at the Faculty of Law, Lund University.

** I am indebted to Peggy Oscarsson for translating parts of this text from an earlier work ('Asylsystemet, migrantnätverk och den informella arbetsmarknaden' ['The Asylum System, Migrant Networks and the Informal Labour Market'], in S Gustafsson, L Oxelheim och N Wahl, *Europaperspektiv 2006. Årsbok för Europaforskning* (Santérus Förlag, Stockholm 2006), pp 125–42). The present text and the arguments made therein is not identical with that earlier work. Thanks are also due to Jennie Magnusson for research assistance.

[1] Regularisation decisions are controversial not least with neighbouring states. Within the EU, the controversy on whether regularisations in one state leads to secondary flows to the next, has led to the adoption of a binding norm stating that 'Member States shall communicate to the Commission and the other Member States information on the measures which they intend to take, or have recently taken, in the areas of asylum and immigration, where these measures are publicly available and are likely to have a significant impact on several Member States or on the European Union as a whole'. (Council Decision 2006/688/EC of 5 Oct 2006 on the establishment of a mutual information mechanism concerning Member States' measures in the areas of asylum and immigration, OJ L 283, 14.10.2006, pp 40–3.)

[2] See FJ Moreno Fuentes, 'The regularisation of undocumented migrants as a mechanism for the 'emerging' of the Spanish underground economy', *Unidad de Políticas Comparadas Working Paper 05–06* (Jun 2005). Regularisation policies are no new phenomenon and account for the presence of sizeable migrant populations in countries such as France, Italy, Spain and Portugal. See UN DESA, World Economic and Social Affairs. International Migration (UN, New York 2004) *UN Doc No E/2004/75/Rev.1/Add.1*, pp 46–7; A Levinson, *The Regularisation of Unauthorized Migrants: Literature Survey and Country Case Studies* (Centre on Migration, Policy and Society, University of Oxford, Oxford 2005).

workers the chance to defend themselves against exploitation in the informal sector.

Many of these workers had made their way as undocumented migrants from North Africa to Spain in open boats under considerable risk to life and limb.[3] To avoid being returned upon coming in contact with Spanish authorities, they regularly applied for asylum upon arrival. However, only a few were recognised as refugees or as other persons in need of international protection. Many of those refused permission for residence managed to remain on Spanish territory. In time they found work, eg in the large greenhouse operations, which provide the tomatoes and cucumbers Europeans would buy in their supermarkets.

The regularisation of undocumented migrants in Spain shows that whether we like it or not, the asylum system and the labour market are closely intertwined. The demand for cheap tomatoes, and cheap labour to grow them, were more important in the decision than international conventions or humanitarian concerns. Traditionally, refugee lawyers have been careful to keep the labour market and asylum conceptually separate, mostly for fear that the grant of asylum will be made conditional on the manpower needs of the labour market. However, this separation has not stopped states from applying a broad range of restrictions designed to make the road to asylum more difficult to navigate. Is it not time to alter our perspective, and ask whether the informal labour market and migrants' own networks in fact provide a fundamental form of protection?

Governments attempting to regulate labour markets and control immigration are confronted with difficult questions. In the past, there was general agreement that the asylum system should not be exploited as a side entrance to the labour market. The two systems—asylum and labour market—were to be planned and maintained separately. But if migration is a prerequisite for asylum, does not increasingly stiffer migration control block escape for those under persecution? Prices for smuggling go up, and smugglers seek new routes, yet irregular migration continues, and the informal labour market flourishes. Here we must ask an irreverent question: is there any point in having both systems? And can the crux of the matter be that both are repeatedly branded as an 'illegal' phenomena which must be 'battled' like enemies?

Or, to combine both questions in one: is the asylum system a way to regulate the informal labour market within the EU?[4]

[3] For an excellent overview, see T Spijkerboer 'The Human Costs of Border Control', Briefing Paper, European Parliament, *IP/C/LIBE/FWC/2005-23/SC1*, quoting one source documenting some 7000 deaths at European borders in the period from 1993–2006.

[4] For a comprehensive overview, see GJ Borjas and J Crisp (eds), *Poverty, International Migration and Asylum* (Basingstoke, Palgrave Macmillan, 2005). On the impact of undocumented migration on domestic labour markets, see J Hjarnø, *Illegal Immigrants and Developments in the Labour Markets of the EU* (Aldershot, Ashgate publishers, 2003).

2. THE ASYLUM SYSTEM: A WINDOW TO THE INFORMAL LABOUR MARKET?

In order to understand the relationship of migration, asylum and labour market, we need to be aware of two simple legal rules. First, all nation states have the right to regulate immigration.[5] This right comprises a state's personal sovereignty and has ancient origins in international law. States are free to allow immigration of foreign labour one day, and prohibit it the next. States can also recruit well-educated labour from abroad, while refusing entry to those with little or no education.

However, by signing conventions on human rights and refugee law, states have come to an agreement for limiting the application of this right. This brings us to the second rule we should remember. Today, personal sovereignty is limited primarily by the prohibition against returning foreigners to countries in which they risk persecution. This rule is well established. It is a fundamental part of international law (the 1951 Refugee Convention[6] and the Convention against Torture[7]), European law (dealt with in a separate section below) as well as Member States' domestic law. The moment a migrant claims that persecution awaits upon return, the state shall evaluate the risk of such persecution before deportation (certain exceptions exist, but these do not detract from the practical significance of the principle). This provides undocumented migrants with a possibility to avoid immediate return to the country of origin by seeking asylum and to wait for a decision in the new country. If we reflect upon the hard lessons of the 1930s and 40s, when refugees from totalitarian states were deported from liberal democracies on the basis of states' personal sovereignty, then we understand why this rule of non-refoulement badly needed to be codified.

During the 50s and 60s, few regarded the prohibition of refoulement as a hindrance to effective immigration control. The Iron Curtain prevented many from leaving their home countries. But there was also a workable alternative to the asylum system: many industrialised countries required

[5] In 1892, the US Supreme Court affirmed that there was 'an accepted maxim of international law, that every sovereign nation has the power, as inherent in sovereignty, and essential to its self–preservation, to forbid the entrance of foreigners within its dominions, or to admit them only in such cases and upon such conditions as it may see fit to prescribe'. (US Supreme Court, *Nishimura Ekiu v United States*, 142 US 651, 659, 1892.) In 1955, Judge Read formulated this right as follows in his dissenting opinion in Nottebohm: 'When an alien comes to the frontier, seeking admission, either as a settler or on a visit, the State has an unfettered right to refuse admission'. (ICJ, *Nottebohm Case*, ICJ Reports 1955, p 46.)

[6] Convention relating to the Status of Refugees, 28 Jul 1951, 189 UNTS 137 [1951 Refugee Convention, abbreviated GC]. In the following, reference to the 1951 Refugee Convention covers the Convention as modified by the Protocol relating to the Status of Refugees, 31 Jan 1967, 606 UNTS 267.

[7] Convention against Torture and Other Cruel, Inhuman or Degrading Treatment or Punishment, GA res 39/46, annex, 39 UN GAOR Supp (No 51) at 197, UN Doc A/39/51 (1984).

foreign labour. However, after the energy crisis this door closed, and only the asylum system remained.

By necessity, the prohibitions of refoulement under international law also offer a shortcut for persons wishing to enter the EU for employment opportunities rather than as forced migrants. Let us look at the example of migrants who arrive in Europe without an entry permit and who support themselves in the informal sector, without seeking contact with the authorities. When such migrants are discovered by the authorities, they might file an application for asylum as a defence against immediate deportation. In cases where these migrants are not taken into custody, there are opportunities to engage again in the informal sector while the application for asylum is processed. Governments usually label this kind of behaviour as 'abuse', but a good market liberal would sooner consider it completely rational behaviour. In addition, the long waiting times inherent in the asylum process encourage such actions. It sometimes takes years to evaluate a case, and in many cases evaluations take at least six months.

However, it is virtually impossible to say anything about how many asylum applicants should 'really' be seen as hidden labour immigrants. Persons who flee to another country must still support themselves and their families, so it is quite understandable that these people seek a place in the labour market. In many cases, it is impossible to isolate the motive for flight from the labour motive. So, statements about pervasive abuse of the asylum system must be taken for what they are: governments' attempts to maximise their own freedom of action while playing down the significance of human rights and refugee law as constraints.

3. CAN THE LAW DO AWAY WITH THE INFORMAL LABOUR MARKET FOR MIGRANTS?

The informal labour market and undocumented migration have one thing in common: we know little about their size. Estimates claim that up to 16 per cent of the EU's gross national product is created in the informal sector,[8] which of course is not only composed of third country nationals without work permits, but also includes citizens and legal residents of the EU. One assumes that most undocumented migrants end up in occupations which do not require formal education.[9] The construction industry, agriculture,

[8] A scientific source estimates the underground economy to account for 16 percent of GDP in OSCE countries (1999–2003). See F Schneider, 'The Size of the Shadow Economies of 145 Countries all over the World: First Results over the Period 1999 to 2003' (2004), *IZA Discussion Paper No 1431*, p 28.

[9] R Black et al, 'A Survey of the Illegally Resident Population in Detention' (2005), *Home Office Online Report 20/05*, p 26.

cleaning and other service occupations are often cited as typical examples. Many migrants have no opportunity to use the education or qualifications they have, since formal rules for recognition of these qualifications and language barriers stand in the way. Also, low-qualification jobs in the EU can offer far better pay than more advanced occupations in the home country.

What do we know then, about what is often termed 'illegal immigration'?[10] The statistical basis is not especially broad. The European Commission asserts that the number of these people entering the EU annually is in six figures, but also warns that no proof exists to support more precise estimates.[11] In addition, nothing is known about undocumented migrants leaving the EU. By consequence, we know almost nothing about the number of undocumented migrants remaining at any given point in time in the EU. Anyone who studies the statistics more carefully, soon realises that it is impossible to track a sufficient number of persons through the entire migration process, to draw more concrete conclusions about what happens after entry.

Public debate tends to overfocus on the number of asylum seekers. The reason that such statistics exist is simply that asylum applicants contact the authorities. Such contacts can be counted. But these figures say very little about undocumented migration as a whole. A good number of asylum seekers enter the country with some kind of visa, and can hardly be considered 'illegal immigrants'.[12] Regardless of whether entry occurs with or without the necessary travel documents, asylum applicants who receive residence permits for protection reasons, should also be removed from the statistics. But what happens to those who are denied asylum? Some leave the country voluntarily, and some by forced deportation. Some go 'underground', which can mean either that they are still in the country, or that they have travelled to another country, where authorities once again count them as asylum seekers, or regard them as 'undocumented immigrants. While there is a risk that some undocumented migrants are amongst us without anyone noticing, there is also a risk of counting some twice.

[10] I shall not use this terminology of 'illegal migration', since there is a human right to leave any country, including one's own, and there is a right to apply for asylum, even when one does not possess an entry permit. Rather, I shall use the terminology of the 1990 Migrant Workers Convention and term migrants who enter or remain in a destination country, without being allowed to do so, as 'undocumented migrants'.

[11] European Commission, *Communication from the Commission on Policy priorities in the fight against illegal immigration of third-country nationals*, COM(2006) 402 final, 19 Jul 2006, Annex.

[12] In a recent UK study, based on interviews with 83 migrants detained between Dec 2001 and Mar 2002, 60% had entered illegally. This leaves a good number of legal entries. Given the limited size of the sample, I would like to warn from any extrapolations. In particular, it cannot be inferred that some 40% of all third country nationals entering the EU with a valid permit will eventually become undocumented migrants. R Black et al, 'A Survey of the Illegally Resident Population in Detention.' (2005), *Home Office Online Report 20/05*, p 20.

Since it is so difficult to count migrants, perhaps we should calculate the revenue they generate. Both immigrants with residence permits and undocumented migrants send part of their earnings to family members remaining in the country of origin. Altogether, these so-called 'remittances' form the second most important source of income for many states in the south and are exceeded only by foreign direct investments (FDI).[13] They are more important than international aid, which comes in third place.[14] In 1999 remittances to less developed countries amounted to 60 billion dollars.[15] Therefore, an emigration country in Sub-Saharan Africa would be foolish in preventing its citizens from travelling to and working in the EU so a Member State such as Italy could more easily control immigration. It would be a net loss, because remittances from its citizens would drop significantly. While dramatic increases have occurred in recent years, it is politically improbable that the EU will increase aid to a level tantamount to 'buying out' the value of remittances in the foreseeable future. Therefore, we may draw the conclusion that the EU and the Member States do not necessarily possess the economic muscle required to match that of migrant networks. This fundamental fact is often forgotten in 'the fight against illegal immigration'.

Neither liberalisation nor control can do away with undocumented migration and informal labour markets. Let us look at liberalisation first. Would it not be wise to allow more people to migrate in order to 'dry up' undocumented migration and the informal labour market for migrants? It is unlikely that this strategy would succeed. First of all, we must realise that the EU will continue to attract migrant workers for quite some time. The differences between migrants' countries and the EU in terms of employment opportunities and the protection of human rights are so great that it would require an indefinite amount of time to balance them, in the perspective of increased legal migration. The economic integration which took place recently within the EU after new members' entry seems like a fresh breath of air compared to the long-term and very complex redistributions that integration between

[13] 'International remittances received by developing countries—expected to reach $167 billion in 2005—have doubled in the past 5 years as a result of (a) the increased scrutiny of flows since the terrorist attacks of Sep 2001, (b) changes in the industry that support remittances (lower costs, expanding networks), (c) improvements in data recording, (d) the depreciation of the dollar (which raises the dollar value of remittances denominated in other currencies), and (e) growth in the migrant stock and incomes. However, records still underestimate the full scale of remittances, because payments made through informal, unrecorded channels are not captured. Econometric analysis and available household surveys suggest that unrecorded flows through informal channels may conservatively add 50% (or more) of recorded flows.' (World Bank, *Global Economic Prospects. Economic Implications of Migration and Remittances*, (Washington 2006), p xiii.)

[14] N Nyberg-Sørensen, N Van Hear, P Engberg-Pedersen 'The Migration-Development Nexus Evidence and Policy Options State-of-the-Art Overview' (2002), *International Migration* 40 (5), pp 3–47, at p 19.

[15] *Ibid.*

the EU and migrant countries would require. The conditions for allowing free labour immigration *within* the EU and EEA are therefore completely different from those for allowing free labour immigration *to* the EU and EEA. In migration research, the relationship between income adjustment and migration is described as 'the migration hump': as long as significant differences in income persist, many people will migrate. It is only when differences are evened to the level between, say Sweden and Poland, that the number of migrants will be reduced to the trickle we now celebrate as a great victory for integration within Europe. Only then have we overcome the 'hump' and the migration curve flattens out. From a purely political point of view, the migration hump stands in the way of an extensive legalisation strategy, since we as citizens of the EU rightly suspect that a large, income-equalising, global migration will result in consequences for our own privileges.

And what about more extensive migration control? First of all, we must remember that the Member States and the EU have invested heavily in such controls. Institutionalised sharing of information and practices amongst Member States began as early as the 1990s, and military resources have become involved in border control in maritime surveillance operations. With FRONTEX, an EU border control agency has been created. Each time controls increase at one point of a border, the flow of migrants moves to another point of entry. And each time new control techniques are put in place, smugglers and migrant networks respond with counterstrategies. These cat-and-mouse tactics can have grim results. When the Member States began to collect fingerprint information for undocumented immigrants and make them accessible in an intrastate database, reports surfaced describing how asylum seekers burned their fingers for fear of being returned to another EU country which would reject their application.

We must also remind ourselves that an unduly strict immigration policy has economic repercussions in the EU. In order to develop its economy, the EU must allow people to move back and forth over Union borders with a minimum of bureaucratic hassles. Visa rules must not be too restrictive, since we would risk losing valuable business opportunities as well as technology and knowledge exchange. In other words, immigration control allows a kind of protectionist balancing act, and this has effects on integration policy. If we see that people are mistreated and discriminated against at the border, then, yes, they will be mistreated and discriminated against in the community as well. This in turn can undermine the EU as an attractive workplace for highly educated and trained persons.

4. WHAT IS THE EU DOING?

Up to this point, I have described the issue at hand more from the perspective of a single nation state perspective than the EU perspective. I think this approach continues to provide a more accurate picture: the issue is really between the nation state and migrant networks. However, reality has become more complicated now that the EU increasingly profiles itself as a driving force in immigration and asylum issues.

We all know why. During the 90s, the EU began to take seriously the right of free movement for persons within the internal market, and removed the inner barrier preventing this movement. At the same time, governments did not wish to give asylum seekers and undocumented migrants the possibility to use this freedom of movement. One could say that the rubble remaining after the old barriers were torn down was used to build higher, more impassable outer barriers. In addition, governments established administrative control measures which allowed the Member States to track how asylum seekers and other migrants moved within the EU. It was this European integration process—and thus migration *within* EU—which forced the Union to address migration *to* the EU, including asylum issues. The outer barrier surrounding the external borders of EU and its 'flanking measures' in the domain of law, offer abundant evidence that the Union considered the primary issue to be the right to freedom of movement for EU citizens.

If we examine this process more closely,[16] we find that it is a patchwork quilt of national law, international law, and, slowly but surely, EC law. The Member States were eager to preserve personal sovereignty, and retained a hand on the controls. The result has been an imbalanced and inconsistent policy on the part of the EU. True enough, it has produced a vast quantity of instruments through the years, but most of these have been non-binding. With the exception of the 1990 Dublin and Schengen Conventions and binding visa requirements incepted in 1995, the integration process has begun in earnest only after the adoption of the Amsterdam Treaty in 1999. With this, EC law could be established on a larger scale, thereby allowing norms to be set which have a good chance of being accepted in Member States' domestic legal systems. Many of the EC instruments, however, are relatively new, and it is too early to draw conclusion about their effects on Member States' law and practice.[17]

The image of strict dictate from Brussels is therefore unjustified for the issue at hand. The laws the EU has produced are hallmarked by an attitude of respect for domestic legislation, cautious harmonisation is preferred over aggressive unification: the first step merely acts to create a 'level playing field' with minimum norms requiring little change in Member States' law and practice. In the next step, which has just started at the time of writing,

[16] See chs 4–8 in G Noll, *Negotiating Asylum. The EU acquis, Extraterritorial Protection and the Common Market of Deflection* (Martinus Nijhoff Publishers, The Hague, 2000).

[17] At the time of writing, the European Commission has commissioned a study of the transposition of 10 directives in the asylum and immigration fields, accepted to be finalised in early 2008.

the legislative work is intended to be more ambitious. The long absence of the European Court of Justice (ECJ) as a driving force in the field of immigration and asylum is very evident. Why has the ECJ been so silent? Because the Member States quite simply have not given it the same competence within the area of undocumented migration as for other integration issues. It is only since the Treaty of Amsterdam that the ECJ has been empowered to make preliminary rulings in this subject matter.[18]

Let us look more closely at the most important components of EU policy and legislation. If we consider immigration, we can quickly state two things. The Union has invested considerably in shared control of its external borders. Common databases (the Schengen database SIS and the fingerprint database Eurodac), common standards for border control, and the obligation upon Member States which have been remiss in their control to take back immigrants, are some of the major elements. But in the question of which persons the Union shall allow to enter, we have received only negatively formulated answers: no asylum seekers, and no undocumented migrants. Only during recent years have laws been passed which facilitate certain foreigners' movement into and within the EU. What is remarkable is that these rules apply to a kind of upper class among migrants, a class consisting mainly of researchers and students. The EU has also managed to draw up binding norms on family reunification[19] and long-time resident third country nationals.[20] Both of these, however, diminish Member States' right to decide who may enter and remain on their territory only in quite marginal ways.

An ominous silence surrounds the issue that interests us most: how shall the EU approach less qualified immigrants—those who typically find themselves in the informal sector? This is the point on which it is most difficult to agree. In 2001 the European Commission proposed a directive on this exact issue.[21] It was quickly rejected by Member States in the Council. To put it in a nutshell: a migration control policy exists, but a policy for migration is noticeably absent. We can agree that borders must be controlled, but we cannot agree on who should be allowed to cross these borders.

What does current asylum policy look like? Since 1999, a Common European Asylum System (CEAS) has been established, which provides a binding minimum regulation.[22] Among other things, the system will provide

[18] Compare the limitations in Art 68 ECT with the standard formula of Art 234 ECT.

[19] Council Dir 2003/86/EC of 22 Sep 2003 on the right to family reunification, OJ L 251, 3.10.2003, pp 12–18.

[20] Council Dir 2003/109/EC of 25 Nov 2003 concerning the status of third-country nationals who are long-term residents, OJ L 16, 23.1.2004, pp 44–53.

[21] Proposal for a Council Dir on the conditions of entry and residence of third-country nationals for the purpose of paid employment and self-employed economic activities, COM/2001/0386 final, OJ C 332E, 27.11.2001, pp 248–56.

[22] The initiative stemmed from the 1999 European Council at Tampere (Finland). See Tampere European Council, *Presidency Conclusions*, 15 and 16 Oct 1999, Section A.

answers regarding who shall receive protection, and what rights this protection affords (both aspects are discussed in the so-called Qualification Directive of 2004[23]) and minimum standards for the reception of asylum seekers[24] as well as for the asylum procedure.[25] The most powerful legislation today is the 2003 Dublin Regulation, which allocated state responsibility for processing asylum claims on the assumption that all Member States offer approximately the same level of protection[26]. The Dublin Regulation has been sharply criticised, since in fact the Member States show considerable differences in their protection systems. In addition, it creates a skewed distribution which is a disadvantage to states possessing land or maritime borders also serving as outer borders for the EU. The regulation is perhaps the apparent example of how protection interests have taken a back seat to calls for control.

But despite EU legislation and restrictive policies on the part of the Member States, undocumented migrants continue to make their way into Europe. Indeed, it is possible that even those who would have valid reasons for demanding protection choose the informal sector over the asylum system, and avoid contact with authorities as much as possible. In this respect, we see a *privatisation* of the protection system. Partly, the welfare state is replaced by well-intentioned individuals, who conceal undocumented migrants, and who arrange food, living quarters and health care on a precarious philanthropic basis. Also, the formal labour market is replaced by the informal sector. Furthermore, the economic contributions of migrants remain unseen, since they cannot be measured in regular ways, such as tax revenues. Sociologist Anja Weiss has described EU migration and asylum policy in considerably harsher terms, namely as a way to keep the low-qualification labour cheap.[27] Undocumented migrants cannot claim any rights or make any demands, because then they will be sent back. In the next section, we shall study whether this explanation really holds water.

[23] Council Dir 2004/83/EC of 29 Apr 2004 on minimum standards for the qualification and status of third country nationals or stateless persons as refugees or as persons who otherwise need international protection and the content of the protection granted, OJ L 204/24, 30.9.2005, pp 12–23.

[24] Council Dir 2003/9/EC of 27 Jan 2003 laying down minimum standards for the reception of asylum seekers, OJ L 31, 6.2.2003, p 18–25.

[25] Council Dir 2005/85/EC of 1 Dec 2005 on minimum standards on procedures in Member States for granting and withdrawing refugee status, OJ L 326, 13.12.2005, p 13–34.

[26] Council Reg (EC) No 343/2003 of 18 Feb 2003 establishing the criteria and mechanisms for determining the Member State responsible for examining an asylum application lodged in one of the Member States by a third-country national, OJ L 50, 25.2.2003, pp 1–10.

[27] A Weiss, 'Raumrelationen als zentraler Aspekt weltweiter Ungleichheiten,' *Eurozine* 2002, available at <http://eurozine.com/pdf/2002-04-25-weiss-de.pdf> (last accessed on 15 Feb 2007).

5. THE HIDDEN PRODUCTIVITY OF ASYLUM LAW

Must we have such a confusing and contradictory system? EU institutions and Member States see themselves as confronted with a substantial dilemma. States cannot admit to their citizens that they are unable to fully regulate immigration, and that migrant networks exert considerable control over it. In many election campaigns, the fear of immigration plays a decisive role and can be exploited to win votes, even when the candidate has no real will or desire to bring about significant change in the system. What politician and what state would really want to be seen as building a new Berlin Wall around Europe, and order border police to use firearms to turn away asylum seekers and undocumented migrants? Do politicians really want to tell consumers that food and living costs will increase, since the authorities are going to prosecute business owners who employ illegal labour? It seems the political advantages of maintaining the status quo tip the scales.

At the same time, technical solutions are available that could be applied without having to revolutionise the state or the welfare society. Economically, states would benefit from hiring more asylum processing staff and thereby significantly shorten the asylum process. This in turn would result in reduced costs for housing and custody, and ensure that the asylum seeker would not suffer emotionally from prolonged uncertainty while waiting for a decision (the occurrence of severe withdrawal behaviour amongst asylum-seeking children in the Swedish system is one of the most drastic examples of this problem)[28]. In Sweden this has been suggested repeatedly, but the asylum system has not received additional funds for processing asylum applications. How do we explain this?

Another technical improvement is the proposal to let asylum seekers contact the Member State embassies in their home region and file an application for asylum (so-called Protected Entry Procedures).[29] Primary advantages would be that the smugglers' monopoly on information would be undermined, and applicants would receive authoritative answers regarding their chances of receiving protection *before* any migration decision is made. The proposal was discussed on the EU level, but received a lukewarm response from the Member States. Why? Here are two examples of clearly irrational behaviour on the part of the Member States—examples in which rhetoric and action are in glaring contrast. How can we explain such contradictions?

There are two approaches—one economic and one related to the politics of identity. The economic approach sees the asylum system as a doorway to

[28] See the *Report of the Special Rapporteur on the right of everyone to the enjoyment of the highest attainable standard of physical and mental health, Paul Hunt. Mission to Sweden.* UN. Doc. No. A/HRC/4/28/Add.2, 28 February 2007, p 20–22.

[29] G Noll, J Fagerlund and F Liebaut, *Study on the Feasibility Of Processing Asylum Claims Outside the EU Against the Background of the Common European Asylum System and the Goal of a Common Asylum Procedure* (Luxemburg: European Communities, 2003).

the illegitimate sphere of our economy. Irregular migrants end up outside official minimum wage mechanisms and work for far lower wages than legal residents and citizens. They comprise a labour reserve that can be dispensed with when it is no longer needed, something both employers and the welfare state can use to their advantage.[30] All this presumes that the official immigration policy is very restrictive. The system filters away the majority of migrants and guarantees that the informal labour market is not flooded with too many immigrants. The asylum system then becomes the door that stands ajar, letting in a small number of immigrants, with the blessing of the state and employers, and under the guise of human compassion. The number of immigrants can vary, but the main thing is that the infrastructure is maintained: authorities judge applicants' cases and accommodate asylum seekers during the process, and the migrant networks send some of these persons into the informal sector. Immigrants finance the journey themselves and take all the risks. The mechanism is distinguished by a surplus, since migrants know that the majority of applicants will be refused a residence permit, and will be removed from the country if apprehended. Immigrants have no chance of creating a base for renegotiating these conditions, such as, say a union. The illegal aspect is therefore a crucial tool, both for keeping wages low and for limiting the number of people in the informal sector, while silencing questions about legitimacy. After all, the official position is that the informal sector must be eradicated, and that rejected asylum seekers will be deported.

The system appears to prioritise young, single men: they are best at coping with the physical hardships of smuggling and can quickly assimilate themselves in the informal sector without having to consider the needs of an accompanying family. Since the informal sector primarily recruits uneducated labour, long years of study are not an advantage. This can be another reason why older persons are less interesting. Lengthy processing times in the asylum process are necessary in order to give the informal labour market a chance to absorb a certain amount of asylum seekers, and to ensure that uncertainty of the outcome will diminish migrants' wage expectations. Offering asylum via embassies merely complicates matters and brings up the question of who shall pay for the journey. In this way, long processing times and the refusal to allow asylum granted via embassies indicate how humanitarian objectives have been subordinated to labour market policy. From an economic perspective, it is rhetorically wise to preserve a strict division between labour market policy and asylum policy. As soon as the interaction of migration, the informal labour market and asylum becomes apparent, it becomes impossible to exploit immigration issues in an election campaign. The concept of a

[30] This would neatly posit such persons in a 'glocalised' underclass, characterised by its immobility in terms of entitlement. See A Weiss, 'The Transnationalization of Social Inequality: Conceptualizing Social Positions on a World Scale' (2005), *Current Sociology*, Vol 53, No 4, pp 707–28.

regulated, completely legal labour market reveals itself to be an illusion equal to that of a thoroughly non-political and humane asylum policy.

Does the economic theory provide a fair picture? It cannot provide a comprehensive explanation. Its underhanded objective—cheap labour—could be realised through a more humane asylum system. The uncertainty and waiting during a long asylum process overwhelm some asylum seekers, and such persons are now allowed to stay for humanitarian reasons developed during the application process. From a purely economic perspective, this is rather pointless and costly for the welfare state. This is where the identity-political approach comes in. The basis for this thesis is that a community does not constitute itself once and for all, for everyone, for example through a document as a form of government, but instead constitutes itself continually. A typical question of constitutional character is who is a member of the community, and who is outside the community. The Member States must quite simply establish a certain level of tangible exclusion in order to constitute themselves, and thereby the EU.

This exclusion occurs more seldom at the Member State's border: controls have been reduced by the free internal market, and the flanking measures such as increased EU border control cannot be pushed too far for fear of damaging trade. In a time when the physical migration control meets with such problems, governments merely move the exclusion from country borders to other fora—such as the asylum process. We might experience such exclusion as brutal and unfair—the so-called apathetic children come to mind—but even in the most disturbing cases it serves a purpose: it demonstrates the state's unlimited power over membership in the community. How could refugees believe they could put themselves above the law of the national state? In the asylum process, such persons are put back in their place in the national state system, either by being returned to the country of origin, or by becoming part of the asylum country's community. If necessary, the monopoly of violence is validated in the deportation process. This is made all too clear when police forcibly remove deportees from a church where the congregation has offered protection, or when deportees are injured or even die during enforced return.

From an economic standpoint, it is difficult to explain the use of violence, especially when used against deportees. Here, it seems as if the informal economy and the politics of identity are in symbiosis. Those who claim the asylum system to be merely a concealed labour policy or merely a protection mechanism for the persecuted, are mistaken and miss its performance of communal identity.[31]

[31] The violent aspects of the asylum system can be meaningfully analysed by drawing on the theory of imitative violence developed by René Girard. The scapegoat is sacrificed to avert the spread of violence in a community, and the sacrificial violence is presented as a divine command. See R Girard, *Violence and the Sacred* (John Hopkins University Press, Baltimore 1977).

6. CONCLUSIONS

Can we progress away from this symbiosis between market and identity? I doubt it. Those who believe the problem can be solved by increasing legal immigration of labour ignore the fact that a working permit makes the migrant visible and a possessor of certain rights, and therefore more expensive. Even the most generous programme for legal immigration or for normalisation of existing undocumented labour runs out at some point. In addition, such programmes run out before the demand is satisfied, since the need for labour in the north is not so great that the surplus from the south will diminish in the foreseeable future. As such there will always be room for a new informal labour market beside the formal one. A radical measure would be to deregulate the labour market completely, and allow free labour immigration to the EU and its Member States. However, this contradicts the idea of a united welfare community within the national state or attempts to develop such a community within the EU. Hoping that new demographic needs will open the door for new immigration is hoping for too much. As Jan Ekberg's research has shown, immigration can address the problem of an aging European population only to a small extent.[32]

And those who insist in the traditional manner that the asylum system must be completely separated from the informal labour market are on thin ice. Australia has put such a separation into practice, isolating asylum seekers who arrive without entry visas in closed compounds while they wait for a decision. Of course, asylum seekers in custody cannot be recruited by the informal labour market. The price in terms of human suffering is indeed high. This might raise issues under human rights law.

Some hope perhaps that increased control on the EU level will help. I am sceptical in this case as well. First, we ought to recall that all significant changes on policy for migration and asylum must be accepted by a qualified majority in the EU Council of Ministers. Within the EU, the Member States hold very divergent opinions about the issue. Some countries are more dependent upon foreign labour in the informal sector than others. Their geopolitical situation also plays a role: Malta has different interests than those of Sweden, and Poland concerns itself with other threats than does France. It has been a long road to agreement on the watered-down minimum norms we have today, and more substantial changes in course are unlikely. Secondly, no real reasons exist to bring about a radical shift in policy. EU sees itself as under great pressure from the competition from other regions in the global market. Why should the EU act differently from a country that wished to maximise its ability to compete? Thirdly, the EU desperately needs an identity. If the real power

[32] J Ekberg, 'Kan invandrare underlätta försörjningen av en åldrande befolkning?' [Can immigrants facilitate support of an ageing population?] in *Ekonomisk Debatt* nr 4 (2004).

over the asylum process and deportations were in fact delegated to the EU, EU representatives would likely reproduce the states' behaviour, but on the Union level. In other words, the system would be presented with a certain amount of arbitrariness to demonstrate both internally and externally who is sovereign.

Is it possible to think beyond the existing system? We could start by openly discussing our dependence upon the informal sector and in particular the networks of foreign employees in this sector. We could exert pressure on employers in the illegal labour market, while making clear for consumers that the price of their tomatoes, pizza, monthly rent or office cleaning is too low to be based on legal labour. These are extremely unpopular political measures, but they would have far more potential change than further militarisation of migration control. We would also need to speak openly about the downsides of our prioritisation of civil and political human rights. In particular, their priority over economic human rights in asylum law is arbitrary, considering the indivisible nature of human rights. Migration can reveal itself to be a stronger force for realising human rights than all monitoring bodies, courts, and overseas development assistance programs combined.

Another alternative is to have EU Member States set unified quotas for legal labour migration, thereby transforming parts of the existing illegal labour market for unskilled persons to a legal one. This is no trivial demand, because the EU competes with other states using disenfranchised labour to reduce costs. The EU must then establish itself as an accessible presence in migrant's home regions and, when possible, inform potential migrants about available opportunities for asylum and if it will be possible for them to work. This would establish an authoritative, reliable source of information which would effectively contradict smugglers' false information. However, the effects of a legal labour immigration programme and protected entry procedures should not be overestimated.

The real challenge lies in the next step: the creation of transregional mechanisms which link employment, welfare and political representation. It is here that our political creativity will be tested to its limits.

A beginning would be the creation of a permanent system of negotiation for the liberalisation of migration, in tandem with the WTO process. According to Professor Dani Rodrik's calculation, greater economic potential would be realised through temporary working permits for persons from the Global South, than through the liberalisation of trade we see happening now.[33] Lastly, we would need to include migrant networks in the political

[33] D Rodrik, 'Comments at the Conference on "Immigration Policy and the Welfare State"' (Trieste, Jun 23, 2001), available at http://ksghome.harvard.edu/~drodrik/Comments%20on%20Immigration%20Conference.doc> (last accessed on 15 Feb 2007).

process around immigration and integration. These networks have proven that they can surpass the state when it comes to organising freedom of movement, employment and basic protection of its members. Keeping them outside the political process will perpetuate the problems I have described here. Inviting them into the debate would endow EU policies with a badly needed dose of legitimacy.

2

European Legal Strategies to Global Environmental Cooperation

JONAS EBBESSON*

1 MULTILATERALISM PREFERRED

As a part of the industrialised world, and a region with one of the highest levels of consumption and economic standard in the world, the 'footprints' of the EU on the global environment, ecosystem services and natural resources are immense. Counted per capita, the environmental impact of the EU is greater than that of most other regions of the world. This said, the EU has also shown an engagement for global environmental policy-making and cooperation which is unparalleled in any other region of the world. Environmental cooperation on a global scale would be poorer and most global environmental agreements more diluted without the engagement of the EU. Some of the environmental agreements adopted in the last decade would not even have been realised without the influence of the EU. With the exception of some smaller individual countries, no other political force among the industrialised countries is currently pushing for global environmental cooperation and the development of international rules for the protection of health and the environment to the same extent as the EU.

This essay aims at detecting and shedding light on some of the features in the EU approach to global environmental cooperation and international law, which differ from those of other industrial regions. While linking the approach of the EU to its own legal structure, the main issues in this sketch are the endorsement of multilateralism and internationalism, and the promotion of precaution as a legal and political principle in international environmental governance. This attitude and strategy to global

* Professor of Environmental Law at Stockholm University. This article draws on a previously published article, in Swedish, J Ebbesson, 'Bräckligare internationellt miljösamarbete utan EU', in P Cramér, S Gustavsson and L Oxelheim (eds), *EU som aktör i världen: Europaperspektiv 2007* (Santérus, Stockholm, 2007). Thanks to Veit Koester for useful input.

environmental cooperation differ sharply from that of the USA. Although contrasting the position of the EU to that of the USA is not the main purpose of the article, some such comparison is unavoidable.

Singling out the EU as the main driver in the development of global environmental cooperation requires some proviso and clarifications. First this position of the EU has not been achieved only by virtue of its own merits. To a considerable degree this is also due to the near complete lack of interest of the current federal administration of the USA to actively promote such cooperation and development; or, perhaps more correctly, due to its failure of perceiving environmental issues as something international. The political approach of the US federal administration has not only become increasingly introvert, but in some cases also directly confrontational to the development of international law concerning environment protection. This is most apparent in the climate change negotiations, maintained by the EU and consistently opposed by the US federal administration. Of course, the development of global environmental regimes is not the result of the EU alone. The activity and influence of most developing countries has been critical for the legitimacy of the global legal frameworks in a North-South context.

Moreover, appearing as the most environmentally engaged political force in the industrial world does not exclude selfish interest behind certain actions and proposals of the EU, so as to set aside global concerns and North-South justice when acting globally. In some areas, for instance fisheries outside the coastal areas of the EU Member States,[1] the EU has on good grounds been criticised for not acting towards sustainable management of natural resources,[2] and for acting contrary to the objective of sustainable development, as set out in the treaties establishing the EU.[3]

With these qualifications, and despite considerable internal conflicts of interest between the European Commission and the Member States as well as among the Member States, the EU remains able to define a common international environmental policy in several areas, which is more ambitious than that of most other industrial states and regions.

[1] One such case was revealed in the conflict between the EU and Canada concerning fisheries outside Canadian waters, described eg by CH Joyner, 'On the borderline? Canadian Activism in the Grand banks' in S Stokke (ed), *Governing High Seas Fisheries* (Oxford, Oxford University Press, 2001), pp 207–33. The EU has alse been criticised for the European fisheries outside the African coast.

[2] Yet another example, with repercussions in the field of the environment and management of natural resources, was the condemnation by many non-governmental organisations of the EU for being too Eurocentric in the negotiations with developing countries under the General Agreement on Trade in Services concerning trade liberalisation in the World Trade Organization (WTO).

[3] Consolidated Versions of the Treaty on European Union, Art 2, and of the Treaty Establishing the European Community (EC Treaty), Arts 2 and 6; [2006] *Official Journal* (OJ) C321E, p 1.

Throughout this essay, for reasons of simplicity, unless the issue concerns the power relation between the European Community (EC) and the EU Member States, I mostly refer to the environmental policies and actions of the EU although formally speaking environmental policies and lawmaking are EC matters. In the same vein, international agreements are entered into by the EC, not the EU. While the Community does not have exclusive competence in this field vis-à-vis Member States, the supranational structure of the EC and the role of the Commission (and the European Judiciary) are still essential elements also when acting internationally.

2 SOLID MANDATE FOR EUROPEAN ENVIRONMENTAL POLICY

One cannot separate the external activities of the EU in environmental matters—neither in international cooperation nor in the development of international environmental law—from the internal aspects, ambitions and handling of these same matters. Today, there is a solid legal and political mandate for the EU to pursue environmental and health issues 'domestically' as well as externally. The more than 50 international environmental agreements to which the EU (EC) has consented reveal that this mandate has also been utilised.

Initially the Rome Treaty Establishing the European Economic Community (EEC) did not provide any such explicit mandate, and environment protection was not an obvious task for the Community. Even so, the EEC adopted its first environmental action programme in relation to the first UN conference devoted to environmental issues (Stockholm Conference on the Human Environment) in 1972. Cooperation with international organisations, such as the OECD, the UN and the Council of Europe, was emphasised already in the first action programme. The notion of international cooperation has been repeated, in different ways, in the following five environmental action programmes (the 6th Action Programme covers the period of 2002–12), thus giving a solid political mandate for the EU to engage itself in international environmental cooperation and lawmaking.

Although the action programmes are important platforms for the environmental strategies and undertakings by the EU, legally speaking the mandate given in the Treaty Establishing the European Community—setting out that the European Community *shall* engage itself internationally in order to promote the protection of the environment—is even more important.

The 1987 Single European Act not only introduced in the EC Treaty an explicit mandate for European Community measures to address environmental issues. It also established environment protection as an important policy area of the EC, and endorsed international cooperation to pursue this policy. Since then, the EC Treaty provides competence to the Community and sets out the basis and direction for Community environmental policy, as well as the guiding principles for this policy:

> 1. Community policy on the environment shall contribute to pursuit of the following objectives:
>   — preserving, protecting and improving the quality of the environment;
>   — protecting human health;
>   — prudent and rational utilisation of natural resources;
>   — *promoting measures at international level to deal with regional and worldwide environmental problems.*
> 2. Community policy on the environment shall aim at a high level of protection taking onto account the diversity of situations in the various regions of the Community. It shall be based on *the precautionary principle* and on the principles that preventive action should be taken, that environmental damage should as a priority be rectified at source and that the polluter should pay.
>
> . . .
>
> 4. Within their respective spheres of competence, *the Community and the Member States shall cooperate with third countries and with the competent international organisations.* The arrangements for Community cooperation may be subject to agreements between the Community and the third parties concerned.
>
> The previous subparagraph shall be without prejudice to Member States' competence to negotiate in international bodies and to conclude international agreements.[4]

Of course, it is not possible to deduce directly from such treaty texts the actual measures taken or the engagement of the EU in the field of health and the environment—normative texts cannot be taken as a pretext that it 'is' as it 'ought to be'. Still, the impact of the drafting of the EC Treaty on the international environmental policy should not be underestimated. The clearly defined mission of the Community to act internationally and promote measures at the international level has a solid base in the quoted provision its practice of international environmental cooperation is also affected by the mixed competence of the Community and the Member States, to act in international fora and to conclude international agreements in the field of the environment. Finally, the international activities and arguments of the EU have on several occasions been tainted by the notion that environmental policy and law should be based on the precautionary principle, as set out in the quoted provisions, in the consideration of risks and uncertainties.

In Community law, international environmental agreements are 'mixed agreements'.[5] Thus, the EC participates in international environmental

[4] EC Treaty, Art 174; *ibid.* Emphasis added.

[5] A Rosas, 'Mixed Union—Mixed Agreements', in M Koskenniemi, *International Law Aspects of the European Union* (Kluwer Law International, The Hague, 1998) 125–18, makes the useful distinctions between 'parallel' and 'shared' competences, where the latter implies some sort of division of the rights and obligations contained in the international agreement.

cooperation and is a party to multilateral agreements in parallel with the EU Member States (all or some of them).[6] Despite significant coordination of activities between the EC and the Member States, the mixed competence can be frustrating for the rest of the world. First, mixed competence may confuse other parties as to who will actually negotiate a specific issue. Second, mixed competence complicates the assessment of who is legally responsible for the implementation of the agreement; the EC or the Member States? The described complexity has been considered in some agreements. Thus, according to the 1997 Kyoto Protocol (further discussed below), if the EC fails to meet its total reduction as set out by the protocol, responsibility will be transferred to each Member State.[7] In other cases, for example, the Convention on Biological Diversity, the EC and the Member States are obliged to clarify the allocation of responsibility to the other parties of the convention.[8]

In other areas, such as trade and fisheries, the allocation of competence between the Community and the Member States is different. While fisheries policy is formally part of the Community's exclusive competence, international agreements on fisheries may also pertain to issues which remain within the domain of the Member States, such as enforcement. For this reason, the 1995 Agreement Relating to the Conservation and Management of Straddling Fish Stocks and Highly Migratory Fish (to UNCLOS)—one of the major global agreement on fisheries—was also mixed (although on different legal grounds), and ratified by the Community as well as the Member States.[9]

Although the Community has exclusive competence also in the area of trade, when international agreements contain elements on environment and health as well as trade (which is the case in agreements concerning trade in chemicals, wastes, genetically modified organisms, and endangered species), the Community institutions and the Member States may have different mandates for different parts of the agreement. This requires further collaboration and clarification of competence and responsibility of the Community and the Member States, before and during the negotiations. Confusion and

[6] As observed by A Rosas, *ibid*, the 'mixity' may take different forms also with regard to international agreements with bearing on the protection of the environment. For accounts of the external competence of the EC in environmental contexts, see also J Jans, *European Environmental Law* (Amsterdam, Europa Law Publishing, 2000), pp 69–98; D Thieme, 'European Community External Relations in the Field of the Environment', in *European Environmental Law Review* [2001], pp 252–64; and G Loibl, 'The Role of the EU in the Formation of International Environmental Law,' 2 *Yearbook of European Environmental Law* (2002), 223–40.

[7] Kyoto Protocol, Art 6.

[8] Convention on Biological Diversity, Art 34.

[9] To this end, the EC made a declaration to the 1995 Agreement, clarifying the different competences, which is also relevant for the responsibility of taking the necessary measures of implementation. The case was different with the 1993 Agreement to Promote Compliance with International Conservation and Management Measures by Fishing Vessels on the High Seas. This Agreement was only ratified by the EC, but not by the Member States (Sweden and Cyprus are also parties, but they both ratified the agreement before joining the EU).

different political intentions also lead to legal disputes between the European Commission, the Council, the European Parliament, and individual Member States, eg concerning the legal basis for Community engagement.[10]

While the situation is formally different in negotiations where there is no mixed competence, collaboration of course still takes place between the Community institutions and the Member States. When the Commission proposes to enter into international negotiations, it needs the approval of the Member States, in the Council, and thus must act in concert with the Member States. The Community's ratification of the agreement is also decided by the Member States in the Council. Even so, with legal backing of the EC Treaty the Commission can push for measures to protect the environment even when some Member States put on the brakes, as long as there is a qualified majority in favour of the action among the Member States.[11]

The described disagreements among the Member States and in relation to the Commission before and during negotiations should not be underestimated, and they do require much coordination and collaboration. On the other hand, the EU has the advantage in international environmental negotiations and meeting of parties, of bringing huge delegations with representatives not only from the Commission and the Presidency of the Council, but also from the other Member States. In these cases, the representatives of the Member States will have to coordinate the work for their respective government with that of the EU. This need for coordinating the activities in negotiations has the positive effect, from the Member States' point of view, of giving more weight and substance to their argument—not least in relation to the USA, but also to other states—than if each Member States had acted unilaterally in the negotiations. In the same vein, if the EU Member States manage to agree and act in concert, they usually have better chances of influencing the legal development than if the they acted without such institutional coordination and cooperation. The back-flip of the coin, from a Member States perspective, is of course that it has to compromise and may not only pursue its own policy agenda.

3 MULTILATERALISM IN ENVIRONMENTAL COOPERATION

The main feature of the EU approach to international environmental concerns is not that it repeats the same arguments or concepts in each and every context. Rather, it is found in its consistent backing and promotion of *internationalism and multilateralism* as such. In the field of

[10] See for instance European Court of Justice, Opinion 2/00 [2001] *European Court Reports I* (ECR:I) 9713, concerning the 2000 Cartagena Protocol to the Convention on Biological Diversity; and C-94/03, *Commission v Council*, [2006] ECR:I 1; and C-178/03 *Commission v Parliament and Council*, [2006] ECR:I 107, concerning the 1998 Rotterdam Convention.

[11] EC Treaty, Arts 175 and 251.

the environment, the approach of the EU has also been to endorse legal structures and frameworks for such international cooperation; ie a kind of internationalism under 'the rule of law'.

Today, with some expectations, the EU participates in the most relevant global and regional multilateral arrangements. The topics of these agreements concern, inter alia, pollution of the atmosphere, the sea and fresh water, the control of hazardous chemicals and pesticides, genetically modified organisms and wastes, fishery, protection of nature and biodiversity,[12] as well as more horizontal issues, such as environmental decision-making and information, and environmental impact assessments. The EU is absent only in one area, viz oil pollution from ships. For a long time, it was controversial as to what extent the EU (EC) had any lawmaking competence, or possibility of participating in international cooperation concerning issues outside the territories of the Member States. Today, it is quite clear that the EU can be active internationally also in the field of oil pollution from ships.[13] Still, the EU is not a party to any agreement of global application, administered by the International Maritime Organization (IMO), with detailed regulations concerning oil pollution from ships. On the other hand, the EU participates, for instance, in the following agreements of global reach:[14]

1992 UN Framework Convention on Climate Change (UNFCCC), and the 1997 Kyoto Protocol
1985 Vienna Convention for the Protection of the Ozone Layer, and 1987 Montreal Protocol on Substances that Deplete the Ozone Layer (as amended)
1992 Convention on Biological Diversity (CBD), and 2000 Cartagena Protocol on Biosafety
1989 Basel Convention on the Control of Transboundary Movements of Hazardous Wastes and their Disposal
1998 Rotterdam Convention on the Prior Informed Consent Procedure for Certain Hazardous Chemicals and Pesticides in International Trade
2001 Stockholm Convention on Persistent Organic Pollutants
1982 UN Convention on the Law of the Sea (UNCLOS)
1994 UN Convention to Combat Desertification in those Countries Experiencing Serious Drought and/or Desertification, Especially Africa (CCD)

[12] For formal reasons, the EU has not been able to accede to the 1973 Convention on International Trade in Endangered Species of Wild Flora and Fauna. More than 20 years since the amendment of the convention was adopted, which would allow for such organisations to be a party, it still has not entered into force.

[13] J Jans, *European Environmental Law* (Groningen, Europa Law, 2000), pp 69–89.

[14] A useful link to the listed agreements is found at UNEP, www.unep.org//law/ (visited 18 May 2007).

1995 Agreement Relating to the Conservation and Management of Straddling Fish Stocks and Highly Migratory Fish (to UNCLOS)
1980 Convention on the Conservation of Antarctic Marine Living Resources
1979 Convention on the Conservation of Migratory Species of Wild Animals

Some of these agreements embrace more than 150 countries, which makes them truly global, while others have fewer parties, but from most regions. The 'global' character also differs from one regime to the other. Some agreements are concerned with problems which really are global in scope, for example climate change and ozone layer depletion. Others apply to issues which are not in each case global in scope, but which can be found in most parts of world. While the EU (EC as well as most of its Member States) participates in all these regimes, the USA is only involved in a few of them, relating to the Antarctica, the ozone layer, desertification, straddling fish stocks and climate change (only the 1992 UNFCCC, but not the Kyoto Protocol). In addition to the agreements of global application, the EU participates in numerous regional environmental agreements. The more restricted geographical applications have not prevented some of these agreements from being of global relevance. In a few cases where the agreements deal with politically interesting matters—eg public participation in environmental decision-making, environmental impact assessments, and the control of high risk installations—they have had some repercussions also outside Europe, eg by inspiring measures, action programmes, and discussions in other parts of the world.

An evident case of a regional environmental agreement reaching outside its defined area of application is the 1998 UNECE Convention on Access to Information, Public Participation in Decision-making and Access to Justice in Environmental Matters (Aarhus Convention). As the title of the convention indicates, the 40 parties (states in Europe, and North and Western Asia plus the EU) are obliged to ensure citizens' right to access to information, to participate in decision-making and to access to legal review procedures in environmental matters. This is a unique agreement, by defining at the international level what can be perceived as minimum standards of environmental democracy. The Aarhus Convention has laid bare further differences of Europe (including the EU) and the USA in the attitude to international law. As a member of the UN Economic Commission for Europe (UNECE), the USA can be a party to the Aarhus Convention, but it has decided not to join. Rather than encouraging the work within the Aarhus Convention, the USA expressed its dissatisfaction with parts of this regime, although the USA would comply better with the convention, had it been a party, than many of the existing parties.

Generally speaking, there is a greater trust and expectation in the EU Member States than in the USA of what the state can and should do; and this notion has rubbed off on the EU level and on its external activities and policies as well. Thus, there is an expectation in the EU that welfare issues should not only be dealt with by the Member States, but also at Community level, and this matters for its international activities concerning health and the environment. To this account should be added the far greater confidence in international solutions and international cooperation, as such, in the field of health and the environment in the EU compared with that of the US federal administration. Moreover, it is obvious that the action and attitude of the USA as such—its resistance to strengthening international environmental law and, as in the climate negotiations, to actually ruin international environmental cooperation—has contributed significantly to uniting the EU Member States.

4 COOPERATION WITHIN LEGAL STRUCTURES AND FRAMEWORKS

The described, confident approach of the EU to international environmental cooperation in general is accompanied by a preference to conducting this cooperation in legal forms and within legal structures and frameworks. This 'rule of law' ambition is not all that apparent or consistent. Still, it is reflected in the support for the adoption of multilateral agreements in general, and also by the promotion of the development of rules and institutions, which provide for legal structures in the agreements. One such example is the development of review procedures through compliance committees which now operate in several international environmental regimes and are standard elements in new regimes of a global scale (and in some regional regimes).

The establishment of compliance committees in the various environmental regimes can be seen as a soft, quasi-judicial substitute for more traditional dispute settlement or as a quasi-judicial means of dispute avoidance. Such committees have been set up eg under the 1997 Kyoto Protocol, 2000 Cartagena Protocol (trade in genetically modified organisms), Basel Convention (transboundary movements of hazardous wastes), 1987 Montreal Protocol (ozone layer depletion), and some regional conventions in Europe, such as the Aarhus Convention (public participation). Compliance committees do not operate as courts; they make no legally binding decision and they are not intended to resolve disputes in more traditional judicial ways. Still, they may contribute to clarifying if a state has failed to comply with the requirements of environment protection measures set out in the treaty in question. They may also help to clarify the interpretation of the agreement.[15]

[15] See generally G Ulfstein, T Marauhn and A Zimmermann (eds), *Making Treaties Work: Human Rights, Environment and Arms Control* (Cambridge, Cambridge University Press, 2007); and, with regard to state responsibility and compliance committees, M Koskenniemi, 'Breach of Treaty or Non-compliance? Reflections on the Enforcement of the Montreal Protocol', 3 *Yearbook of International Environmental Law* (1992), p 125.

Existing compliance committees operate with different degrees of independence, and with different degrees of activity, in relation to the parties to the agreement. The most independent compliance committee thus far operates under the Aarhus Convention. Drawing in part from committees under some international human rights regimes, the Aarhus Convention Compliance Committee makes its review of compliance independently from the parties, and it also examines compliance issues based on complaints ('communcations') from members of the public, ie from individuals and non-governmental organisations.[16] It communicates directly with the parties concerned and reports to the meeting of the parties about the parties' compliance with the requirements set out in the convention.[17]

The proceedings when the Compliance Committee of the Aarhus Convention was to be established, at the first Meeting of the Parties, in 2002, give an illustration of the different views of the EU and the USA about such an independent review body, with the mandate of also examining compliance on the basis of communications from members of the public. The USA, without being a party to the Aarhus Convention (but as a member of the UNECE), and thus with no possibility of blocking the decision on the compliance committee, made a statement that it would not recognise the compliance rules under the Aarhus Convention to be a precedent for compliance procedures in other multilateral environmental agreements. The EU reacted by expressing its support for the compliance mechanism and its conviction that it was fully compatible with international law.[18]

This incident is not just anecdotal; it also indicates different attitudes of the EU and the USA, although the USA has not generally blocked the establishment of compliance commitments in other regimes. The concern of the USA was rather the possible political impact of arrangements under the Aarhus Convention on other, globally applicable, environmental agreements. The EU favours the establishment of compliance committees in international environmental regimes, but it does not push for the Aarhus structure in other international environmental agreements. The composition and mandate of the compliance committee will depend on the content of the agreements and the geopolitical composition of the parties.

There are many possible explanations as to why the EU promotes a more 'legalistic' approach in international contexts. One such explanation can be found in the domestic experience of the EU itself, when adopting as well as

[16] The Compliance Committee was established by Decision I/7, at the first meeting of the parties in 2002. See *Report of the First Meeting of the Parties to the Aarhus Convention*, UN Doc ECEMP.PP/2 (17 Dec 2002), available at www.unece.org/env/pp/ (visited 25 Feb 2007).

[17] V Koester, 'The Convention on Access to Information, Public Participation in Decision-making and Access to Justice in Environmental Matters (Aarhus Convention)', in G Ulfstein et al, above n 15, p 193.

[18] V Koester, 'Review of Compliance under the Aarhus Convention: a rather Unique Compliance Mechanism', 2 JEEPL (2005), p 31.

applying environmental legislation. Community environmental policies are frequently expressed through legislation, and usually in the form of directives. Directives resemble international treaties by being addressed to the (Member) States and obliging them to fully implement the prescribed measures and restrictions. Hundreds of cases concerning the interpretation and application of environmental rules and principles have been decided by the European Court of Justice; and the Community institutions as well as the Member States are used to this method and form of cooperation in the EU. In the continuous legal processes before the European Court of Justice, the Member States and the Commission often disagree and side by either of the parties to give their support to the one or the other interpretation. Despite the differences in the international context, the notion of conducting international cooperation and policy development within legal frameworks and institutions, and under the rule of law, is not that unfamiliar for the EU. Rather the contrary.

The support of a legalistic, rule of law approach to international environmental cooperation is also in line with a more general conviction of the EU, on how to handle international issues and promote global governance. This is shown eg in its support of the Rome Statute of the International Criminal Court, ratified by all the EU Member States, but not by the USA.[19] Some see in this European attitude to international law and internationalism a sign of European 'weakness' and lost global power in its relation to the USA.[20] However, the present article shows the irrelevance of such a realist analysis with regard to global environmental concerns, including ecological security matters. One can of course discuss the success and effectiveness of some of the existing global environmental arrangements. Still they are the result of the efforts of the EU and likeminded states to establish global environmental regimes, by multilateral treaties, despite the opposition of the USA. Whatever the assessment, crude force would hardly have achieved more.

5 PRECAUTION AS A LEGAL PRINCIPLE

Each global environmental agreement may be unique in terms of objective, rationale and/or geographical scope, as well as its content, but certain structures, basic concepts and principles still recur in international agreements and policy documents. If such concepts and principles are endorsed by a great majority of states in various regimes of global application, they indicate a more general policy shift and may even imply a change in

[19] The international criminal court does not come under the Community competence in the EU, but under the common foreign and security policy. See, however, Council Common Position 2003/444/CFSP of 16 Jun 2003 on the International Criminal Court; 2003 OJ L150, p 67.

[20] See eg, R Kagan, 'Power and Weakness', *Policy Review*, June 2002.

general international law, thus reaching beyond the agreements in question. In accordance with the 'precautionary principle', as set out in the EC Treaty, the EU has in several international contexts pushed for the development of precaution as a principle in international law.

The precautionary principle pertains to the considerations of risks and uncertainties; ie standard concerns in most environmental contexts. Should an activity or a pesticide be allowed unless it is shown by 'full scientific certainty' that the activity or substance is harmful? Or, should it be possible to restrict the use or to impose safety measures, trade restrictions or even to prohibit an activity or substance if there are uncertainties as to its impact or risk indications about adverse effects? In most countries with some developed environmental legislation, safety measures can be requested already at the stage of risk, ie when there are indications that an activity or substance may or is likely to cause certain harmful effects. Yet, the ways of balancing risks and uncertainties against the costs of safety measures and restrictions may differ greatly.

No definition of the precautionary principle is given in the EC Treaty, nor is the principle clearly and consistently set out in Community legislation or in the jurisprudence of the European judicature.[21] However, the Commission has endeavoured to defining the scope of the precautionary principle more generally, and also attempted to clarify the impact of the precautionary principle for the EU common fisheries policy.[22]

The precautionary principle has been properly summarised as a 'principle for action in the face of uncertainty'[23] ie as a requirement to take preventive measures—including, if feasible, the ceasing or banning of an activity or substance—on the basis of risk calculations, even if no harm has yet occurred.

The precautionary principle can be implemented procedurally, eg when placing the burden of proof, whether a substance or an activity is harmful, on the person who wishes to use the substance or carry out the activity. In other contexts, applying the precautionary principle may result in stricter requirements of prior assessments and evaluations about the substance/activity, and in yet other cases it may lead to strict conditions

[21] See *Communication on the Precautionary Principle*, COM (2000) 1 (final), where the Commission holds that measures based on the precautionary principle should be proportional, non-discriminatory, consistent with similar measures taken, based on a cost-benefit examination, subject to review, and capable of assigning responsibility for the production of scientific evidence.

[22] Commission *Communication on the Application of the Precautionary Principle and Multiannual Arrangements for Setting TACs*; COM (2000) 803 (final).

[23] N de Sadeleer, *Environmental Principles: from Political Slogans to Legal Rules* (Oxford, Oxford University Press, 2002), pp 91–223 (quote at 221), describes the development of the precautionary principle, and analyses the concept and its practical applicability. The status of the precautionary principle is also discussed in N de Sadeleer (ed), *Implementing the Precautionary Principles: Approaches from the Nordic Countries, EU and USA* (London, Earthscan, 2007).

and restrictions imposed on the operator as soon as there is a sufficient indication of a risk.[24] Crucial in this regard is the required level of identified risk to justify an interference or a prohibition. For example, is some basis in scientific findings needed before it can justify restrictions? Or contrarywise, can an activity or the use of a chemical be banned or restricted until it is shown with sufficient degree of certainty that it is not harmful?

There would not be so much controversy if the application of the precautionary principle did not have any transboundary repercussions, but it does. It is not surprising that the disputes concerning the legal status of the precautionary principle arose mainly in relation to international trade. It is in this particular context that the EU and some other countries, among them Canada and the USA, have disagreed on whether the precautionary principle is a general principle of international law or a part of customary law; thus also embracing (and binding) states which are not parties to the agreements concerned. The main issue in these cases has been whether certain measures supposedly taken to protect the health and the environment violate international trade law.

The relation between international environmental law and trade law achieved a great deal of attention in the early 1990s, not least in relation to the finalising of the negotiations to establish the World Trade Organization (WTO). The issue was also discussed at the 1992 UN Conference on Environment and Development, in Rio de Janeiro 1992. The Rio Declaration sets out two relevant principles, which relate to environment protection and international trade:

> In order to protect the environment, the precautionary approach shall be widely applied by States according to their capabilities. Where there are threats of serious or irreversible damage, the lack of full scientific certainty shall not be used as a reason for postponing cost-effective measures to prevent environmental damage (Principle 15).
>
> Trade policy measures for environmental purposes should not constitute a means of arbitrary or unjustifiable discrimination or a disguised restriction on international trade. Environmental measures addressing transboundary or global environmental problems should, as far as possible, be based on an international consensus (Principle 12).[25]

The first item is an expression of the precautionary principle, the second of multilateralism in cases of conflict between environment protection measures and international trade. Both issues have been addressed in disputes under the WTO as well as in international environmental negotiations, not least between North America and Europe.

[24] E Rehbinder, 'The Precautionary Principle in an International Perspective', in EM Basse (ed), *Miljørettens grundspørgsmål* (Copenhagen, GEC GAD, 1994), p 91.

[25] UN Declaration on Environment and Development (Rio de Janeiro, 4–13 Jun 1992, reprinted in 31 *International Legal Materials* (1992)), p 876.

In 1996, in the *Hormone Meat* Case, the USA and Canada brought the EU (EC) to the mandatory dispute settlement procedure in the WTO, and asked the Dispute Settlement Body to declare that the Community rules on the prohibition of import of meat and meat products treated with hormones for growth purposes were in violation of the WTO Agreement on the Application of Sanitary and Phytosanitary Measures (SPS Agreement).[26] The SPS Agreement is intended to prevent the WTO members from invoking sanitary or phytosanitary measures when the real reason behind the trade restrictions is to protect the domestic producers and products from imports. To this end, it sets out when the WTO members may take sanitary and phytosanitary measures, with potential effects on trade, for the protection of human, animal or plant life or health. No WTO agreement contains any explicit reference to the precautionary principle, but the SPS Agreement allows the WTO members to take safety measures affecting the import provided they are based on scientific findings. They may also introduce temporary trade restrictions if they think that existing scientific material is incomplete. Thus, some fragments of the precautionary principle are reflected in the WTO.

However, the EU (EC) had asked the Dispute Settlement Body in its defence to consider the precautionary principle which, according to the EU, was part of customary international law. The USA and Canada opposed the statement that the principle was part of general international law, and thus applicable also to states not parties to the relevant environmental agreements. According to the Appellate Body of the Dispute Settlement Body, it was 'less than clear' whether the WTO members considered the principle a part of general or customary international law. However, there was still a possibility for the EU to base its defence on the SPS Agreement. The problem for the EU—and its credibility—was that it did not succeed in presenting one single document to prove the risk for health from meat or meat products treated with hormones for growth purposes (moreover, hormone treatment of meat was allowed in the EU for other purposes than growth). The EU lost the case, but the Appellate Body in many ways interpreted the relevant WTO agreements in a rather environmental way. It recognised that WTO members may introduce sanitary measures with trade implications based on proper risk assessment, and that they may apply a higher standard of sanitary protection than set out in international standards and

[26] WTO Appellate Body Report, *EC Measures Concerning Meat and Meat Products (Hormones)*, WT/DS26/AB/R and WT/DS48/AB/R, 16 Jan 1998. Precautionary measures and risk assessments were also part of other WTO disputes, eg WTO Appellate Body Report, *Australia—Measures Affecting Importation of Salmon*, WT/DS18/AB/R, 20 Oct 1998; and *Japan—Measures Affecting Agricultural Products*, WT/DS76/AB/R, 22 Feb 1999. Cases available at www.wto.org (visited).

guidelines. Yet a WTO member cannot abstain from proper risk assessment by determining its own appropriate level of protection to be 'zero risk'.[27]

The EU faired slightly better in promoting the precautionary principle in the global environmental agreements negotiated after the WTO *Hormone Meat* Case. The principle was one of the core issues in the negotiations of the agreement concerning safety and trade in certain ('living') genetically modified organisms; what was to become the 2000 Cartagena Protocol on Biosafety to the CBD. One of the reasons why these negotiations were postponed was a disagreement about risk assessments and considerations. While the USA did not formally participate in the negotiations (not being a party to the CBD), it had a great impact on the negotiations through 'allies'. Finally, the agreement was clearly influenced by the precautionary principle, as proposed by the EU. The Cartagena Protocol sets out that, while subject to certain procedures, the parties may prevent the import of genetically modified organisms covered by the agreement (pharmaceuticals, for instance, are not included). According to the Cartagena Protocol—which again is the most comprehensive treaty on trade in genetically modified organisms (with more than 130 parties)—'in accordance with the precautionary approach contained in Principle 15 of the Rio Declaration', the objective is to contribute to an adequate level of protection in the field of safe transfer, handling and use of living modified organisms. It also provides for a certain form and procedure of the risk assessment.

Once new legal concepts become generally accepted and established in international environmental documents, they tend to rub off on other, newer treaties as well. Thus, the 'succeeding' global environmental agreement—the 2001 Stockholm Convention on Persistent Organic Pollutants—also provides that 'mindful of the precautionary approach as set forth in Principle 15 of the Rio Declaration on Environment and Development, the objective of this Convention is to protect human health and the environment from persistent organic pollutants'. Just like the Cartagena Protocol, the Stockholm Convention has achieved a large number of parties (more than 130 states and the EU). The USA signed the Convention, but at the time of writing had not ratified it.

These and other developments, eg the 2002 Johannesburg Plan of Implementation of the World Summit on Sustainable Development,[28] indicate that the EU and likeminded parties have been able to establish precaution as core concept in international environmental law and policy. While the concept was not included in the 1998 Rotterdam Convention

[27] N de Sadeleer, *Environmental Principles*, above n 23, pp 105–7.

[28] 2002 Johannesburg Plan of Implementation of the World Summit on Sustainable Development, Paras 23 and 109, endorsed by the UN General Assembly in its Resolution 57/353 of 20 Dec 2002.

concerning trade in chemicals and pesticides, adopted prior the Cartagena Protocol, it came into light in some European environmental agreements (concerning the marine environments of the Baltic Sea, North-East Atlantic, and Mediterranean) to which the EU is a party.[29] There has not yet been any further clarification by the WTO Dispute Settlement Body about the application of the precautionary principle,[30] but the given developments in global contexts suggest that it be considered also in WTO disputes. According to the WTO Dispute Settlement Body, it may not apply other international treaties agreements than those covered by the WTO in its decision-making, but it is bound by general international law. Reinforcing the precautionary principle in international environmental law and policy increases the scope of states for taking safety measures, unilaterally or multilaterally, also when affecting trade on the basis of risk for harm to health and the environment.

6 CLIMATE CHANGE NEGOTIATIONS—THE ACID TEST

The climate change negotiations, before, during and after the 1997 Kyoto Protocol, have probably been given more attention than any other global environmental negotiations. They have also come to symbolise the diverging views on global environmental problems and cooperation of the EU and the USA. The climate change regime involves all elements characterising global environmental concerns, eg uncertainties as to certain causal links as well as social and economic consequences, the North-South dimension, and strong lobbying. The uncertainty is not centred around the question of whether human activities have added to the concentration of carbon dioxide in the atmosphere, or whether human activities have contributed to the greenhouse effect and the increasing temperature—they have.[31] There are disagreements as to the likely consequences of these changes.

[29] The precautionary principle is also essential in the 1995 Agreement Relating to the Conservation and Management of Straddling Fish Stocks and Highly Migratory Fish, Arts 5 and 6.

[30] In the *Biotech Products* Case, WT/DE291-293 (29 Sep 2006) Canada and the USA claim that the EU rules on biotech products affect the import of agricultural products in a way which is not compatible with the WTO. In its report (of more than 1000 pp), the Panel held that the Community rules and measures violate the WTO in several ways. In particular, the decision concerns the moratorium of permits for biotech products in the EU, and whether individual Member States had scientific ground for their prohibitions, but it does not clarify the status of the precautionary principle in international law.

[31] According to the Intergovernmental Panel on Climate Change, *Climate Change 2007: The Physical Science Base. Summary for Policymakers* (Paris, Feb 2007), global atmospheric concentrations of various greenhouse gases have increased markedly by human activities in the last centuries, leading to '*very high confidence* that globally averaged net effect of human activities since 1750 has been one of warming, with a radiative forcing of +1.6 [+0.6 to +2.4] W m^{-2}' .

Despite increasing consensus as to the contribution of human activities to climate change, there are also scientific and economic uncertainties in the calculations.

The scientific uncertainties were even greater in 1992, so it is not surprising that the 1992 UNFCCC was structured as a framework convention with no precise commitments on how to cut down the introduction of green house gases. The EU, the USA and more than 180 states ratified the UNFCCC. Rather than committing themselves to targets or reduction quotas, however, the parties mainly recognise that climate change is a common concern, and that the parties have common but differentiated responsibility to protect the climate system. The precautionary principle is set out among the principles of the 1992 UNFCCC.[32] It was made clear already in 1992 that several states wanted the framework convention to be followed up by a protocol with binding commitments (as was done in the 1987 Montreal Protocol to the 1985 Vienna Convention for the Protection of the Ozone Layer).

The 1997 Kyoto Protocol specifies the obligations of the industrial countries to cut down emission of greenhouse gases. The EU is obliged to reduce its emissions by 8 per cent and the USA (provided it acceded) by 7 per cent. If the prescribed reduction levels are complied with by all industrial states (including the USA), the calculated total reduction of emissions of green house gases by these states is about 5 per cent in the period of 2008–12. This is far from the reduction levels needed to stabilise the concentration of the carbon dioxide in the atmosphere.

However, the American Senate declared already in 1997, before the Kyoto Protocol was adopted, that the USA would not ratify a climate agreement unless it set out some commitments also for the developing countries. Despite this act of the Senate, the federal administration of president Bill Clinton did sign the protocol, but never submitted it for ratification by the Senate, since it was not going to be approved. After the shift of power in the US federal administration, George W Bush stated that the USA was not going to ratify the Kyoto Protocol, but instead intended to withdraw its signature of the protocol. The reason, according to him, was that the Kyoto Protocol was 'fatally flawed in fundamental ways', not least because neither India nor China were subject to commitments in the Protocol.[33] Many feared at the time that the Kyoto Protocol had come to a dead end, partly because the USA is an important player in global negotiations in general, partly because the US withdrawal made the entry into force of the protocol more complicated.

[32] Art 3(3).

[33] Speech given by President George W Bush 11 Jun 2001. http://www.whitehouse.gov/news/(visited 22 Feb 2007).

Quite possibly, the US decision to withdraw from the Kyoto Protocol spurred the public and the political segment of the EU, because the EU actually increased its engagement at this time in order to get other states to ratify it. This was important from a legal point of view, since the Kyoto Protocol, with all its shortcomings, was the only climate change accord present, and it would take much effort and time to draft a new treaty. The symbolic and political value of keeping the Kyoto Protocol was equally important from the EU position, since it showed the capacity to mobilise other states despite the US withdrawal and, indeed opposition. The ratification of Russia finally made it possible for the Kyoto Protocol to enter into force in 2005.

In the meantime, the signatories negotiated on a number of issues to improve the compliance with the Kyoto Protocol, eg by the establishment of a Compliance Committee, and the development of the different flexible mechanisms, aiming at reaching the prescribed levels of reduction in a cost-effective way. Although it is still far from sure that the parties will achieve the reduction levels set out by the protocol in the period of 2008–12, discussions have commenced on commitments beyond 2012, when the first commitment period ends. As pointed out, stabilisation of greenhouse gases in the atmosphere would require much greater reductions by Europe, the USA and other industrialised countries than some 5 per cent. It would also need to somehow involve the developing countries. At the time of writing (November 2007), the EU has not yet taken a common position on the objective beyond 2012, and is even further away from defining its means.

The climate change negotiations nevertheless confirm the approach of the EU to multilateralism. They also illustrate the preference of the EU to maintaining international negotiations and cooperation within legal frameworks; with legally binding commitments. This can be compared with the contrary position of the US federal administration, as shown eg in the Asia-Pacific Partnership on Clean Development, launched by the USA, in part as a means to address climate change, but with no legal commitments for the states concerned. Finally, the climate change negotiations reveal a greater sensitivity of the EU than the USA to the situation and arguments of the developing countries. The far greater contributions by the industrialised countries, in terms of per capita emissions, compared to most developing countries explain why the Kyoto Protocol, in this first phase, only prescribes reduction levels for the industrialised countries. The Kyoto Protocol thus reflects the principle of common but differentiated responsibilities, set out in the UNFCCC, and some degree of distributive justice. Without focusing on the industrialised countries only in this first phase, the Kyoto Protocol would not have achieved the required number of approvals and the legitimacy of the developing countries.

7 IMPLEMENTATION OF INTERNATIONAL COMMITMENTS IN THE EU

The credibility of the EU in international environmental contexts is highly dependant on the measures taken by the EU and its Member States back home, to comply with the international agreements. Generally speaking, the Community structure as such, with supranational legislation and a relatively effective judicature, add to the effective compliance by the EU members states with international agreements. For several EU Member States, their environmental law is a direct result of European environmental legislation, and some Member States would hardly have any such law at all without Community legislation. Moreover, the Community structure adds to the implementation of international environmental agreements also by Member States with developed environmental laws and functioning environmental administrations.

Most European environmental legislation is made in the form of directives, to be transformed into national laws by the Member States, in order to be applicable to national courts and authorities, individuals and corporations. In terms of content and structure, while directives resemble international treaties, Community law in some cases (but not always) is more ambitious than the underlying international accord. Still, the main difference between an international agreement and the supranational structure of the EU (EC) is institutional. Even though Community environmental law and policy suffer from many shortcomings in terms of implementation deficit, the rules and principles on environment protection are surrounded by institutions, players and procedures which, in all, provide for more effective implementation than institutions of international law.

Despite the various compliance committees and reporting systems set up in most regimes of global reach, the poor means available for requesting independent reviews of compliance remain a weak spot in international environmental cooperation. Once the EU (EC) is a party to an international treaty and has adopted legislation for its purpose, the Commission may supervise the implementation of the Member States. If they fail, which is quite common, the Commission can push them to comply better, by bringing them to the European Court of Justice. In addition, national courts may ask the European Court of Justice for interpretive instructions (preliminary ruling) concerning the application and implementation by the Member States of Community legislation and international agreements. This gives the European Judiciary an important role in the application of European law. Lacking an international forum for reviewing compliance with the international agreement, the European Judiciary may also take on that function with regard to the EU Member States.

In addition to considering international obligations indirectly, when interpreting and applying Community legislation, the European Court of Justice has taken an active and direct role to effectively implement and enforce international environmental agreements. This is shown in cases where the Court considered and referred to international environmental agreements, in support of trade-restricting measures taken by a Member State.[34] The Court has also asserted a conformist interpretation of European Community law in light of the international obligations.[35] Finally, the European Court of Justice has held that, in some cases, international environmental treaties to which the Community is party shall be 'directly' applied and interpreted by national courts and authorities. [36] It follows that, where the relevant treaty provisions fall within Community competence, the European Judiciary may add to the implementation of international obligations by EU Member States. In so doing, the Court assesses whether the Member State has taken sufficient measures to fulfil the international obligations. Its jurisprudence also provides for national courts to be more active in the direct application of international treaties, when the state in question has not taken sufficient measures to adequately implement the treaty provisions.[37]

The activities of the Commission, the European Court of Justice, the national courts and the members of the public, in trying to have international agreements applied in domestic cases, are not sufficient to ensure compliance with international law. Yet, they may contribute to strengthening the implementation of the agreements and thus to approaching the agreed objectives.

8 STRATEGY CHOICE

There are many reasons for comparing the different strategies of the EU and the USA to global environmental cooperation, one of them being that the strategy choice matters for the development of international environmental law. However, in assessing the attitude and strategy of the EU to global environmental cooperation, such a comparison is not really relevant, since the EU and the USA are not aiming in the same direction. A shift in the EU to a more inward-looking approach, in line with that of the USA, would not only amount to a shift of strategy, but indeed to a shift of policy; in this case a considerable reduction in the ambition. Therefore, without such an indication of policy shift (of which there is none at the time of writing), a comparison of strategies makes little sense. Deciding on the priority and relative weight of environmental and health concerns vis-à-vis other issues is a political rather than legal matter, but a policy shift in the EU towards

[34] See C-2/90,*Commission v Belgium* (Vallonian Waste Case) [1992] European Court Reports I (ECR:I) 4471, and C-67/97, *Ditliv Blumhe* (Danish Bees Case) [1998] ECR:I 8033.

[35] C-341/95, *Gianni Bettati v Safety Hi-Tech Srl* [1998] ECR:I 4355; see also C-284/95, *Safety Hi-Tech v S&T Srl* (1998) ECR:I 4301.

[36] C-213/03, *Syndicat professionnel coordination des pêcheurs de l'étang de Berre et de la région v Electricité de France* [2004] ECR:I 7357.

[37] See also C-239/03, *Commission v France* [2004] ECR:I 9325.

that of the USA would actually also trigger legal considerations. While the Community legislature retains quite a leeway in striking the balance between the different objectives and principles set out in the EC Treaty, the Treaty nevertheless implies some legal constraints,[38] eg by prescribing a high level of environment protection and active international cooperation as a means for dealing with regional and worldwide environmental problems.

An assessment of the EU strategy for international cooperation and multilateralism should rather look at what has been achieved. Although it is difficult to generalise, the climate change negotiations reveal the relative strength of the European strategy in pushing and keeping an important regime alive; in this case despite the complexity of the issue at stake and despite the opposition of the USA. One explanation for this achievement is, again, the relative sensibility of the EU to the arguments and views of developing countries. Without this attitude, developing countries would have been less convinced about the merits of approving the Kyoto Protocol. There are other examples where the EU has been slightly more sensible than other industrialised regions to justice arguments from developing countries, for instance in the negotiations on access and benefit sharing of genetic resources in the framework of the Convention on Biological Diversity.

Such attitudes matter in international environmental law- and policy-making. Despite economic globalisation and the continuous discourse on the withering of the state, global environmental cooperation is still much carried out in the form of intergovernmental arrangements and multilateral agreements, with all related weaknesses and shortcomings. Non-governmental actors and actions have become more significant in international environmental collaboration, but in many cases these activities are also somehow related to intergovernmental institutions and agreements. When drafting these agreements and establishing cooperative structures, states are, formally speaking, participating on a voluntary basis, and they only become bound by agreements to which they consent. There are of course informal means to bring pressure to bear on states or to entice states to participate in the agreement; and some countries and regions also have greater influence on the negotiations than others. Even so, the voluntariness of entering into environmental agreements implies that all concerned parties must perceive that they benefit from joining the venture, or at least that they are worse off outside. While voluntariness adds to the legitimacy of international environmental law, it also makes international governance a tardy matter.

Provided a sustained ambition of EU environmental policy, lacking more effective global institutions—whether supranational or otherwise beyond the Westphalian state paradigm—there is nothing to indicate that, from a European position, cutting down the degree of international cooperation or

[38] Cf C-284/95, *Safety High-Tech* [1998] ECR:I 4301; and C-341/95, *Gianni Bettati* [1998] ECR:I 4355.

neglecting the views of the South would be rational. Rather, exactly these attitudes seems to have had an important impact in the negotiations. While the choice of policy and strategy reveals the approach taken to global concerns and solidarity, even a realist reading of the European approach seems to support—at least in some cases—the international strategy taken by the EU so far. As a general approach to international environmental law, a more coercive strategy would hardly have been more successful.[39]

This assessment does not suggest that the EU has done 'enough' or that the measures taken are sufficiently effective or fair to promote the objective of sustainable development, as set out in the treaties establishing the EU. As already mentioned, there are many examples of how the EU has taken up a hard stance when negotiating with developing countries in environmental matters, and cases where the environmental ambitions of the EU surrendered in favour of strong economic interests (fishery), where the EU has promoted selfish interests rather than environmental considerations (GATS negotiations), and where the arguments and measures allegedly taken to promote the environment rather covered up for protectionism. Despite these observations of internal conflicts, clashes of interests, compromises and self interest, it remains remarkable that the EU stands out as being able to push for a more active, and sometimes radical, international environmental policy than most industrialised countries and regions.

One can always wish for more: more resolute international measures to avoid negative environmental impacts, more effective control systems to achieve compliance, greater sensitivity towards developing countries, and so on. Still, without the impact of the EU on global environmental agreements so far, many of them would be even less resolute than today, the control would quite likely be worse, and the sensitivity of the industrialised countries to the views of developing countries would be even weaker. International environmental cooperation is already poor, but it would be even poorer without the EU. The political and legal structure of the EU has contributed to the strategy and positioning of the EU in global environmental contexts. While the EU may provide a useful model for environmental cooperation in other regions of the world,[40] it is difficult to foresee an analogous development of a supranational structure or institution for global environmental cooperation. In the short term perspective, however, the strategic choice and policy choice of the EU itself—whether it will reduce, maintain or increase its international commitments—will be instrumental for the future direction of global cooperation and international environmental law.

[39] It is quite another matter, that in individual cases, where the activities of/in one state seriously threaten another state, coercive measures may be more relevant.

[40] For a discussion, whether the EC offers a model for global environmental cooperation, see L Krämer, 'The EU: a Regional Model?' in G Winter (ed) *Multilevel Governance of Global Environmental Change* (Cambridge,Cambridge University Press, 2006), pp 333–57.

3

The Complications of Formulating a National Environmental Action Plan

FILIP BLADINI*

1 INTRODUCTION

DIFFERENT ASPECTS OF sustainable consumption and concern for the environment give rise to a flood of initiatives for change, not only in Sweden but also all over the world. These initiatives dominate the political agenda and produce schemes for practical change in the form of political proposals, action plans, research projects etc. They come in such vast numbers it is difficult for the general public to evaluate them and keep them apart. Among these initiatives and proposals *government authorities and government inquiries* stand out, as we have reasons to believe that their opinions and proposals are well considered and have noteworthy democratic support. However, this does not mean that they are politically uncontroversial. But in a political democracy the majority rules.

Proposals for domestic legislation within the European Union should not only fulfil national political goals, if applicable they must also respect EC law principles. Particularly principles connected to the four freedoms play an important role in the debate of what is considered to be in accordance with EC law or not. When policies for a sustainable development are to be broken down into concrete and practical measures Member States face many challenges. Governments wanting to take the lead for change by using sharp and radical measures stand an apparent risk of coming into conflict with EC principles. Perhaps this is not surprising; it is a known phenomenon throughout history. However it is remarkable that many proposals for a switch-over to a more sustainable society are inadequately assessed from an EC law perspective.

* Associate professor in private law and a senior lecturer at the School of Business, Economics and Law, Göteborg University.

For the purpose of this article, I will use the proposals from the so-called Edman inquiry suggesting an action plan for sustainable consumption for the household sector in Sweden.[1] Mr Stefan Edman, who led the inquiry, is a biologist and author of many books about the environment and society. He is a former political adviser on environmental issues to Sweden's prime minister and ministers for the environment. The inquiry was finished in May 2005 and the proposals were generally discussed in Swedish media. The Edman inquiry is chosen because of its wide scope of proposals relating to many sectors of Swedish society and hence also to a number of EC law principles. Even though the starting point is a Swedish perspective, the analysis has general implications for all Member States formulating environmental actions plans, showing many pitfalls which may lead to infringements of EC law. It seems like these pitfalls are not always fully realized.

With the proposals of the inquiry as a background, the article will look into the nature of environmental law discourse in relation to contemporary societal crossroads having to do with sustainability in a broad sense. A frequent and recurrent theme is the delicacy of 'trade offs' between different interests. But what is a greater problem—and not emphasised enough—is the division in two arenas, making the discourse compartmentalised. In one arena environmental experts dominate without deeper preference or knowledge of legal perspectives of free movement of goods. In the other arena we find experts on the economic side of law, like internal market law, trade and competition law. If we want results, one cannot exist without the other. Yet, each arena seems to stick to itself, not taking the other side seriously. This is a crucial obstacle on the way towards a more sustainable society, particularly as trade related objections normally work as trump cards, overriding environmental concerns. The aim of this article is not to deliberately take sides, but merely to give a practical example of this process from a Swedish perspective. It will show that discrepancies between law and policy on the community level seldom resolve themselves as intended on the national arena. Instead the same inconsistencies are transferred to the national level, leaving the crucial issues just as they were at the beginning.

To begin with, I will outline the rationale behind initiatives for sustainable consumption in relation to trade and market obstacles. Policy declarations from the community level are scrutinised, as are how these policies have been understood by Swedish authorities. Policies focusing on trade and competition are not always commensurable with those referring to sustainable

[1] The inquiry presented two reports, one in Dec 2004, Official Report SOU 2004:119 Uthålliga laster. Konsumtion för en ljusare framtid (Sustainable Burdens—Consumption for a brighter future) and a second one with proposals in May 2005, Official Report SOU 2005:51 Bilen, Biffen, Bostaden. Hållbara laster—smartare konsumtion (The car, the beef, the house. Sustainable Burdens—Smarter consumption). The latter is used for reference in this article.

development. Hereafter, the main proposals of the Edman inquiry are presented, with emphasis on proposals affecting public procurement, product labelling of origin, VAT levels and State Aid. Subsequently these themes will be analysed under separate headings, focusing on reactions from government authorities to the proposals in the light of EC law principles, with finally, some concluding remarks.

2 TRADE AND THE ENVIRONMENT—FROM COMMUNITY TO DOMESTIC LAW

Regulatory as well as policy initiatives taken by governments and international organisations on the topic of environmental issues and sustainable development are vast and cover so many aspects that it is difficult to get an accurate overview of the area. It stretches from declarations by bodies like The World Commission on Environment and Development (the Brundtland Commission) all the way down to national action programmes with suggested measures for an ecological, social and economical sustainable consumption. In between we find policy declarations as well as regulatory instruments in specific areas, such as trade, energy, transport, consumer policy etc. To further complicate the picture this takes place in different regulatory levels; ie global, regional and local level.

A recurring theme in this article is the legal definitions used to classify on the one side products and on the other side production processes and methods. Distinctions like these are important as one way or another, they will separate what are considered to be sustainable products from non-sustainable ones. The theme is recurring in the sense that the initial question of separating one product from another is the same, however as we will see, the legal technique for doing so is different depending on the applicable legal construction. An example, which will not be further dealt with in this article, is found within the framework of WTO and the Agreement on Government Procurement (GPA).[2] Community membership include an obligation to follow the agreement. Even if it is reasonable to believe that harmonised measures on Community level, eg for organic production, makes it possible to define such products as products of their own if they comply with the Directive, it is uncertain whether the same conclusion

[2] WTO Members are, under GATT, free to favour domestic products in the context of government procurement, thereby allowing discrimination on ground of nationality. This is an exemption from the important principle of Most Favoured Nation treatment that requires that an advantage granted to any product, shall be accorded to *like products* originating in or destined for the territories of any other Member. Art III of the GPA restores the balance by establishing the principle of non-discrimination, ensuring national treatment and Most Favoured Nation treatment to all products. See further P Van den Bossche, *The Law and Policy of the World Trade Organization, Text, Cases and Materials,* (Cambridge University Press 2005) p 478 f.

is likely under the GPA. In this context the term 'like products' is decisive and it is not evident that the production method is included at all in this assessment.[3]

A suitable starting point for analysis is Article 6 of the EC Treaty that states that 'environmental protection requirements must be integrated into the definition and implementation of the Community polices and activities referred to in Article 3, in particular with a view to promoting sustainable development'. This obligation on horizontal integration was introduced into EC law through the Amsterdam Treaty, entered into force in 1999.[4] Article 6 limits the discretionary margin of the institutions when legislating and in their decision-making.[5] Furthermore, it should be mentioned that the wording of Article 6 implies that only the institutions of the Community are concerned and thus leaving environmental initiatives of Member States outside the scope of Article 6. This is of course true, but in areas which have not been harmonised it is possible to recognise an obligation, based on Article 6 and the principle of Community loyalty in Article 10 ECT as 'a (passive) obligation to refrain from adopting policies which could complicate or hinder the (future) achievement or observance of the principle in Article 6'[6]. According to this statement Article 6 becomes both a facilitator of environmental protection as well as an obstacle for Member States that want to move forward in a faster pace.

After the Amsterdam Treaty the fundamental rules on Community policy on the environment are found in Article 174 ECT. In Article 174 (1) we find the objectives to preserve, protect and improve the quality of the environment and protect human health, as well as a careful utilisation of natural resources and measures to deal with regional and worldwide environmental problems. Further on, in Article 174 (2) a number of important principles are laid down, such as the precautionary principle, the principle of prevention, the polluter pay principle and that damages should primarily be rectified at the source. Finally in Article 174 (3) we find obligations for the Community to take into account a number of circumstances when preparing its policies, such as available scientific and technical data,

[3] However, the notion of distinguishing between products on the basis of their production method as being GATT-illegal has been challenged. See R Howse and D Regan, 'The Product/Process Distinction—An Illusory Basis for Disciplining Unilateralism in Trade Policy' (2000) (11) *European Journal of International Law*, pp 249–89.

[4] Treaty of Amsterdam amending the Treaty on European Union, the Treaties establishing the European Communities and related Acts, Official Journal C 340, 10/11/1997.

[5] Some commentators consider horizontally applicable clauses as the result of an inflation process and as political declarations of little material impact. However, it has been argued that Article 6 should be taken more seriously than other horizontal clauses, because of its well-defined requirements, specific aim, elaborative context, strong wording and exceptional place in the Treaty. N Dhont *The Integration of Environmental Protection into other EC Policies*, (Groningen, Europa Law Publishing, 2003), p 27 and p 108.

[6] N Dhont *The Integration of Environmental Protection into other EC Policies, ibid*, p 38.

existing environmental conditions, potential benefits and costs of both actions and lack of actions.

The legal relevance of Article 6 and Article 174 seems to be heavily debated. Different views are represented, everything from that they are merely political guidelines to binding norms which if violated would render the Community Act invalid.[7] In his monograph on the Integration of Environmental Protection into other EC Policies, Nele Dhondt penetrates the relevant literature and the applicable case law. His conclusion is that Articles 6 and 174 are not applicable in an all-or-nothing fashion, but rather point to a certain direction, and that the institutions have a wide discretion when applying these provisions. He points out that it's not a question of a mechanical approach and in a situation of conflict with other rules or principles, these conflicting rules in a given situation could be given priority, making the application of the integration principle impossible.[8]

Now then, if it is from time to time argued that environmental law principles are not taken seriously, the opposite is at times said about free-trade-related legal instruments. In the strive for the creation of a single European market, trade and competition law in a wide sense have always been very important. The rules relating to the free movement of goods and particularly the interpretation of the provisions for the elimination of non-tariff barriers to trade in Article 28 to 31, guarantees the free flow of goods, securing it from restriction or other quantitative measures taken by Member States.

From an economic perspective the principle of integration could be understood as a requirement of internalising external costs, like environmental costs, into the total cost of a product. Through this operation the price of a product will reflect the true impact on the environment. This logic results in the effect that the more environmentally friendly the product is, the cheaper it becomes. Hence, the trick is to add all costs from a non-sustainable production into the product's price. This would also be in accordance with the polluter pays principle. However, this theory does not seem to be confirmed by empirical evidence. Environmentally friendly products, eco-labelling etc, always seem to make products more costly and policy instrument often focus on how to inform consumers, creating an environmental awareness and thereby a demand for environmentally friendly products.

A competitive market presupposes a variety of market actors, which implies both market harmonisation to create equal opportunities to compete, but also market differentiation as an incentive to develop the economy further. This reveals the double sided nature of EC trade and competition law. On the one hand it promotes standardisation and streamlining of

[7] N Dhont, *ibid*, p 182 and there cited literature.
[8] N Dhont, *ibid*, p 182.

products, setting foreseeable rules for competition favouring the most efficient market actors. This process would make non-sustainable products more costly and the sustainable and environmentally friendly ones less expensive. This side of efficiency is normally called production efficiency, as it favours actors who attain more output at the same level of input, or increase output with the same input of resources. This supply side perspective makes it easier to compare prices and hence reward the most efficient producers. The theory of production efficiency also goes hand in hand with general principles of EC law regarding the elimination of non-tariff barriers to trade in non-harmonised areas according to Articles 28–30. Domestic environmental requirements on products will easily be targeted as quantitative restrictions or measures having equivalent effect. Even though harmonisation and internalisation of environmental costs could be said to be the ultimate goal of EC trade and environmental law, the road to the goal is long and winding. The barriers to achieve harmonisation on environmental standards on products or production are extensive, balancing the opinions of different lobby groups up to the point where political consensus is reached.

On the other hand economic theory says that markets function best with as little government involvement as possible. Deregulation, or rather re-regulation has been a world wide trend since the late 1980s, advocating abolishment of state control and ownership, opening up new markets for competition. In theory a regulated market will disturb the proper communication between producers and consumers which supposedly automatically decides demand and supply according to the principle of the invisible hand. Of course, this is an oversimplified analysis but it highlights another important aspect of the concept of economic efficiency: allocation efficiency. A market is an unwieldy organism and consumer demand will allocate the resources to production of what the market wants. It doesn't matter how efficiently you produce if there is no demand for your product. By affecting the demand side it could be said that it is an outflow of allocation efficiency to refrain from standardising product markets and instead promote increasing demand for environmentally friendly products as well as facilitate production and distribution of such products.

It seems to be a political consensus to strive for ways of integrating sustainable development into practical concepts on the national level. The Commission's Communication on an Integrated Product Policy (IPP),[9] stresses the importance to work with consumption and to give consumers, including industry and public administration, access to information which is relevant, trustworthy and easy to understand. The Commission also points out that it is up to the Member States to decide what is needed to

[9] COM (2003) 302 final. Brussels 18 Jun, 2003.

achieve the level of consciousness necessary for consumer to take their full responsibility in the process of adapting environmentally friendly products. Late in 2003, the Council welcomed the conclusion of the Communication and encouraged Member States to implement national strategies.[10] IPP outlines a strategy for reducing the negative environmental impacts of products throughout their lifecycle. IPP aims to improve coherence within the economic and legal framework, strengthen access to life-cycle information and eventually by 2007 lead up to identification of products that have the greatest potential for environmental improvement.[11] Obviously harmonisation would be the most effective way of implementing an IPP policy, which also is underlined by the Commission in its Green Paper from 2001. Still, Member States are expected to drive the process forward, with the Commission in a supporting role. In Sweden a number of research reports have been produced focusing on legislative matters, highlighting the diminishing national scope for regulating products, but also the considerable uncertainty even in harmonised areas.[12]

So what do the Swedish experiences tell us so far? In a report from 1998 named 'Environment, Trade and Competition—rules for effective markets',[13] three Swedish agencies; the National Board of Trade,[14] the Swedish Competition Authority and the Agency for Economic and Regional Growth,[15] evaluated the domestic environmental legislative process as well as put forward recommendations for a future course of action. The report is often cited by authorities in the comprehensive Swedish system of referral, which takes place when proposals for legislation are submitted for consideration to authorities concerned. Depending on the agency's impact these considerations will be of great importance for the further implementation of regulative proposals.

The report points to several examples where schemes to impose technical environmental standards passed almost through the whole legislation process, only to be stopped at the last moment due to EC rules of free movement of goods. One example discussed is the Swedish regulation for producer responsibility for end-of-life vehicles, which was implemented

[10] Council Conclusions on the Integrated Product Policy 14405/03 (12/11 2003).

[11] See European Commission Joint Research Center on Environmental Impact of Products. (2006) *Analysis of the life cycle environmental impacts related to the final consumption of the EU-25*. EUR 22284 EN.

[12] See the Swedish Environmental Protection Agency. (2004) *Lagstiftningens roll i den integrerade produktpolitiken*, Rapport 5412 and the Swedish Environmental Protection Agency. (2003) *An integrated Product Policy in the EU—some legal conditions*. Rapport 5338.

[13] The National Board of Trade. (1998) *Miljö, Handel och Konkurrens—Spelregler for effektiva marknader*. Rapport 1998:2. Konkurrensverkets rapportserie 1998:1. NUTEK, Info. 025-1998.

[14] Kommerskollegium, the central administrative body in Sweden dealing with foreign trade and trade policy. The Board provided the Government with analysis and recommendations.

[15] NUTEK is Swedens's national public agency for economic policy issues.

before the EC directive on the subject was finalised.[16] The proposal was said to be encouraged by the Commission pointing at good examples where Member States are forerunners, implementing regulations in spirit of a proposed EC directive. In addition, such procedures speed up the process of getting the directive accepted. This line of action caused quite an administrative process, including efforts to convince the Commission to frame the final proposal in accordance with the Swedish regulation as well as defending the domestic regulation from criticism from both industry and the Commission. Reading between the lines a friction between the National Board of Trade and the Ministry of Environment is detectable. It is noted in the report that the Ministry persisted to implement a domestic regulation in spite of a recommendation of the National Board of Trade not to go along with a domestic regulation; instead it advised the Government to prioritise efforts to accomplish a directive on a Community level.

In the final recommendations of the report, it is discussed whether Sweden should refrain from domestic environmental regulation in favour of rules laid down on the European level.[17] It is noted that the Commission Directorate for the Environment as well as the Swedish Ministry of Environment and the Swedish Environmental Protection Agency, on several occasions have emphasized the strategy of Member States acting as forerunners in the strive for sharpening environmental protection rules. In this respect, it is often referred to the success of the directive on packaging[18] and the influence played by the pre-existing domestic German rules on the subject. However, it is pointed out in the report that from an environmental perspective it is better for the environment to attain environmental protection rules applicable in all Member States. It is further noted that such a strategy is uncertain, and normally would require an influential Member State or at least an alliance with such states. Finally, the three Government authorities conclude that elaborating new proposals in the environmental area often is ineffective. You stand the risk of having to do the job twice and waste resources on proposals that cannot be carried out. Furthermore, if proposal must be re-designed or withdrawn it creates an indistinct and instable perception of the rules of the game. Hence, authorities and inquiries exploring new proposals for environmental legislation must take on the responsibility to clear these with EC law.[19]

To summarise, the simple conclusion is that the tension between trade and environmental considerations can be solved in either two ways. First,

[16] Eventually implemented by Dir 2000/53/EC on end-of-life vehicles.

[17] Miljö, Handel och Konkurrens, above, n 13, p 118 f.

[18] Dir 1994/62/EC of the European Parliament and the Counsel on packaging and packaging waste.

[19] The National Board of Trade. (1998) *Miljö, Handel och Konkurrens—Spelregler for effektiva marknader*, above, n 13, p 129.

in non-harmonised areas by using the free-trade provisions of the Treaty by placing limits on the ability of Member States to enact legislation restricting trade. Second, the Community can set common environmental standards for all Member States. Referring to the above mentioned remedy for combining market logic with environmental considerations by integrating environmental costs in the price of a product, leads us to the conclusion that proper integration of environmental costs can only be done within the second one. In non-harmonised areas measures to increase demand could be used as well as the use of exemptions, however it implies a delicate appraisal of a number of EC law principles.

So if this is history; what has happened since? In the following section I will move on to the example of the Edman inquiry and the proposals for a national action plan for sustainable consumption.

3 THE EDMAN INQUIRY

To begin with it should be pointed out that the inquiry worked only for about a year and a half, setting together a proposal for a large scale policy covering a wide area of society. More than 50 concrete and practical initiatives are presented, divided into three areas—eating, housing and transport. In view of this fact it might be unfair to use this inquiry as an example of how EC law aspects are integrated. However, the overall approach of the inquiry makes it noteworthy as it covers sustainable consumption initiatives from global to local level into practical suggestions within one Member State. Such an approach is often pointed out as desirable by policy makers, in contrast to more fragmented and narrow fields of vision. Furthermore, the general scope reinforced the media impact which lead to broad attention in society as a whole. The implications, much wider than normally taken in official reports makes it its strength as well as its weakness.

The reports set out from the fact that aggregate production and consumption today is estimated to exceed the earth's long-term ecological sustainability by about 25 per cent and the richest 14 per cent of the worlds population consume 56 per cent of the global consumption. This calls for major changes towards a greener consumption. Furthermore, it is denied that from sustainable consumption must necessarily follow a general risk for reduced economic growth and less material prosperity. Instead it is pointed out that information efforts will shape greener consumers who will ask for environmentally friendly products, thereby changing the supply on the market. Another important starting point is that when a household economy permits increased consumption space, it should be concentrated on immaterial consumption, primarily services. The logic being that an increase in welfare shouldn't be spent on products that exhaust resources. Sustainable consumption presuppose greener purchases from consumers as well as a gradual reduction of the proportion of goods in our household budget in favour of consumption of services that limit the use of resources. Proposals are given under three titles; Eat sustainably, Live sustainably and Travel sustainably, representing foodstuffs, housing and transportation.

The inquiry contains many relevant proposals not mentioned here. Focus at this point is on a couple of aspects relating to the free movement of goods, as these often will become insuperable barriers for implementation of the proposals. To overcome this gap is one of the great challenges for environmental law if we should succeed in changing our path towards a sustainable development.

According to the Government's terms of reference to the inquiry, EC law principles on free movement of goods and services should be taken into account.[20] From a Community law perspective many of the proposals are unproblematic, eg making consumer science a core subject in schools or strengthening the Swedish Consumer Agency's role in stimulating sustainable development. However, some of the suggestions with potential great impact on society involve a wide range of aspects that move along a grey zone challenging the borders of EC law rules and principles derived from the free movement provisions in the EC Treaty. Some of these conflicts are explicit, while others are more vague as details are not specified, hence making assessments of equal treatment and non-discrimination difficult to estimate. A general theme throughout the inquiry is to let public authorities and undertakings set good examples, primarily by claims on how to carry out purchases. I have chosen to discuss some of these proposals from a trade/free movement perspective.

3.1 Public Procurement

One of the more important measures suggested by the inquiry is an obligation to perform public procurement in the best quartile of the product assortment, taking balanced sustainability perspectives into account. Within this framework the Swedish Environmental Management Council (SEMC) would act as a national body for knowledge management, analysis and the training of public procurement officers. This would, due to big volumes, stimulate an environmentally friendly production for both internal consumption and export markets. Based on market surveys of market output SEMC would identify and describe products according to their environmental standards in 25 per cent clusters.

Yet another proposal from Mr Edman is a target of 25 per cent organic food purchased in the public sector by 2010, which would put pressure

[20] Kommittédirektiv 2004:37. En handlingsplan för hållbar konsumtion—för hushållen (An action plan for sustainable consumption—for the households).

on food and packaging industries, wholesale and distribution as well as restaurants.

Moreover, Central Government and authorities should serve as a good examples and procure only fair trade produced coffee, tea and bananas not later than 2007. Municipalities and county councils should be encouraged to buy the same products as well as inform about the possibilities to purchase fair trade produced.

3.2 Labelling of Origin

According to the Edman inquiry Swedish farming and domestically produced foodstuff holds a high international standard, compared to quality, environment, animal protection and care of the landscape. He concludes that a continuing high share of Swedish produced staple food, like bread, butter, milk, fish, and vegetables will facilitate and speed up attainment of the Swedish goals for sustainable development. Among other things, he mentions better opportunities for employment, living rural areas as well as less effects from transport emissions. Furthermore, 86 per cent of Swedish consumers want to know where a product is produced and 56 per cent how it has been produced. Finally, this leads up to a proposal for a law on general origin labelling on staple food.

3.3 VAT

In order to stimulate a more sustainable consumption the inquiry discussed the possibility of lowering VAT rates for both organically produced and fair trade products. Concerning fair trade products, a halving of VAT is proposed while a reduction is suggested for organic products, at least for a limited time. Here the inquiry makes a counter attack on the conclusion of a previous survey on this topic performed within the Ministry of Finance. This report clearly advised against such differentiation of VAT levels, primarily due to incompatibility with EC principles. However, Mr Edman calls for a re-examination of the conclusions.

3.4 State Aid

Due to changes in the EC agriculture policy 2003 a decrease of Swedish beef production is anticipated. From a sustainability perspective the inquiry sees this as a threat to the efforts to keep the rural landscape open. Grazing cattle is an effective way to prevent the landscape becoming overgrown and in addition has the potential to produce healthier meat. As a result the inquiry proposed financial investment support to Swedish produced so called 'Health meat' in cattle ranches, which is considered as a condition for attaining profitability. Financially this could be achieved by funds on support for rural development from the European Agricultural Guidance and Guarantee Fund.[21] Finally the cost for being environmentally certified is discussed and support to farmers and restaurants for such expenses are proposed.

Under the title 'Travel sustainably' the inquiry proposed a number of different measures, like premiums for people who buy lighter cars, imposing a purchase tax related to emissions of CO_2/km,[22] and premiums for early scrapping of older vehicles.

4 PUBLIC PROCUREMENT

In the Swedish debate the new directives on public procurement have partly been understood as a widening of the scope of applying social and environmental criteria for decisions on public procurement.[23] It refers to the integration of social and environmental aspects in the fulfilment of a contract, using such considerations as award criteria. The preliminary Government Bill to Parliament[24] explicitly referred to the directive and stressed that under Article 6 of the Treaty, environmental protection requirements are to be integrated into the definition and implementation of the Community policies and activities.[25] Furthermore contracting authorities that wish to define environmental requirements for the technical specifications of a given contract may lay down the environmental characteristics, such as a given production method, and/or specific environmental effects of product groups or services.[26] Moreover the Bill emphasises the various possibilities to encourage a greener procurement process as given in the directive.[27]

[21] Reg 1257/1999 on support for rural development from the European Agricultural Guidance and Guarantee Fund.

[22] See Official Report SOU 2004:63 Vägtrafikskatteutredningen and the Swedish Road Administration. (2004) *Vägverkets klimatstrategi*. Publikation 2004:102.

[23] Dir 2004/17/EC of the European Parliament and of the Council of 31 Mar 2004 coordinating the procurement procedures of entities operating in the water, energy, transport and postal services sectors and Dir 2004/18/EC of the European Parliament and of the Council of 31 Mar 2004 on the coordination of procedures for the award of public works contracts, public supply contracts and public service contracts. Both directives basically apply the same procedures.

[24] The two directives are not yet implemented, though the deadline for implementation was 31 Jan 2006. (See Dir 2004/17/EC, Art 71 and Dir 2004/18/EC, Art 80.) The government Bill is still not yet presented to the Parliament, but referred for consideration in May 2006 to the Council on Legislation, which is a division within the Supreme Court. the Council on Legislation performs a judicial preview of certain bills, primarily with focus on constitutional questions and compliance with EC law. The opinion of the Council was not made official before this article was submitted.

[25] Dir 04/18/EC, Recital nr 5.

[26] Dir 04/18/EC, Recital nr 29.

[27] See Dir 04/18/EC, Art 48.2 f, 50 and 53.1 a.

However, it is questionable whether the directives really introduce any new elements. From a legalistic point of view it's more a codification of what already has been established by the ECJ in several cases. Nonetheless case law opens up for a wide range of interpretations (see below).

The present version of the Government Bill neither prescribes an obligation to observe environmental considerations, nor any form of recommendations to do so. In this aspect the Swedish legislation is drawn up closely along the lines of the directives, ie it is possible for procuring bodies to consider environmental aspects. But in the legislative process preceding the Bill, a Governmental Inquiry discussed whether to introduce an obligation for procuring bodies to include social and environmental requirements in the process when possible, or at least that they *ought* to do so.[28] This final report from the Inquiry was not finished in time to be considered in the Government Bill and was subsequently not included. But the issue will be reconsidered by the government in the near future. The Inquiry discussed both a compulsory requirement (that procuring bodies, when appropriate, shall require an obligation relating to the environment) as well as a recommendation (that procuring bodies, when appropriate, ought to lay down obligations relating to the environment). References are made to other Member States where such requirements more or less already exist, eg Belgium, Denmark and Norway. The Inquiry concludes that a recommendation is preferable.[29] Nonetheless, different views are reflected in the Inquiry and we find reservations from both members representing industry as well as from members representing environmental groups. The latter stressing the implications of Article 6 of the Treaty, while industry interests emphasise the precedence of Community law and the risks of procuring bodies going farther that EC law permits if explicitly encouraged to require environmental considerations.[30]

The immediate and practical effect of the different positions above is difficult to assess. In essence, the stated views can be considered as mere claims in the processes of gradually narrowing down the allowed room for manoeuvre for environmental considerations. In the end all parties underline the importance of procedures being in accordance with the principles of transparency, non-discrimination and equal treatment. But how these

[28] Official Report SOU 2006:28 Nya upphandlingsregler 2.

[29] Official Report SOU 2006:28 Nya upphandlingsregler 2, p 232.

[30] In this respect the report received mixed reactions. The National Board for Public Procurement (NOU) welcomes provisions that encourage tenderers to require environmental standards. However, NOU would like to see the provisions elaborated more clearly. (Opinion 2006-08-23. Dnr 2006/0091-22.) The Swedish Competition Authority rejects mandatory provisions to require environmental standards. The authority is also sceptical to the recommendation as it in practice would increase the risk of tenderers setting up trade barriers and discriminatory requirements in violation of EC rules. Particularly standards that lack the relation to the subject matter of the procured product (Opinion 2006-06-27 Dnr 301/2006).

standpoints in practice relate to the principles is difficult to say. In addition, the chances of the proposal reaching Parliament as a Bill is probably considerably less after the social democratic government lost the election in September 2006.

4.1 Swedish Green Procurement

In December 2005 the Swedish Environmental Protection Agency proposed an action plan for greener public procurement.[31] The report was performed within the above mentioned IPP project where Member States are requested to take a number of measures to strengthen green public procurement.[32] According to a survey performed by the Agency, 60 per cent of central government, regional and local agencies regularly stipulate environmental requirements in their procurement procedures. Nevertheless, in one third of the cases these requirements are framed in such a way that they have no effect on purchases, implying a lack of knowledge of how to express environmental requirements. The target for the future, apart from achieving properly formulated requests, is to increase the current level up to 80 per cent. The Agency points out that public procurement is one of the more important driving forces for companies to improve their environmental performance of products and services.[33]

Previously, the Swedish Competition Authority expressed their concern about the IPP policy and how it would affect competition. Environmental instruments should be addressed directly towards the undesired effect and not regulate technical solutions as this removes the incentives for competition on technical improvements. A full internalisation of environmental costs would increase prices and in the short term would strain the economy, with vast social costs to follow. Furthermore, according to the Authority, public procurement as a mean to achieve environmental goals has several shortcomings. Increased environmental standards raises entry costs for new companies leading to fewer market actors and small companies would have difficulties in adapting.[34]

When the action plan for a greener public procurement was presented, the Authority put forward the same type of criticism. According to the Authority the report has many weaknesses, eg if Authorities should require higher environmental standards than those which follow from applicable

[31] The Swedish Environmental Protection Agency. (2005) *En mer miljöanpassad offentlig upphandling—förslag till handlingsplan*. Rapport 5520. The report is still under consideration by the Government.

[32] Council Conclusions on the Integrated Product Policy 14405/03 (12/11/2003).

[33] The Swedish Environmental Protection Agency. (2005) *En mer miljöanpassad offentlig upphandling—förslag till handlingsplan* above, n 31, p 9.

[34] The Swedish Competition Authority. Opinion 2003-09-01. Dnr 702/2003.

law, and if so how will competition be affected, not only by such requirements but also by requests related to production processes and methods. Again the Authority points to the dangers of environmental requirements being in violation of procurement law and making the procurement process more complicated.[35]

4.2 The Edman Inquiry on Public Procurement

As noted above the proposals from the Edman inquiry on public procurement relates to three areas. First of all, an obligation to perform public procurement in the best quartile of the product assortment, taking balanced sustainability perspectives into account. Secondly, a target of 25 per cent organic food purchased in the public sector by 2010. Finally, a proposed obligation to procure only fair trade produced coffee, tea and bananas not later than 2007 for the central Government and its controlled agencies.

The best quartile system would mean an obligation to purchase only within the best quartile of environmental friendly products. It is suggested that SEMC should be given more resources to act as a national body for knowledge management, analysis and the training of public procurement officers. Based on surveys of market output, SEMC would identify and describe products according to their environmental standards in 25 per cent clusters. The overall aim of the activities of SEMC is to help and support private and public organisations to implement and carry out systematic and progressive environmental work, towards a sustainable development.[36] The Board has the responsibility for the so-called EKU-instrument; a Swedish instrument for ecologically sustainable procurement. SEMC improves and develops the EKU-instrument in cooperation with enterprises in order to widen the use in the private sector.[37]

The SEMC response to the proposals of the inquiry is ambivalent; on the one side the Board recognise the importance of offering tenderers information about how to express environmental performance in different product groups, but on the other side the method requires great resources with frequent updates of both product groups and verification criteria.

[35] The Swedish Competition Authority. Opinion 2006-01-10. Dnr 994/2005.

[36] SEMC (Miljöstyrningsrådet) is a company owned jointly by the Swedish Government, the Confederation of Swedish Enterprises and the Swedish Association of Local Authorities and Regions.

[37] EKU is internet based and provides suggestions for environmental requirements when preparing specifications for the tenders. The purpose is to serve as a voluntary guideline that could be used as support in making environmental considerations when purchasing goods, services and contract services. The defined environmental requirements are divided into compulsory requirements and non-compulsory as well as evaluation requirements. (http://www.miljostyrning.se and http://www.eku.nu.)

Furthermore, SEMC stresses the difficulties of fulfilling this task according to principles of equal treatment, non-discrimination and proportionality and finally questions whether the Board with its obligations to be impartial and neutral is the appropriate body for the job.[38] But promoting the EKU-instrument too much also has side effects. The Environmental Protection Agency points to the fact that the EKU-instrument generally has lower environmental requirements than many of the existing eco-labels on the market. This might lead to a decreasing interest from suppliers to Eco-label their products, hence having a negative impact on the environment in general.[39]

NOU is much more critical towards the Edman inquiry and underlines that every procurement is unique which will require a natural relation between the specifications of the tender and the subject matter and that these are proportional to what is procured.[40] An unreflected precedence of environmental performance will be illegitimate according to NOU. Moreover, if selection among products is done beforehand, these lists of approved products will guide procurers only to already assessed products thereby excluding competition for the latest development on the market. NUTEK points to the consequences for small companies when procurement procedures get more complicated making it more difficult for them to participate.[41]

4.3 Procuring Organic and Fair Trade Products—Obstacles or Possibilities?

When turning to the next step of the proposals referring to organic and fair trade products it is important to outline the different steps in the procurement procedures. In principle the following stages can be distinguished. The choosing of the subject matter of the contract, which means that the product, service or work of the contracting authority wishes to procure is decided. Next, the technical specifications and contractual parameters for the product or service which are the subject matter of the contract must be drawn up. After that and once the bidders have presented their tenders, but before they are opened, the contracting authority must select the companies which have the economic, financial and technical capacities to perform the contract. Finally, the award process take place. The contract will be

[38] The Swedish Environmental Management Council. (Miljöstyrningsrådet) Opinion to the Ministry of Agriculture 2005-10-26.

[39] The Swedish Environmental Protection Agency. Opinion 2005-11-03. Dnr 632-4272-05Hm.

[40] The National Board for Public Procurement. (NOU) Opinion 2005-10-17. Dnr 2005/0163-22. Similar views are expressed by the Swedish Competition Authority, Opinion 2005-02-24, Dnr 26/2005 and Opinion 2005-10-31, Dnr 698/2005.

[41] The Agency for Economic and Regional Growth. (NUTEK) Opinion 2005-10-28. Dnr 013-05-3027.

awarded to the bidder who complies with all the technical specifications and has offered either the lowest price or the economically most advantageous tender from the point of view of the contracting authority. If the economically most advantageous offer is used, transparency, equal treatment and non-discrimination in the award process is required. Various criteria having to do not only with the price but also with quality, technical merit, aesthetic and functional or environmental characteristics etc can be taken into account. Award criteria must be linked to the subject matter of the contract and, as well, each criterion must be allocated a relative weighting. Furthermore, the contracting authority has to be able to verify the accuracy of the information supplied by the bidders. Obviously this makes the award process a delicate procedure.

Nonetheless, it follows from the directive that production methods are within the scope of procurement. 'Contracting authorities that wish to define environmental requirements for the technical specifications of a given contract may lay down the environmental characteristics, such as a given production method, and/or specific environmental effects of product groups or services'.[42] Specific details concerning the specifications are drawn up in Articles 23 (3) (b) and (6), and concerning the performance of the contract in Article 26.

Even though there is a legitimate ground in EC law for green (and social) public procurement, interpretations of how it should be performed are debated and positions within a wide spectrum are found. An array of arguments based on general EC law principles makes the borders of green public procurement fuzzy. The text of the Directive, Commission standpoints and case law, are easily challenged by objections referring to principles of equal treatment, non-discrimination, mutual recognition, proportionality and transparency.

I will not go into details of this discussion as it would require more space than is offered in this article. However, a couple of reflections are appropriate. An essential question is whether a production method has anything to do with the subject matter of the procured product, ie the product itself. Is an organic potato a different sort of potato to a regular one? Or is fair trade coffee a different sort of coffee to regular coffee? Many would argue that it is the same thing, but the Commission states that a product could 'differ(s) from identical products in terms of its manufacture or appearance (whether the differences are visible or not) because an environmentally-sound production process has been used, eg organically grown foodstuffs, "green" electricity'.[43] Although green electricity is not physically different from

[42] Dir 2004/18, Recital 29.

[43] Interpretative Notice 1.2. Commission Interpretative Communication on the Community law applicable to public procurement and the possibilities for integrating environmental considerations into public procurement (2001) 274 final.

conventional energy, the nature and value of the end product has been modified by the process and production method. In the *Buying Green Handbook* the Commission focuses on eco-labels, organic foodstuffs, green electricity and timber.[44] However, it is not obvious why these products would qualify for special treatment compared to other environmentally friendly produced products.[45] As we can see the referred discussion is similar to the one above mentioned in Section 2, relating to WTO and the GPA agreement about 'like products', although the outcome would not necessarily be the same and hence giving rise to potential inconsistencies.

As noted above, using soft values like environmental or social consideration as award criteria in a selection process based on most advantageous offer will evidently complicate the procurement, particularly as award criteria must be both ranked and given a relative weighting.[46] Many commentators have pointed out the technical/legal difficulties linked to this process. In last years edition of this book Henriksson analyses case law and argues for a restrictive use of award criteria.[47] His position appears to be narrower in scope than the above referred standpoint of the Commission. He stresses the risk that procuring entities would go beyond what is required by the contract, assessing all sorts of environmental aspects unrelated to the procuring products.

The proposals of the Edman inquiry on organic and fair trade products could of course avoid some of the mentioned difficulties by primarily using mandatory or *absolute* criteria, ie conditions related to the contract that must be fulfilled. If the procuring product is *organic foodstuff* or *fair trade coffee* the question is whether tenders fulfils the technical specifications or not. Hence, using lowest price as award criteria makes it easier, as long as a legitimate subject matter of the contract is used, technical specifications are objective and non-discriminatory and linked to the subject matter; the contract must be awarded the bidder who fulfils all the relevant technical criteria and offers the lowest price. Still, such a procedure could be challenged from several perspectives, like the right of establishment, the freedom to provide services or discrimination on grounds of nationality. Obligations in a procurement process which can be simply satisfied by national bidders and only with difficulties for tenderers from other Member States will be

[44] The text backed up with references to case law, primarily the Wienstrom Case, Case C-448/01 *EVN, Wienstrom v Austria* [2003] ECR I-14527 and Concordia Bus Case, Case C-513/99 *Concordia Bus Finland Oy Ab v Helsingin kaupunki and HKL-Bussiliikenne* [2002] ECR I-7213.

[45] JE Falk, 'Miljökrav vid upphandling' (2002) (1) *Europarättslig Tidskrift*, pp 45–56.

[46] Dir 2004/18 Art 53(2).

[47] L Henriksson, 'Restrictive Use of Award Criteria in Public Procurement' (2006) (1) *Swedish Studies in European Law* (Oxford and Portland Oregon, Hart Publishing, 2006). Henriksson argues that secondary policies are better dealt with by the legislator on a national level or at the Community level.

considered discriminatory.[48] But the question remains; if general EC law principles are respected, can you avoid the difficulties with performance conditions linked to the award process by using absolute criteria? It seems to be an open case whether conditions like these are permissible or not.[49] But it could be noted that the European Fair Trade Association in a legal report recommended procuring entities to define the purchase as 'fair trade supply of', thereby making the product itself the subject-matter of the procurement.[50]

Nevertheless the question whether public procurement, apart from being an instrument to get best value for money, should also perform secondary objectives is debated. The pressure to recognise 'soft' considerations, like social and environmental aspects has gradually increased. In many ways there is no longer a question of whether these aspects are relevant or not, but more how it could or should be done. Some say that this would include an exercise of public authority, shifting focus from purchasing for the authority's own needs to also include prioritised societal goals.[51] Slavicek argues that this development is not in accordance with principles guiding domestic and international rules on public procurement. All the same you can observe an increasing desire to fulfil these secondary objectives. In many Swedish municipal assemblies, political parties demand a widening use of the public's buying power to encourage the course for a sustainable development. Strangely enough you will find both adherents and opponents leaning on legal advice from municipal civil servants to support their standpoint.[52]

The above mentioned proposal for a general requirement in the Swedish Public Procurement Act for authorities to lay down obligations relating to the environment, would be a step towards clarifying this question. With legal authority in the Public Procurement Act and an instruction from Government to buy organic products, a legitimate relation between the contract and the subject-matter would be secured. However, with the new centre-right Swedish Government it is not likely that this proposal ever will reach the stage of a bill to Parliament. But even if there weren't any domestic legal hinders, EC law considerations must be made. If public

[48] Case 31/87 *Gebroeders Beentjes BV v State of the Netherlands* [1988] ECR 4635, paras 29–30.

[49] L Henriksson, 'Restrictive Use of Award Criteria in Public Procurement' above, n 48, p 188.

[50] European Fair Trade Association. (2005) *Fair Procura: Making Public Authorities and Institutional Buyers Local Actors of Sustainable Development.*

[51] See eg, M Slavicek, 'Upphandlingens olika ansikten' (2002) (1) *Europarättslig Tidskrift*, pp 15–34.

[52] Similar reports from several municipal councils, eg the cities of Uppsala and Sundsvall. Another example is 'My tax money', a national campaign for promoting fair trade in the procuring process initiated by one of the major Swedish Unions (SKTF) and several fair trade organisations.

procurement was to be done predominantly for organic products, trade restrictions would most likely occur. This would lead us to a test for assessing whether it is legitimate or not. Hence, first the objective sought must be demonstrated to serve the environmental goal, eg established environmental targets. Secondly, a causal link is required between the measure adopted and the environmental objective, avoiding speculations and hypothetical positive impacts on the environment. Thirdly, an environmental measure that restricts trade or competition, can only be justified if it cannot be achieved by a less restrictive measure, and finally there must be a balance between the measure and its objective, making the restriction proportionate to the environmental benefits of that measure. Clearly, this would be a tough test to pass and even more so for fair trade products, in absence of concrete fair trade goals established on Community level.

To summarise: the Edman inquiry proposed an obligation to perform public procurement in the best quartile of the product assortment from a sustainability perspective, a target of 25 per cent organic food purchased and an obligation to procure only fair trade produced coffee, tea and bananas for the central Government and its controlled agencies. From the discussion above, it follows that these proposals face several problems. First of all it is clear that all of the proposals will require high standards in the administrative process; where the subject matter is well defined, the technical specifications described in detail and award criteria are thoroughly ranked and weighted. But even then the lawfulness will be uncertain, disclosing a wide margin of appreciation. Public procurement law is characterised by a requirement of transparency, where every detail must relate to legitimate objectives applicable to the circumstances in each case. This makes the legal construction ill suited and easy to challenge when performing goals which primarily have to do with setting good examples for the future. Furthermore, it has been questioned whether an extensive use of the public procurement instrument to promote organic and fair trade products is an effective way to convert society towards a sustainable consumption. An escalating demand for such products will most likely lead to increased use of definitions and demarcation lines derived from Community level, like the European Union Eco-Label[53] or the directive on production and labelling of organic products[54], thereby creating less interest for established national marking schemes that go further than those on the EC level. Even if more products sold are classified as green products, it might lower the incentive to produce and buy products with even better environmental performance. Public procurement will be one of many instruments used to convert to a greener society, however I must conclude, sad at heart, on a rather

[53] The EU-flower. Reg 1980/2000 on a revised Community Eco-Label Award Scheme.
[54] Reg 2092/91 on Organic Production and labelling of Organic Products.

pessimistic point. The law of public procurement is primarily designed to open national markets for competition from all over the Union as well as to promote economic efficiency, and getting best value for tax money. In such a legal construction, green procurement on the sole ground to take the lead by good example in the process for change towards a sustainable development, will be constantly challenged on grounds of legality.

5 LABEL OF ORIGIN ON FOODSTUFFS

As previously mentioned, one of the suggestions from the Edman inquiry is a proposal to the Government to test the possibility to extend the rules on labelling of origin to all foodstuffs, not only beef and eggs sold to consumers. As a parallel strategy it is suggested to pursue a policy for a labelling system on a voluntary basis, if the legislative road to success should fail.[55] The justification for this proposal is the high international standard of Swedish foodstuffs concerning quality, environment, animal protection and care of the landscape. As consumers seem to prefer to know where a product is produced, this implies they also favour domestically produced products, which leads to the conclusion that a high demand for domestic products promotes a more sustainable consumption.

It is enough to be vaguely familiar with EC law and the provisions regulating the internal market and the free movement of goods to realise that these suggestions are likely to infringe fundamental principles of EC law. To expect success with schemes that favour products on grounds of nationality is almost like raising a red rag to a bull; it's asking for trouble. Articles 28 to 30 of the Treaty, provide for the elimination of non-tariff barriers to trade in non-harmonised areas. The abolition of quantitative restrictions and measures having equivalent effect has been one of the fundamental aims of completing the internal market. It is well known that Article 28 has been applied in a wide range of circumstances, catching also national legislation that hasn't been introduced for trade related reasons, but potentially affects the free movement of goods. Among those areas affected are those concerning consumer protection or the protection of the environment, even if applied equally to imported goods and domestic goods.

The extensive case law of Article 28 starts with the Dassonville case,[56] where the Court states that 'all trading rules enacted by Member States which are capable of hindering, directly or indirectly, actually or potentially, intra-Community trade are to be considered as measures having an effect equivalent to quantitative restrictions'. Based on guidance from the

[55] Edman inquiry, p 59.
[56] Case 8/74 *Procureur du Roi v Dassonville* [1974] ECR 837.

Commission[57] and case law the division between 'distinctly applicable' measures and 'indistinctly applicable' measures is made.[58] Distinctly applicable measures are those that treat domestic products differently from imported ones, including measures which make imported products more difficult or costly than the disposal of domestic production. The distinctly applicable measures would normally be discriminatory having an equivalent effect contrary of Article 28. Such discriminatory measures could be justified under Article 30.

Measures which are equally applicable to domestic or imported products classify as indistinctly applicable measures. Such measures can escape the effects of Article 28 if reasonable and necessary in order to satisfy *mandatory requirements*. This follows from the so-called Cassis doctrine[59] where Article 28 and the Dassonville formula has been elaborated to the extent that Member States still have the power to lay down rules governing the composition, manufacture, 'after packaging', and presentation of goods. However, they are required to admit to their territory any goods lawfully produced and marketed in the other Member States. In the absence of harmonisation import can *only be restricted*, if such rules:

— are necessary in order to satisfy *mandatory requirements* such as the effectiveness of fiscal supervision, the protection of public health, the fairness of commercial transactions and the defence of the consumer,
— are proportionate to the desired objective, and
— are the means of achieving that objective which least hinders trade.

The mandatory requirements that follow from the Cassis doctrine, are generally understood as a non-exhaustive list of exemptions from the applicability of Article 28, while the provisions in Article 30 are perceived as an exhaustive list of grounds to justify discriminatory measures (distinctly applicable), thereby highlighting on the one side the difference between a discriminatory and non-discriminatory measure caught by Article 28 and on the other side, those discriminatory measures excused under Article 30. As only the indistinctly applicable measures fall within the Cassis exception, this will limit the scope of the mandatory requirements as means to legalise Member State actions that impede the free movement of goods compared to Article 30. In the Danish beer bottle case, the Court confirmed that the protection of the environment constitutes a mandatory requirement under Article 28. The case concerned the requirement under Danish law that beer and soft drinks be sold in reusable containers and be made subject to a

[57] Commission Dir 70/50 EC, although no longer in force often cited in the literature.
[58] Introduced in the case *Cassis de Dijon*, Case 120/78, below.
[59] Case 120/78 *Rewe-Zentral AG v Bundesmonopolverwaltung für Branntwein* [1979] ECR 649.

deposit. The Court held that this was justified on environmental grounds to ensure that containers were in fact reused. It was therefore proportionate to the aim of protecting the environment.[60]

It is not obvious that an obligation to make a declaration of origin would qualify for an assessment under the Cassis test under Article 28 as an indistinctly applicable measure. Its effects might very well lead to importation obstacles of a practical nature or higher costs, thereby considered as a distinctly applicable (discriminatory) measure and as such assessed under Article 30. However, the relation between the two Articles has been debated and whether the exemptions in Article 30 really are exhaustive has been questioned.[61] It has been argued that the same justification should be applicable irrespective of whether the measure is discriminatory or not. If the ECJ created an open ended list of mandatory exceptions to Article 28, why would it not be legitimate for the ECJ to read Article 30 to include matters such as the environment, asks Craig and de Búrca.[62] Whether this is important or not could be discussed; as Vedder declares, environmental protection will almost never lead to or require a discriminatory measure.[63]

In relation to the proposal of the Edman inquiry there are substantive limitations for Member States to introduce indistinctly applicable measures within the framework of Article 28. A British regulation requiring certain goods, such as clothes and textiles, to indicate their country of origin was in breach of the Article.[64] The British government argued it was justified in the interest of consumers as an indication of quality, but the Court pointed out that quality could be indicated on the goods themselves or their packaging. The general principle is that products must compete on their own merits and not on basis of national origin.[65]

We have strong reasons to believe that a State imposed obligation to make a declaration of origin constitutes a measure of equivalent effect contrary to Article 28. However such an obligation may be justified if consumers might otherwise be mislead by packaging or labelling of the product. It is in this spirit we must understand the Directive relating to the labelling, presentation and advertising of foodstuffs.[66] It follows from the Directive that information in certain areas must be included, concerning for example ingredients,

[60] Case 302/86 *Commission v Denmark* [1988] ECR 4607.

[61] Advocate General Jacobs in PreussenElectra, challenging the reasoning in the Walloon Case. See further P Craig and G de Búrca, *EU Law, Text, Cases, and Materials,* (3rd edn, Oxford University Press 2003) p 634 f.

[62] P Craig and G de Búrca, *ibid,* pp 635 and 661.

[63] H Vedder, Competition Law and Environmental Protection in Europe; Towards Sustainability? (Groningen, Europa Law Publishing, 2003) p 418.

[64] Case 207/83 *Commission v UK* [1985] ECR 1201.

[65] Case 113/80 *Commission v Ireland* [1981] ECR 1625 .

[66] Dir 2000/13/EC on the approximation of the laws of the Member States relating to the labelling, presentation and advertising of foodstuffs.

net quantity, minimum durability, language information etc. Furthermore, Member States may not forbid the sale of foodstuffs which comply with the Directive, unless it is due to the protection of public health or indications of provenance, registered designations of origin or prevention of unfair competition. This would also be in accordance with the protection of designation of origin and geographic indications of a number of named products, like Champagne, Gorgonzola or Feta Cheese etc.[67]

It should be noted that even engagement in a process to encourage a policy for a labelling system on a voluntary basis stands the risk of being caught by Article 28. A state measure in a wider sense may very well include the activities of a government-sponsored body. In the case Buy Irish, activities of the Irish Goods Council to promote Irish goods by advertising on the basis on Irish origin were in breach of Article 28.[68] It didn't matter that the body was merely government-sponsored, it still fell under the definition of 'Member State'. Furthermore, although measures were not binding nor successful, they were considered to influence traders' behaviour and thereby challenging the goals of the single market. It is also worth mentioning that even though the Buy Irish campaign was assessed under Article 28, the Court noted that financing of such a campaign should have been notified under the provisions in the Treaty regarding State Aid. The fact that national rules might be regarded as aid within the meaning of Article 87 cannot exempt them from the prohibition set out in Article 28. The same conclusion also follows from the Du Pont case where the Court otherwise stated that public procurement cannot be structured to reserve a certain part of purchases to national territories or regions.[69]

The proposal from the Edman inquiry is easily challenged from many perspectives. First of all the sustainable aspects on grounds of nationality is doubtful. Even if we should accept that Swedish produced products hold a higher environmental standard, proportionality aspects would disqualify a general obligation to make a declaration of origin as a method for selection. It is also likely that a positive assessment under Article 28 would require that there are no other better methods to achieve the same goals. Secondly, the objective appears to be the promotion of Swedish produced products and facts are not presented to support the casual link between nationality and environmental sustainability. In summary, it seems particularly ill-considered to suggest laws or other State measures to increase the use of declarations of origin and specially so if it is to be done on the grounds of nationality. Compulsory EC systems for marking of origin has so far only taken place where regional outbreaks of disease has threaten to knock out

[67] This procedure is laid down in Art 17 of Reg 2081/92 supplementing the Annex to Reg 1107/96 on the registration of geographical indications and designations of origin.

[68] Case 249/81 *Commission v Ireland* [1982] ECR 4005.

[69] Case C-21/88 *Du Pont de Nemours v Unità sanitaria locale* [1990] ECR I-889.

a whole industry, as in the case of BSE.[70] In this case a label of origin has reassured consumers and upheld demand for beef from non-infected areas.[71] Similar aspects are found behind the marketing standards for eggs.[72]

6 DIFFERENTIATION OF VAT FOR ORGANIC AND FAIR-TRADE PRODUCTS

The Edman inquiry discuss the possibility of lowering VAT rates for organically produced and fair trade products, where a 50 per cent cut of VAT is proposed for fair trade products while a reduction during a limited time is suggested for organic products. As mentioned above, in 2002, a working group within the Ministry of Finance had already explored the question of lowering VAT for organically produced products.[73] The report advised against a differentiation of VAT levels, primarily due to incompatibility with EC principles. But the Edman inquiry wants a re-assessment of the conclusions in the report.

Over the years the ECJ has come to rule on a number of cases in the VAT area. The case law has had great influence over the design of domestic rules in Member States. An important reason for the attention given to VAT by the Court is the effects these taxes have on the proper function of the internal market. The starting point in the legality assessment is whether the principle of equal treatment in Article 90 of the Treaty permits a differentiation between products on ecological grounds. In the ruling of the Outokumpu Oy case the Court states that Member States have the freedom to establish a tax system which differentiates between certain products, even products that are similar within the meaning of Article 90, on the basis of objective criteria, such as the nature of the raw materials used or the production processes employed. However such differentiation will only be accepted if it doesn't discriminate, directly or indirectly, against imports from other Member States.[74] In addition, the Court has repeatedly stressed that a tax differentiation which lead, if only in certain cases, to higher taxation being imposed on imported products will not be in accordance to Article 90.

In the process of looking into the question of lowering VAT on organically produced products, the Ministry of Finance working group had

[70] BSE (bovin spongiform encephalopati) known as 'Mad Cow Disease' and believed to cause Creutzfeldts-Jacobs disease.

[71] Reg 1760/2000 establishing a system for the identification and registration of bovine animals and regarding the labelling of beef and beef products and Commission Regulation 1825/2000 for more detailed rules for the application.

[72] Reg 1028/2006 on marketing standards for eggs.

[73] Official Report Ds 2002:51 Mervärdesskatten på ekologiska livsmedel. (VAT on organically produced foodstuffs.)

[74] Case C-213/96 *Outokumpu Oy* [1998] ECR I-1777, in para 30.

informal contacts with civil servants within the Commission. From the discussions that followed the civil servants were sceptical of the idea of using VAT as a means to promote environmentally friendly produced products.[75] VAT is an effective way for getting revenues from taxation, but as an economic instrument of control other taxes serve the purpose better. In the report it is also referred to the 6th Directive on VAT and provisions regulating the use of lower VAT on certain products, but the Directive is silent if a Member State wants to apply two different lower tax levels within one product area, eg foodstuffs. The admissibility of such a procedure will in the absence of an explicit rule be assessed under the principle of equal treatment.[76] The report concludes that a differentiation between organic and ordinary foodstuffs would first of all require that the tax levels applied were on the approved levels, secondly that imported products are not in any way discriminated against and finally that the principle of equal treatment is upheld.

In the analysis the working group points to the key question: whether two seemingly similar products can still classify as non-similar within the meaning of Article 90, hence making VAT differentiation possible. The crucial question is; is there is a common market for the two products and thus factual competition between them? In a VAT context the question is: does the tax differentiation affect the choice of consumers? Or in other words, differentiation could be permitted if it is without relevance as a mean for competition between the two products. This approach was affirmed fully in a case where France upheld different tax levels on reimbursable and non-reimbursable pharmaceutical products.[77] Fiscal neutrality prevents treating similar goods, which are thus in competition with each other, differently for VAT purposes, and as the two categories of pharmaceutical products were considered not to be in a situation of competition, the difference in the rates of VAT was irrelevant.

The question of finding ways to introduce tax relief is taken seriously by the working group and they add that the differences in production costs between organic and non-organic production, eg reflected by the financial support given to organic production by EU institutions, indicates such differences between the functioning of this market compared to the ordinary market of foodstuffs, that a direct competition between the two doesn't exist.[78] However, the explicit intent of the suggestion to lower VAT levels on organic and fair trade products is to increase demand and the market share of such products at the expense of ordinarily produced products. It

[75] Official Report Ds 2002:51, above, n 74, p 63.
[76] Official Report Ds 2002:51, above, n 74, p 55.
[77] Case C-481/98 *Commission v French Republic* [2001] ECR I-3369.
[78] Official Report Ds 2002:51, above, n 74, p 61.

is also evident that the object of the proposal is to ease the cost burden of organic production. An EC law compatible strategy might work if the object was to make consumers choose organic carrots when corresponding potatoes were too expensive, but not if the aim was to motivate consumers to choose organic potatoes instead of ordinary ones.

The working group come to the conclusion that differentiation of VAT would most likely come into conflict with the principle of equal treatment. It continues to examine whether a tax differentiation would come within the framework of the provisions of State Aid in the Treaty. Similar criteria as discussed above reappear, but the conclusion is that tax differentiation very well may require a notification under Article 88.3. In this case however, a differentiation of VAT would escape the condition of being *selective*. In order to fall under the notion of State Aid in the Treaty the aid must favour an industry, certain companies or certain production. A reduction in VAT will gain consumers on a general level and thereby escapes the criterion of being selective. However, as stated above the working group makes an extensive analysis, including not only a legal analysis, but also of the administrative and practical obstacles. Against this background the group, perhaps even more convincingly, advises against a differentiation of VAT levels. It refers to high control costs in order to uphold a differentiated system. In addition, it is stated that a tax reduction through the means of VAT would be misdirected, primarily due to that the only legitimate ground for separating organic from non-organic products would be the Regulation 2092/91 on Organic Production and if so many organically produced products wouldn't qualify. Neither would it encourage furthering enlargement and improvement of environmental performance of products. Finally the working group states that a VAT differentiation doesn't comply with the PPP principle as it implies that costs should increase for those who contribute to reducing environmental effects and not relaxation for those who don't.[79]

The impression from the report is that lowering VAT levels for organic and fair trade products is a blunt instrument not likely to fully hit the target, which also is pointed out by tax experts saying that VAT is ill-suited to direct consumers' behaviour. The conclusions in the report give a solid impression and it is puzzling what makes the Edman inquiry want to reconsider it. Normally, I would be reluctant to mention the patronising comment from the National Board of Trade to the Edman inquiry, but in this case it is relevant. The Board makes the laconic statement that EC law, just like other parts of law, is not possible to re-interpret because other conclusions would be preferable.[80]

[79] Official Report Ds 2002:51, above, n 74, p 60.
[80] The National Board of Trade. Opinion 2005-10-31. Dnr.154-2006-05.

7 STATE AID

Many of the proposals in the Edman inquiry concern financial support from the Government to facilitate a more sustainable production and consumption. Among other things a program for establishing cattle ranches for grazing livestock is suggested. This would increase Swedish beef production, which the inquiry considered to be healthier than other foreign beef, and in addition conserve traditional landscapes by keeping the countryside open. In order to promote this production different investment subsidies are proposed. In this connection, it specifically pointed to support for rural development from the European Agricultural Guidance and Guarantee Fund.[81] Furthermore, subsidies to farmers and restaurants for costs relating to environmental certification are suggested.

In the referral process following the inquiry, several of the above mentioned Government authorities indicated that the proposals were not detailed enough to be assessed on grounds of compatibility with EC rules on State Aid.

The rules on State Aid are an important tool to uphold the free movement of goods. Systematically Articles 87–89 on State Aid are found under the competition provisions of the Treaty, but the line between State Aid, quantitative restriction and discriminatory taxation is far from obvious as they all, in one way or the other, relate to the free movement of goods or services. Aid granted by a Member State or through State resources to certain undertakings of products will subsidise these subjects, and they will automatically be favoured before their competitors and hence create a distortion on the market. Only under certain circumstances will State Aid be permissible, which is drawn up in Article 87 (2) and (3). Furthermore, it should be noted that the Commission normally plays a special role regarding State Aid. As the initial decision maker they form and develop a substantial policy through their individual decisions and other instruments, such as formal legislation and informal rule making. As an example, environmental aids can be authorized under Article 87 (3) (b) and (c). Already in 1974 the first set of Commission Guidelines on State Aid for environmental protection was issued and the ones presently in force from 2001[82] will expire on 31 of December 2007.[83] The current Guidelines lean on Article 87 (3) (c) and are basically divided into three categories. First of all *investment aid*, which refers to measures which help firms to adapt their facilities to new environmental standards or to reach such standards,

[81] Council Reg (EC) No 1257/1999 on support for rural development from the European Agricultural Guidance and Guarantee Fund.

[82] Community guidelines on State Aid for environmental protection [2001] OJ C 37/03.

[83] For the review of the Guidelines, States and other parties were invited to answer a questionnaire before Oct 2005. The answers are now accessible on the Commissions home page.

secondly *aid for horizontal measures*, which enables aid to encourage R&D of technologies that cause less pollution, technical information, consultancy services etc, and thirdly *operating aid*, which comprise aid in the form of grants, relief from environmental taxes or charges and aid for the purchase of environmentally friendly products. However, these guidelines as well as other guidelines such as on de minimis aid,[84] training aid,[85] or exemptions from the obligation to notify for certain SMEs,[86] are of little importance here. The mentioned proposals from the Edman inquiry are from a State Aid perspective, not handled in accordance with ordinary Commission procedures in State Aid matters. In this case the suggestions refer to State Aids in the agricultural sector that are under the responsibility of the Directorate General of Agriculture. This means that there is yet another layer of formal Commission legislation and Guidelines that apply to the agricultural sector.

Article 33 of the Treaty defines the objectives of the common agricultural policy. In working out the agricultural policy and the special methods for its application, account has to be taken of the particular nature of agricultural activity, which results from the structural and natural disparities between the various agricultural regions and the fact that agriculture constitutes a sector linked with the economy as a whole. The Guidelines for State Aid in the agricultural[87] sector provides a framework for the different types of State Aids allowed, the guidelines take particular account of the developments in agricultural policy and especially of the need, on the one hand, to improve and promote the quality of agricultural products and, on the other hand, to preserve the environment and the traditional heritage in the countryside. Aid for investments on farms can be permitted up to a certain percentage, inter alia for investments linked to the preservation of traditional landscapes, to the improvement of the environment or animal welfare.

The proposals from the Edman inquiry are not detailed enough for a reliable assessment of whether they would comply with the State Aid provisions in the Treaty. However, the Swedish Board of Agriculture points out that the European Agricultural Guidance and Guarantee Fund is not designed

[84] Commission Reg 1998/2006 on the application of Arts 87 and 88 of the Treaty to de minimis aid.

[85] Commission Reg 68/2001 the application of Arts 87 and 88 of the Treaty to training aid.

[86] Commission Reg 70/2001 on the application of Arts 87 and 88 of the EC Treaty to State Aid to small and medium-sized enterprises. Prolonged by Commission Reg 1976/2006 amending Regs 2204/2002, 70/2001 and 68/2001 as regards the extension of the periods of application.

[87] Commission Guidelines for State Aid in the Agriculture and Forestry Sector 2007 to 2013 (2006/C 319/01). In Dec 2006 the Commission adopted new rules on State Aid in the agricultural sector which allow Member States not to notify State Aid given to small and medium-sized undertakings and in addition present guidelines that complement the regulation and lay down rules applicable to notified aid.

to support beef production, which seems to be the aim of the inquiry, but rather an environmental goal for a rich flora of cultivation, eg conservation of traditional landscapes.[88] Furthermore, the Board points out that several of the proposals for financial support for environmental certification costs, either already exist or concern areas where there are no such costs.

A concluding remark is that even though investment subsidies as well as support for environmental efforts are possible, the problem seems to be that the crucial object of the measures proposed is to stimulate Swedish beef production and as such make it questionable. A general observation is that it is one thing to admit State Aids to compensate for competitive *disadvantages*, and another to admit State Aid to achieve competitive *advantages*. Generally the Commission would not contribute to worsen existing problems or to transfer them from one area to another by strengthening undertakings in one area on behalf of others competing in intra-Community trade.

8 CONCLUSION

In the first part of my final remarks I will summarise my conclusions on each of the above-analysed areas of EC law and hopefully some of the observations can serve as a memento for future authors of environmental action plans. I will continue with some reflections on whether product harmonisation is the only solution to a consistent and practical policy on sustainable consumption. In the second and last part of my conclusion I will say something about the prospects of bringing trade and sustainable development together. Can we look to the future with confidence or despair?

In the area of public procurement we have seen progress over the last few years. Gradually environmental as well as social values have worked their way into the complex procedures of public procurement law. Even though it exists, there are noteworthy arguments not to complicate the process further, namely the practical difficulties of balancing competing aims like efficiency and cost savings on the one side and environmental goals on the other. Although we should recognise this dilemma, we will most likely have to get used to it. Claims of what are acceptable criteria in the procuring process will slowly change predominant conceptions and at times show a rather fragmented image, but eventually the picture will stabilise. The key factor in this process is the formulation of a common product classification system, that holds the desired values, taking methods of production into account, and making it possible to distinguish one product from another.

[88] The Swedish Board of Agriculture. Opinion 2005-10-27. Dnr 39 6513/05.

Certain routes appear to lead towards more dead end streets than others. The proposal for a law on labelling origin on foodstuffs seems to be of that nature; contrary to everything that EC law stands for if using nationality as a marker. Possibly a more realistic suggestion would be a common labelling system showing the environmental impact of the product, which would include effects from transportation. This is easier said than done. We have a long way to go before we can agree on common denominators indicating environmental impact as it will include difficult trade offs, eg between transportation distance and energy consumption for the production. For now, let us just say it is a bad idea to advocate compulsory labelling of origin.

At first glance the proposal to lower VAT on organic and fair trade products appears an excellent suggestion to stimulate a more sustainable consumption. One of its advantages being that the effect only occurs on the consumer level and in this manner makes it neutral in relation to the producers. Nevertheless, this suggestion has been scrutinised thoroughly within the Swedish Ministry of Finance and several good arguments for not going along that line have been presented. Even if the above mentioned question of a common product classification could be overcome, such differentiation would be discriminatory from an EC law perspective at least if used as a mean to subsidise organic products at the expense of traditionally grown foodstuffs. In addition, the analysis points to questionable environmental effects as well as VAT not being a suitable regulative tool to steer consumer behaviour.

Implementing new policy goals normally means pressure on governments for financial support as a stimulus for change. During the last couple of years a great deal of attention has been given to the provisions on State Aid in the Treaty. The Commission drive this process by constantly increasing the number of Regulations, Notices and other soft-law instruments. Under these circumstances it is not surprising that State Aid arguments pop up, as jack in the box, wherever proposals for increased use of public money are made. The rather unclear border between permissible and prohibited State Aid drawn up in the Treaty in combination with the vast, and many times indistinct, rule making of the Commission makes proposals for new Government spending easy to challenge.[89] As advice to future writers of environmental action plans, it would be wise to design aid directly along the substantial formal and informal output from Commission, using it as a checklist. Even though these rules are possible to challenge, it is preferable from a practical point of view.

[89] I Simonsson, 'On the Emerging Obligation for Member State Authorities to Supervise and Enforce EC State Aid Law, and the Resulting Need to Consider Decentralisation' (2006) (1) *Swedish Studies in European Law* (Oxford and Portland Oregon, Hart Publishing, 2006).

I will now move on, and comment on the prospects of positive harmonisation, ie common environmental standards for all Member States. With positive harmonisation many of the problems connected to the free-trade provisions of the Treaty are avoided.

A harmonisation process revolves around finding criteria and legal techniques that let us identify products with the desired characters and also allow us to assess trade effects when such products are introduced and handled on the market. A far-reaching harmonisation would also internalise environmental costs in accordance with the Polluter Pays Principle. We are looking for instruments that, like a homing robot, hit only the intended target without creating adverse effects outside the object. But as techniques vary as well as a definition of what the target really is, the process becomes highly unpredictable.

However, harmonisation alone is hardly the only answer. A comprehensive product classification system involves a considerable workload, which in a system based on negotiations between Member States normally ends up with the lowest common denominator. Balanced against potential strains of the economies in Member States as well as interests of developing countries in the WTO-GPA sphere it is not likely that definitions become particularly radical. This draws attention to efficiency considerations, whether costs are proportionate to environmental gains.

It must also be noted that a trade system which by means of standardisation separate between variants of similar commodities, must provide a secure control system. Consumers must be able to rely on classifications, and invisible variants like organic products are more costly to handle in a surveillance system than classifications based on visible criteria. The potential free-riding problem will of course increase in relation to the possible financial benefits for free-riders. Lastly, but not least important, harmonised standards will encourage market actors to reach the base line but no further, hence having an adverse incentive on competition for technology development for sustainable consumption. Consequently, product harmonisation is not likely to be the sole answer. Faster and more efficient remedies are also required.

In the introduction to this article it was contended that the legal discourse of internal market law and environmental law was compartmentalised. This observation has a horizontal as well as vertical side to it. The horizontal perspective is found between legal experts working in areas of law on the same level, eg experts on EC internal market law, EC environmental law, EC tax law etc, no matter if they are civil servants or legal scholars. The same horizontal relation could be found on the domestic level. The focus is to deepen the discourse, not opening it into a wider context raising questions of compatibility between legal areas. In many ways the big words on integration of environmental protection into the definition and implementation of the Community polices appear as mere rhetoric. Opinions of the various Government bodies' stays within their own fields of competence and seldom tries to overcome gaps by seriously recognising the objectives of the other side that would require a compromise on both ends. This could be illustrated by the relative silence from the Swedish Environmental Protection Agency or the Board of Agriculture relating to internal market aspects of the proposals from the Edman inquiry. Another aspect of compartmentalisation is found along a vertical line stretching from a global, regional and domestic level. The first found conflict on the WTO or Community level is merely transferred to the domestic level and reappears intact, which is particularly unfortunate as alternative domestic solutions can work as good examples to be followed by others and eventually re-emerge as proposals on the Community level. Sadly enough this creates a deadlock situation with unnecessary red tape slowing down the pace for a sustainable development. In addition, this also puts the Swedish lawyer in a new role. Lawyers must be cautious; they act on a politically soaked arena, where awareness of a balance is crucial. The lawyer's expert role working for foreseeable legal instruments fit for the use must be weighed against respect of democratic decisions and values

Finally, I will give some concluding reflections about the future. The above made observations give little hope for fast change. Soberly analysed, the impression is a split between two camps where little progress is made. Practical proposals for a more sustainable consumption are difficult to coordinate with the legal instruments and logic of internal market law.

So, was the Edman inquiry only a waste of time and money? Hopefully it was not. In a more dialectical approach where interests stand against each other, however on different arenas, a small step from one side will likely have effect on the other. The thoughts of an early constructionist named Ludwik Fleck can illustrate the process. Fleck was a Polish physician and epistemologist who developed his ideas in the 1920s and 30s. Although Fleck's case applied to science, there are close points of similarity between Fleck's description of how changes of scientific beliefs come about and how the concept of law is developed. Fleck considered scientific facts as constructed by groups of scientists, by 'thought collectives'. Each thought collective elaborates a thought-style which contains norms, concepts and practices of that collective. Newcomers to a professional community are socialised into its specific thought style and develop a unique way of viewing the world. Scientific facts produced by a given thought-collective are therefore shaped by that collective's thought style, and are incommensurable with facts produced by other thought-collectives. Fleck's suggestion was that people generally belong to several different thought-collectives, and within each group reliance and trust makes participants lower their guard and listen unreservedly. When moving between collectives, new elaborated ideas are possible to spread to new collectives and also move science forward. This makes individuals, with or without intent, 'ambassadors' bringing new ideas between collectives.[90] Referring to the theme of this article, last years development of public procurement law, which involves lawyers trained in different thought collectives has triggered a shift and actual change has now started.

BIBLIOGRAPHY

Articles and Literature

Craig, P and de Búrca, G, *EU Law, Text, Cases, and Materials* (3rd edn, Oxford University Press 2003).

Dhont, N, *The Integration of Environmental Protection into other EC Policies* (Groningen, Europa Law Publishing, 2003).

Falk, JE, 'Miljökrav vid upphandling' (2002) (1) *Europarättslig Tidskrift*, p 45–56.

Fleck, L, 'The Problem of Epistemology' (1936) in R S Cohen and T Schnelle (eds) *Cognition and Fact—Materials on Ludwik Fleck* (Dordrecht, Reidel, 1986).

Henriksson, L, 'Restrictive Use of Award Criteria in Public Procurement' (2006) (1) *Swedish Studies in European Law* (Oxford and Portland Oregon, Hart, 2006).

Howse, R and Regan, D, 'The Product/Process Distinction—An Illusory Basis for Disciplining Unilateralism in Trade Policy' (2000) (11) *European Journal of International Law*, p 249–289.

Simonsson, I, 'On the Emerging Obligation for Member State Authorities to Supervise and Enforce EC State Aid Law, and the Resulting Need to Consider Decentralisation' (2006) (1) *Swedish Studies in European Law* (Oxford and Portland Oregon, Hart, 2006).

Slavicek, M, 'Upphandlingens olika ansikten' (2002) (1) *Europarättslig Tidskrift*, p 15–34.

Van den Bossche, P, *The Law and Policy of the World Trade Organization, Text, Cases and Materials* (Cambridge University Press 2005).

Vedder, H, *Competition Law and Environmental Protection in Europe; Towards Sustainability?* (Groningen, Europa Law Publishing, 2003).

EU Documents

Regulations

Regulation 2092/91 on Organic Production and labelling of Organic Products.

Regulation 2081/92 supplementing the Annex to Regulation 1107/96 on the registration of geographical indications and designations of origin.

Regulation 1257/1999 on support for rural development from the European Agricultural Guidance and Guarantee Fund.

Regulation 1760/2000 establishing a system for the identification and registration of bovine animals and regarding the labelling of beef and beef products.

[90] L Fleck, 'The Problem of Epistemology' (1936) in RS Cohen and T Schnelle (eds) *Cognition and Fact—Materials on Ludwik Fleck* (Dordrecht, Reidel, 1986).

Regulation 1980/2000 on a revised Community Eco-label Award Scheme.
Regulation 1028/2006 on marketing standards for eggs.

Directives

Directive 1994/62/EC on packaging and packaging waste.
Directive 2000/13/EC on the approximation of the laws of the Member States relating to the labelling, presentation and advertising of foodstuffs.
Directive 2000/53/EC on end-of-life vehicles.
Directive 2004/17/EC of the European Parliament and of the Council of 31 March 2004 coordinating the procurement procedures of entities operating in the water, energy, transport and postal services sectors.
Directive 2004/18/EC of the European Parliament and of the Council of 31 March 2004 on the coordination of procedures for the award of public works contracts, public supply contracts and public service contracts.

Commission Regulations

Commission Regulation 70/2001 on the application of Articles 87 and 88 of the EC Treaty to State aid to small and medium-sized enterprises.
Commission Regulation 68/2001 the application of Articles 87 and 88 of the Treaty to training aid.
Commission Regulation 1976/2006 amending Regulations 2204/2002, 70/2001 and 68/2001 as regards the extension of the periods of application.
Commission Regulation 1998/2006 on the application of Articles 87 and 88 of the Treaty to de minimis aid.

Documents from the Commission

COM (2003) 302, final. Commission's Communication on an Integrated Product Policy (IPP) Brussels June 18, 2003.
Commission Guidelines for State Aid in the Agriculture and Forestry Sector 2007 to 2013 (2006) OJ C 319/01.
Community Guidelines on State aid for environmental protection (2001) OJ C 37/03.
Commission Interpretative Communication on the Community law applicable to public procurement and the possibilities for integrating environmental considerations into public procurement (2001) 274 final.
European Commission (2004) *Buying Green! A handbook on environmental public procurement*. Commission staff working paper.

Swedish Documents

Swedish Government Publications

Kommittédirektiv 2004:37. En handlingsplan för hållbar konsumtion—för hushållen. (An action plan for sustainable consumption—for the households.)
Official Report Ds 2002:51 Mervärdesskatten på ekologiska livsmedel. (VAT on organically produced foodstuffs.)

Official Report SOU 2004:63 Vägtrafikskatteutredningen.
Official Report SOU 2004:119 Uthålliga laster. Konsumtion för en ljusare framtid. (Sustainable Burdens—Consumption for a brighter future.)
Official Report SOU 2005:51 Bilen, Biffen, Bostaden. Hållbara laster—smartare konsumtion. (The car, the beef, the house. Sustainable Burdens—Smarter consumption.)
Official Report SOU 2006:28 Nya upphandlingsregler 2.

Swedish Authorities (Reports)

The National Board of Trade. (1998) *Miljö, Handel och Konkurrens—Spelregler for effektiva marknader.* Rapport 1998:2. Konkurrensverkets rapportserie 1998:1. NUTEK, Info. 025-1998.
The Swedish Environmental Protection Agency. (2003) *An integrated Product Policy in the EU—some legal conditions.* Rapport 5338.
The Swedish Environmental Protection Agency. (2004) *Lagstiftningens roll i den integrerade produktpolitiken.* Rapport 5412.
The Swedish Environmental Protection Agency. (2005) *En mer miljöanpassad offentlig upphandling—förslag till handlingsplan.* Rapport 5520.
The Swedish Road Administration. (2004) *Vägverkets klimatstrategi.* Publikation 2004:102.

Swedish Authorities (Opinions)

The Agency for Economic and Regional Growth. Opinion 2005-10-28. Dnr 013-05-3027.
The National Board for Public Procurement. (NOU) Opinion 2005-10-17. Dnr 2005/0163-22.
The National Board for Public Procurement. (NOU) Opinion 2006-08-23. Dnr 2006/0091-22.
The National Board of Trade. Opinion 2005-10-31. Dnr.154-2006-05.
The Swedish Board of Agriculture. Opinion 2005-10-27. Dnr 39 6513/05.
The Swedish Competition Authority. Opinion 2003-09-01. Dnr 702/2003.
The Swedish Competition Authority. Opinion 2005-02-24. Dnr 26/2005.
The Swedish Competition Authority. Opinion 2005-10-31. Dnr 698/2005.
The Swedish Competition Authority. Opinion 2006-01-10. Dnr 994/2005.
The Swedish Environmental Management Council. (Miljöstyrningsrådet) Opinion to the Ministry of Agriculture 2005-10-26.
The Swedish Environmental Protection Agency. Opinion 2005-11-03. Dnr 632-4272-05Hm.

Other Documents

Council Conclusions on the Integrated Product Policy 14405/03. (12/11 2003).
European Commission Joint Research Center on Environmental Impact of Products. (2006) *Analysis of the life cycle environmental impacts related to the final consumption of the EU-25.* EUR 22284 EN.
European Fair Trade Association. (2005) *Fair Procura: Making Public Authorities and Institutional Buyers Local Actors of Sustainable Development.*

Cases

Case 8/74 Procureur du Roi v Dassonville [1974] ECR 837.
Case 120/78 Rewe-Zentral AG v Bundesmonopolverwaltung für Branntwein [1979] ECR 649.
Case 113/80 Commission v Ireland [1981] ECR 1625.
Case 249/81 Commission v Ireland [1982] ECR 4005.
Case 207/83 Commission v UK [1985] ECR 1201.
Case 302/86 Commission v Denmark [1988] ECR 4607.
Case 31/87 Gebroeders Beentjes BV v State of the Netherlands [1988] ECR 4635.
Case C-21/88 Du Pont de Nemours v Unità sanitaria locale [1990] ECR I-889.
Case C-213/96 Outokumpu Oy. [1998] ECR I-1777.
Case C-379/98 PreussenElektra v Schhleswag [2001] ECR I-2099.
Case C-481/98 Commission v French Republic [2001] ECR I-3369.
Case C-513/99 Concordia Bus Finland Oy Ab v Helsingin kaupunki and HKL-Bussiliikenne [2002] ECR I-7213.
Case C-448/01 EVN, Wienstrom v Austria [2003] ECR I-14527.

4

A European Res Publica

DR OLA ZETTERQUIST*

1 INTRODUCTION

THE NOTION OF *res publica* is often translated as the common good but more properly it is what citizens hold in common and above their own narrow self-interest. *Res publica* departs from an idea of the legal order as a species of moral dialogue based on reason, thereby appealing to the rational assent of its members. Viewed as an ongoing moral dialogue striving for coherence and rationality in the law, *res publica* is better understood as a dynamic concept than as a fixed and unalterable set of values. It may sound like an ancient term today, more appropriate for discourses on classical Roman law than for European community law. Such summary dismissal may, however, deprive us of a useful tool for assessing the constitutional enigma of the European Union (EU)—is the EU a *separate* and *independent* legal order comprising not only states but also citizens as direct subjects. The fundamental enigma challenges our traditional notions of the relationship between law, state and democracy where the two former have often been held to be necessarily dependent on the latter. Hence it is that the EU, which undoubtedly is not a state, has given rise to insoluble constitutional problems prompting many scholars and lawyers to hold that the EU is an organisation sui generis, ie one that defies traditional constitutional models.

Our current constitutional models, not least the parliamentary democracy that is prevalent in many of the Member States (Sweden among these), are very much based on and framed by the idea of the (sovereign) state as it has emerged since the 17th century primarily according to the philosophy of Thomas Hobbes. The basis for the idea of sovereignty is the notion of freedom as non-interference, ie a sovereign state is one that does not take orders from any other state (or other wielder of power) and a sovereign people is, in the same vein, one that is not restricted from taking its own course of action.

* Göteborg University.

My claim is that the conclusion of the EU as a sui generis entity is overly simplistic and too influenced by the model of the sovereign state. The incompatibility between traditional constitutional models and the EU is a conflict mainly on the surface level of constitutional law and one that is largely conditioned by the normative ideals underpinning the idea of sovereignty. This conflict is particularly clear in the Swedish constitutional provision (Instrument of Government (IG) Chapter 10 Article 5) on the relation between Sweden and the EU which is deeply influenced by the Hobbesian notion of sovereignty. If the perspective is changed to a deeper level another picture will emerge where the EU accords well with republican constitutional values and models whereas it is much more difficult to reconcile with the idea of sovereignty (however framed).

The classical notion of *res publica* could, on the other hand, confer constitutional legitimacy on the EU in those places where the traditional democracy defined as majority decision-making obviously fails without having to resort to the notion of the EU as a totally unique creation in the history of legal theory. Put differently, the return to the Roman assessment of the moral quality of the constitution and viewing law as an instrument for achieving non-domination, rather than non-interference, will provide a plausible solution to the constitutional enigma that does not necessarily imply the creation of a European state. There is also something attractive about the idea of the EU as a common good for all European citizens and not simply as a zero sum game of national interests where the legitimacy of the EU is measured solely by the benefits of ones own Member State. There are, however, some obstacles before the EU can be said to accord with the republican ideal of the legal order as a species of moral dialogue endowed with a *res publica* of its own. These obstacles are mainly the result of the current position of the states as intermediary subjects between the EU and her citizens.

2 RULE OF LAW AND *RES PUBLICA*

The origin of the notion of *res publica* and republican constitutionalism lies mainly with the Roman statesman and philosopher Marcus Tullius Cicero (106–43 BC) who held that *legal agreement* and *community of interest* formed the core of the concept.[1] In the Roman constitution *res publica* was incompatible with arbitrary power and the constitution accordingly rested on the principle of separation of powers.[2] Another classic of modern

[1] Cicero, The Republic, in *The Republic and The Laws* (Oxford, Oxford University Press, 1998), p 19. In this passage Cicero can be seen as an early precursor of the core ideas of constitutionalism, the modern heir of the republican ideal—cf P Pettit, *Republicanism—A Theory of Freedom and Government* (Oxford, Oxford University Press, 1997) p 177ff.

[2] Cf Cicero, The Republic, *ibid*, p 71ff.

Western legal theory was also formulated by Cicero in his famous account of law to be viewed as right reason [*recta ratio*] in harmony with nature'[3] and that law must be universalistic (and not limited to a certain community) in its character.[4] Put in different words, there was a difference between (morally) good and bad law in the republican constitution[5] and sharing law also meant sharing justice.[6]

It is no exaggeration to hold that Cicero laid the foundations for the modern ideal of the *rule of law* meaning that law, and not the arbitrary will of men, rules society. The law has ever since been held to be instrumental in relation to some over-arching social good. This social good has typically been either religious or moral in kind, ie the law as a social force cannot be studied without connection with other social factors that make up the deep moral structure of society. More specifically this link between public power, law and public morality has, ever since the days of the Roman republic, been known as the *res publica* or the *common good* of the society from which the constitutional notion of the *commonwealth* derives. The notion meant to the Romans not so much as a republic as the activities of the Roman people.[7] This dynamic concept of the *res publica* is underlined by the fact that the Roman republic did not possess a constitution in the modern sense of a clear set of written rules that defined state institutions and their powers.[8]

The understanding of the social good constituting the *res publica* is of importance for understanding the deep-structure of constitutional law since it is according to the *res publica* that the constitutional law is justified (or critisised). Constitutional institutions are likewise designed in order to give effect to the ideals of the *res publica* thus pointing to the issue of purposeful design. The social good represents the reason (*raison detre*) for which the members of the society in question submit to the authority of the norms and institutions set up by the legal order. The legal and political orders are in this sense the property (*res*) of the people (*publica*).

Historically the *res publica* has seldom been specified beyond the core values of limited government under law with the aim to secure non-domination. The lasting appeal of the notion has rather been found in the fact that it appeals to a universalistic idea of a common good, morally superior to the self interest of the single individual (or group of individuals). Rousseau

[3] Cicero, The Republic, *ibid*, p 68.

[4] Cicero, The Laws, *The Republic and The Laws* (Oxford, Oxford University Press, 1998), p 111.

[5] Cicero, The Laws, *ibid*, p 112.

[6] Cicero, The Laws, *ibid*, p 105.

[7] P Jones and K Sidwell (eds), *The World of Rome* (Cambridge, Cambridge University Press, 1997), p 84.

[8] Still today there are constitutions that develop in the Roman way. The British common law constitution is the most important contemporary example.

famously stated that there was a significant difference between the will of all and the general will, the proper *res publica*:

> There is often a considerable difference between the will of all and the general will: The latter looks only to the common interest, the former looks to private interest, and is nothing but a sum of particular wills.[9]

Even though Rousseau in the end concludes that there is no other viable way of ascertaining the general will than by majority rule, his idea of a distinction between the general will and a cumulated will of all has been quite influential for a modern interpretation of the *res publica*. Much like the idea of a social contract, *res publica* aspires to the assent of rationally thinking individuals by appealing to principles of justice that are shared by most (if not all) individuals. Put in other words one could say that the *res publica* concerns the essence of the moral dialogue that constitutes the core of the moral legitimacy of the legal and political order.

3 *RES PUBLICA* AND DEMOCRACY

Historically there has been a tension between the notions of *res publica* on the one hand and the democratic form of government, understood as the unrestricted rule of the majority, on the other. The Athenian democracy, in perfect formal order sentenced Socrates to death, though he had broken no law of the *polis*. Athens also decided to raze the neutral city of Melos to the ground for the simple reason that it had not deferred to Athenian rule. These two events stained the name of democracy for more than 2,000 years to come when democracy was generally equated with mob-rule. Cicero for example rejected Athenian style democracy as a form of government consistent with *res publica*:

> there is no state to which I should be quicker to refuse the name of republic than the one which is totally in the power of the masses ... there is no public except when it is held together by a legal agreement ... That rabble is just as tyrannical as one man, and all the more repellent in that there is nothing more monstrous than a creature which masquerades as a public and usurps its name.[10]

Cicero on this point aligned his philosophy to the official constitutional name of the Roman republic: The Senate and people of Rome (*senatus*

[9] JJ Rousseau, The Social Contract in *The Social Contract and other later political writings* (Cambridge, Cambridge University Press, 1997) p 60.

[10] Cicero, The Republic, *The Republic and The Laws* (Oxford, Oxford University Press, 1998), p 73. This argument, presumably on the same grounds, is echoed by J Locke: By *Common-wealth*, I must be understood all along to mean not a Democracy, or any Form of Government, but *any Independent Community* which the *Latines* signified by the word *Civitas*, J Locke, *Two Treatises of Government* (Cambridge, Cambridge University Press, 1988), II, p 355, § 133.

populusque Romanus- SPQR), a name that reflected its commitment to a system of power sharing where the senate provided deliberation, wisdom and, presumably, reason to the power wielded by the popular (democratic) assemblies. This idea is underlined by the fact that the senate was nominally only an advisory body having no other authority than its reasoning. A later and telling example of the historically uneasy tension between democracy and *res publica* is to be found in the constitutional debate preceding the American constitution of 1787, one of the first modern constitutions and the oldest written one still in force. The framers of the American constitution were decidedly against the idea of setting up a government based on the principles of Greek democracy holding that:

> In all very numerous assemblies, of whatever character composed, passion never fails to wrest the scepter from reason. Had every Athenian citizen been a Socrates, every Athenian assembly would still have been a mob.[11]

The framers were thus disinclined to believe that the classical democratic form of government could secure *res publica* understood as public reason. The authors of the American constitution therefore deliberately omitted any reference to democracy (which, conspicuously, is not even mentioned once in the entire document) and instead opted for the label republic. Still to this day it is argued that the American constitution is not primarily based on democratic but on republican values. This is what makes its non-democratic features, such as a system of checks and balances guarded by non-elected judges, acceptable even for the current generation.

4 LEVIATHAN—THE CHALLENGE TO THE REPUBLICAN MODEL

The republican model of freedom as non-domination and government characterised by checks and balances should be contrasted with its powerful challenger of the 17th century, namely Thomas Hobbes and his tremendously influential theory of the sovereign state set out in his masterpiece *Leviathan* (1651).[12] This is not the place to give a full account of Hobbes theory but attention will be drawn to the most important contrasts with the republican model.

Freedom, according to Hobbes, is to be understood as the absence of Opposition understood as external impediments of motion.[13] Such a concept entails that freedom is not viewed as a balance of freedoms one against the other as in the case of non-domination where total freedom could not be conceived without this implying domination on some parts behalf. It is

[11] J Madison, The Federalist, no 55 in A Hamilton, J Madison & J Jay, *The Federalist* (London Everymans Library [1788] 1992), p 285.

[12] T Hobbes, *Leviathan* (Cambridge, Cambridge University Press [1651] 1991).

[13] *Ibid*, p 145.

clear that freedom on Hobbes account cannot be equally possessed by all individuals without signifying the much dreaded state of nature, ie anarchy. The crucial point in Hobbes theory is that it is only the sovereign (state) that possesses total freedom otherwise characteristic of the state of nature:

> *The Liberty, which writers praise, is the Liberty of Sovereigns; not of Private men* ... in States and Common-wealths not dependent on one another, every Common-wealth (not every man) has an absolute Libertie, to doe what it shall judge (that is to say, what that Man, or Assemblie that representeth it, shall judge) most conducing to their benefit.[14]

Personal autonomy should not be confused with the autonomy of the state. According to Hobbes there is thus a vast difference between a free state and a free people.[15] In accordance with his idea of liberty as non-interference and ultimate liberty as the prerogative of the sovereign Hobbes also argued that law is, by necessity, a limitation of the original (total) liberty of the state of nature:

> For Right is a Liberty, namely that Liberty which the Civil Law leaves us: But Civill Law is an Obligation; and takes from us the Liberty which the Law of Nature gave us.[16]

The Hobbesian notion of the law proceeds from the assumption that before the law (and the state), everything was liberty in the sense of freedom to choose whatever action that would be considered most appropriate or beneficial for its agent. The introduction of the law into this total liberty introduces something new that cannot possibly be liberty since liberty was there already. Consequently the law takes away the liberty that the state of nature gave. What is not taken away by the law remains free and hence it is not strange that Hobbes idea forms the essence of our modern notion of legality—what is not prohibited by law is permitted.

The civil law furthermore serves the paramount function of distinguishing good from evil:

> the measure of Good and Evill actions is the Civill Law; and the Judge the Legislator, who is alwayes the Representative of the Common-wealth.[17]

According to Hobbes the confusion (of the republicans) of trying to distinguish between good and bad forms of power was indeed to blame for the civil strife and bloodshed that was (and to some degree still is) commonplace

[14] T Hobbes, *ibid*, p 149.

[15] An example of contemporary history could be that of the Soviet Union. The Soviet Union was certainly a free state in the sense that no one could tell the Soviet Union what to do and not to do without this meaning that the citizens of the Soviet Union were free in any sense comparable to their counterparts in the Western world.

[16] Hobbes above n 12, p 200.

[17] Hobbes above n 12, p 223.

in human society.[18] Hobbes strived to eliminate the possibility of assessing law against some (independent) moral criteria and thereby augured the thesis, central to all brands of legal positivism, that there should be a clear distinction as to what the law *is* and what it *ought* to be.

5 COUNTERCHALLENGES TO LEVIATHAN

Hobbes straightforward view of the concept of liberty and its relation to the law was challenged by several contemporaries of a more republican vein. James Harrington for one accepted the Hobbesian challenge by stating:

> to say that a Lucchese [Lucca was an Italian republic, authors remark] hath no more liberty or immunity from the laws of Lucca, than a Turk hath from those of Constantinople, and to say that a Lucchese hath no more liberty or immunity by the laws of Lucca than a Turk hath by those of Constantinople, are pretty different speeches. The first may be said of all governments alike, the second scarce of any two.[19]

John Locke also rejected the Hobbesian notion of freedom and law by affirming that freedom must be understood, in the Roman fashion, as non-domination (i.e. absence of arbitrariness) rather than as simple non-interference. The law, as an expression of public reason, was instrumental in securing the objective of non-arbitrariness:

> *Freedom of Men under Government*, is to have a standing Rule to live by, common to every one of that Society, and made by the Legislative Power erected in it: A Liberty to follow my own Will in all things, where the Rule prescribes not; and not to be subject to the inconstant, uncertain, unknown, Arbitrary Will of another Man.[20]

Furthermore

> *the end of Law* is not to abolish or restrain, but *to preserve and enlarge Freedom*: For in all the states of created beings capable of Laws, *where there is no Law, there is no Freedom*.[21]

Locke in this passage reconnects to Ciceros distinction between just and unjust forms of law by pointing out that there is a qualitative difference

[18] And by reading of these Greek, and Latine Authors, men from their childhood have gotten a habit (under the falseshew of Liberty), of favouring tumults, and of licentious controlling of the actions of their Soveraigns; and again of controlling those controllers, with the effusion of so much Blood; as I think I may truly say, there was never any thing so deerly bought, as these Western parts have bought the learning of the Greek and Latine tounges, Hobbes, above n 12, p 150.

[19] J Harrington, The Commonwealth of Oceana in *The Commonwealth of Oceana and a System of Politics* (Cambridge, Cambridge University Press [1656] 1992), p 20.

[20] J Locke, above n 10, p 284, § 22.

[21] J Locke, above n 10, p 306, § 57.

between law that preserves and enlarges freedom and law that merely restrains.[22] Democracy and freedom are more complex concepts in the republican tradition than a process of decision-making. A decision that has been endorsed by the majority is not necessarily in accordance with the *res publica* if it is not in the interest of the whole of the community but rather a way of the majority dominating the minority.

On the other hand, the advantages of the democratic process for the *res publica* should not be overlooked. It is certainly the easiest and most efficient way to ensure that decisions are taken with a view to the interest of the whole to place the legislative power in the hands of elected representatives rather than in the hands of a few non-elected (often self-proclaimed) experts. The republican ideal of government rejects a Westminster style model of parliamentary sovereignty since such a system does not provide for any safeguard against the possible domination of the majority. It may be very true that a democratically elected assembly does not generally go about enslaving or dominating minorities but the absence of such safeguards means that there will always be a possibility of this happening. As one of the advocates of the American cause had it in 18th century England:

> For by the same power, by which the people of England can compel them to pay *one penny*, they may compel them to pay the *last penny* they have. There will be nothing but arbitrary imposition on the one side, and humble petition on the other.[23]

Even though the latter possibility seems remote in ordinary political life, it is the mere possibility of arbitrary power that is the target of the republican ideal. The other side of the coin is that political, collective, action will be more difficult, even when there is wide support among the general public for such action. Action will thus only be taken when several powers, representing a more qualified support than a single majority, agree on it.[24]

[22] In the same paragraph Locke makes an implicit reference to the Hobbesian concept of law and freedom, for *Law*, in its true notion, is not so much the limitation as *the direction of a free and intelligent Agent* to his proper interest, and prescribes no farther than is for the general good of those under that law: could they be happier without it, the *Law*, as an useless thing, would of itself vanish; and that ill deserves the name of confinement which hedges us in only from bogs and precipices.

[23] J Priestly, *Political Writings* (Cambridge, Cambridge University Press [1769] 1993), p 140, quoted from Pettit above n 1, p 34.

[24] Even though such a system could indicate a state of paralysis, systems that are based on checks and balances are seldom characterised by inaction and impotence. The paradox was formulated by Montesquieu in his classical analysis of the British constitution: The form of these three powers should be rest or inaction. But as they are constrained to move by the necessary motion of things, they will be forced to move in concert. C. de Montesquieu, *The Sprit of the Laws* (Cambridge, Cambridge University Press [1748] 1989), p 164.

6 INTERPRETATION OF THE *RES PUBLICA*

Res publica concerns the interpretation of fundamental (moral) values underpinning the legal order—the reason *why* there is a legal order in the first place. According to the republican theorists of the 17th and 18th century the concept was, along the lines of the Roman understanding of the constitution, more a question of a continuous process rather than fixed and static rules. The connection between the law and the *res publica* is particularly prominent in theories that stress law as a reflection of public reason rather than as command and will. The difference is once again, as Harrington pointed out, between freedom *from* law and freedom *by* law. The republican understanding of law accordingly accepts some interference in personal autonomy without holding that such interference necessarily restricts personal autonomy. Only when such interference is *arbitrary*, ie not in conformity with the *res publica*, is it to be considered as inconsistent with liberty.[25]

Law is on such a view not necessarily a fetter(as Hobbes formulated it[26]) or simply an expression of command but rather a public reason reflecting a civic bond between the individuals belonging to the legal order. In the same vein that Cicero considered that those who share law also share justice Locke argued that law expressed civic morality among the citizens (in their horizontal relation):

> tis in their *Legislative*, that the Members of a Commonwealth are united, and combined together into one coherent living Body. This *is the Soul that gives Form, Life and Unity* to the Commonwealth: From hence the several Members have their mutual Influence, Sympathy and Connexion.[27]

Locke argued famously (in the *Essay Concerning Human Understanding*) that we are born without any intrinsic knowledge and that all knowledge is acquired through experience. The same principle applies in the legal domain; even if we know that the *res publica* entails the liberty and welfare of the individual members of the commonwealth we do not know beforehand the exact content of these concepts. They can only be identified by the collective use of reasoning and the legislative is one of the most important arenas for this activity.[28] Just as the use of reason sets the individual free in the personal sphere[29], reason in the law is crucial for securing political and legal freedom.

[25] This concept is developed by Pettit, above n 1, p 51ff.

[26] T Hobbes, The Citizen, in *Man and Citizen* (Indianapolis, Hackett Publishing [1642] 1991) p 274.

[27] J Locke, *Two Treatises of Government* (Cambridge, Cambridge University Press, 1988 [1689]), p 407, II § 212.

[28] Cf J Waldron, *The Dignity of Legislation* (Cambridge, Cambridge University Press, 1999) p 68ff.

[29] Reason must be our last judge and guide in everything, J Locke, *An Essay Concerning Human Understanding* (Oxford, Oxford University Press [1690] 1975) p 704.

Along the lines of the Lockean argument it is often assumed that the task of public reasoning, ultimately resulting in legal norms, belongs primarily to political assemblies in general and parliaments in particular. The reason for this assumption is that political assemblies reflect all of, or at least most of the, diverse opinions and views found in society. It is from their interaction that a shared notion of social justice can be elaborated. As Burke formulated the idea in his speech to the electors of Bristol on 3 November 1774:

> Parliament is not a *congress* of ambassadors from different and hostile interests; which interests each must maintain, as an agent and advocate, against other agents and advocates; but parliament is a *deliberative* assembly of *one* nation, with *one* interest, that of the whole; where, not local purposes, not local prejudices, ought to guide, but the general good, resulting from the general reason of the whole. You choose a member indeed; but when you have chosen him, he is not member of Bristol, but he is a member of *parliament*.[30]

Parliaments are the places where citizens opinions meet in a free debate and where the end result is likely to improve from the preceding deliberations and to be consistent with a notion of common good rather than as political horse-trading where each group seeks maximum benefit at the others expense.

There are on the other hand limits to what the elected assembly can decide. As already Cicero pointed out, the power held by a democratic assembly can never be thought to be arbitrary in kind, a view later echoed by Locke.[31] Secondly, the legislature cannot give their powers away to someone who is not answerable to the people since this would be tantamount to renouncing ones own reason. Locke formulated this position by stating that the grant conveyed by the people to the legislature can only be to make *Laws*, and not to make *Legislators*.[32]

A republican understanding of the nature of power and law as the instrument for securing freedom obviously calls for a check even on the democratically elected legislature. With the words of the American founding fathers: An *elective despotism* was not the government we fought for.[33] Checks on the legislative power are in modern constitutional law most often entrusted to the judicial power, ie to a court of one kind or another. On the other hand a court will not often, apart from rather extreme cases, be in a position to represent a morally superior position in relation to the elected legislature. A moral dialogue that is conducted exclusively in the

[30] The speech is available at http://press-pubs.uchicago.edu/founders/documents/v1ch13s7.html.

[31] Locke, *Two Treatises of Government*, above n 26, p 357.

[32] Locke, *Two Treatises of Government*, above n 26, p 363. Locke uses the term *legislative* in the original.

[33] J Madison, The Federalist no 48, in A Hamilton, J Madison & J Jay, *The Federalist* above n 11 p 256.

courts would disregard the same activity in the legislative assembly and a court that bluntly insists on imposing its own values over those of the democratically elected bodies will in the end most likely be either wing-clipped or outright abolished.

Still a judicial remedy remains essential for the attainment of non-domination in respect of the public power. The approach taken in the US and Canadian supreme courts is instructive regarding the striking of balance between judicial review and majority decision-making in political bodies. According to this view it corresponds to the political bodies to identify the material values and policies to be pursued by the public authorities while the courts are charged with the duty to ensure that these values are universalistic and applied equally to all without any (conscious or unconscious) bias regarding impact in respect to minorities.[34] The underlying idea is to secure coherence in the law as an analogy to individual reasoning on moral issues where a person is supposed to act on a consistent set of values even if the factual conditions change. Holding that the courts primary objective is to ensure equal and unbiased application of the law can be seen as a transformation from moral philosophy to law of the thesis of *universalisability* which is associated with the philosophy of Richard Hare. Hare formulates this thesis, which also concerns the bridge between *is* and *ought*, in terms of universalising value judgements thereby providing consistency and reason to moral actions.[35] Hares argument prescribes that the person who states a given value judgement is obliged, as a logical consequence, to apply that judgement to all similar cases even if (or especially when) it would affect himself.

If Hares argument is translated to the legal domain the ideal result would be that only legislation based on coherent and unbiased principle, ie that meets the requirement of universalisability, will survive judicial review. The courts participation in the identification of the *res publica* is thus not primarily a question of the judges imposing 'their view' of the morally good on the other branches of government. The ideal of equal protection and rational argumentation amounts to, with the terminology of Dworkin, the concept of *integrity* in the law, meaning that the courts should enforce the law as a coherent and principled whole rather than as isolated *ad hoc* pieces[36] The courts have an important task of interpreting the *res publica* in their day to day business when adjudicating in matters concerning individual rights and freedoms according to the coherent set of principles that make up the *res publica.*

[34] This theory is developed in J Hart Ely, *Democracy and Distrust—A Theory of Judicial Review* (Cambridge, MA, Harvard University Press, 1980).

[35] R Hare, *Freedom and Reason* (Oxford, Oxford University Press 1963) p 30ff.

[36] R Dworkin, *Laws Empire* (Cambridge, MA, Harvard University Press, 1986), p 166f and 254, 258.

7 RES PUBLICA IN THE EC-TREATY AND THE REASONING OF THE ECJ

It is no exaggeration to hold that the ECJ started it all. The ECJ has consistently, since the 1960s, claimed that the EC has a constitutional legal order that is independent from the legal orders of the Member States and that it embraces individuals as well as states. By the same token it is from the status as an independent legal order that the problems associated with the democratic deficit of the EU seek their provenance. The claims of the ECJ correspond fairly well with the republican tradition and a European *res publica* can be advanced on the basis of the Treaty Establishing the European Community ECT and the case law of the ECJ even if there are, as will be seen, some problematic aspects to this argument.

The starting point of the constitutional argument is found in the by now classical statement in the preamble of the ECT that the EC strives to create an ever closer Union among the peoples of Europe. This statement has been said to form the genetic code of the EC.[37] Further guidance could be found in Article 6.1 Treaty on the European Union (TEU) which states that the EU is founded on certain fundamental values (liberty, democracy, respect for human rights and fundamental freedoms and the rule of law) and that these principles are common to the Member States. These constitute the moral foundations of the EU or, put in other terms, its *res publica*—its claim for moral authority.

The ECJ set out its famous arguments for the new legal order of the EC in the seminal *van Gend en Loos* case.[38] One could summarise the argument of the Court as follows: the Treaty provisions could not be understood without an inquiry into its spirit, the general scheme and the wording of [its] provisions. The objective of the Treaty implied that the Treaty did not limit itself to creating mutual obligations between the states but also created rights and obligations for *individuals* which became part of their legal heritage. The Treaties were adopted in legal form and created institutions with state powers. The treaties furthermore made reference to individuals in the preamble and the nationals of the Member States were called upon to collaborate in the functioning of the Community through the European Parliament and the Economic and Social Committee.[39] As a consequence, the Court held that, provided some other conditions are met, rights laid down in the Treaty can have *direct effect* in the Member States. The important constitutional point is that the effect of EC law follows directly from the Treaty and not from the Member States internal provisions. Direct effect

[37] F Mancini & D Keeling, 'Democracy and the European Court of Justice', *The Modern Law Review* [1994] pp 175–90 at p 186.

[38] 26/62, *van Gend en Loos*, ECR [1963] 1.

[39] *Ibid*, p 12.

is in this sense incompatible with the traditional view of the relationship between domestic law and international law since the traditional position is that the internal effects of international law are ultimately determined by the states constitutional provisions.[40]

In the likewise seminal case *Costa v ENEL*[41] the ECJ held that the terms and spirit of the Treaty were accepted by the states on a basis of reciprocity. The executive force of the treaties could not vary between the Member States without giving rise to discrimination between the European individuals. The Treaty, as an independent source of law, could not be overridden without being deprived of its character as Community law and without the legal basis of the Community itself being called into question.[42] The conclusion from this reasoning was that EC law had supremacy over Member State law within the jurisdiction of the ECJ, even in the case where the Member State law concerned was of constitutional character, something which runs counter to the traditional view on the relationship between international and domestic law.

A further paramount step in the development of the constitutional character of the EU was the introduction of protection of fundamental rights of the individual as a part of the general principles of European Community law.[43] Reading a bill of rights into EC law was a very significant step in the constitutionalisation process of the Treaties since it placed a hitherto unprecedented emphasis on the position of the individual in the EC legal order.[44] The Court found that fundamental rights were protected as rights under EC law, rather than as rights of a certain *Member State* legal order. Such protection can be seen as a necessary counterbalance to the principle of supremacy of EC law in relation to national law. If violations, by Community institutions, of fundamental rights of the individual could no longer be checked by national constitutional provisions an alternative protection under Community law would have to be found for the EC to enjoy

[40] Cf inter alia, E Denza, 'The Relationship between International and National law', in MD Evans (ed), *International Law* (Oxford, Oxford University Press, 2006), p 428. This very argument was also put forward in the *van Gend en Loos* case by the Dutch, German and Belgian governments (*ibid,* pp 6–8) and was supported by the Advocate General but not by the Court.

[41] 6/64, *Costa v ENEL*, ECR [1964] 585.

[42] *Ibid,* p 593f.

[43] The ECJ embarked on this path in a string of cases in the 1960s and 1970s starting with the case 29/69, *Stauder*, ECR [1969] 419. The idea was further clarified in the seminal case *Internationale Handelsgesellschaft* where the Court held that respect for fundamental rights form an integral part of the general principles of law protected by the Court of Justice. The protection of such rights, whilst inspired by the constitutional traditions common to the Member States, must be ensured within the framework of the structure and objectives of the Community, 11/70, ECR [1970] 1125 at 1134, § 4. A fuller account of the issue is given in T Tridimas, *The General Principles of EC Law* (Oxford, Oxford University Press, 1999), pp 202–43.

[44] Cf F Mancini, *The Making of a Constitution for Europe*, Common Market Law Review [1989] pp 595–614 at p 608ff.

constitutional legitimacy. To paraphrase Voltaires famous remark on the Deity, one could say that if constitutional rights protection did not exist in EC law before, one would have to invent it.

It is clear from this cursory glance that the ECJ has given an unprecedented importance to the position of the individual in international law and the rule of law in its reasoning on why EC law constitutes a new legal order. The treaties are concluded in legal form and create rights for individuals (although the treaties themselves were concluded by states). This is said to be because of the spirit and general scheme and the objective of the treaty, ie because of its moral *purpose* or *res publica*. Considering the emphasis placed on the rights of the European individual conferred by their common law (the Treaties), the equality of these individuals in regard to these rights and the fact that the ECJ is charged with upholding these rights, one can ague that the reasoning of the ECJ is quite republican in nature.

The EC functions as an important source of genuine rights for European individuals, rights that could not be achieved by the Member States on their own. No state can on its own grant their citizens the right to freely move and reside within other Member States. Even an agreement between two (or more) states on these matters would leave the rights of the individual as, at best, accessory to those of the state in question. What is more; these rights do not only function as a constitutional parameter against ones own state (thereby strengthening judicial protection considerably in states that, like Sweden, previously had a comparatively weak tradition of judicial review), they are also operative against other states as a matter of right and not as concession.

By creating the EU, the rights now held by European citizens have furthermore been set on an independent legal footing which also requires that any claim based on EC law must be arguable in a court of law, ultimately before the ECJ itself.[45] The institutions of the EU can therefore be said to be endowed with a moral authority, a *res publica*, based on these rights. Even though the interest in fundamental rights was to some extent forced on the ECJ by national courts (notably the German constitutional court) the challenge has been readily accepted and the view expressed by one of the Advocate Generals is very much to the point:

> The fundamental principles of national legal systems] contribute to forming that philosophical, political and legal substratum common to the Member States from which through the case-law an unwritten Community law emerges, one of the essential aims of which is precisely to ensure the respect for the fundamental rights of the individual.[46]

Conferring rights on individuals also means that conflicts between different rights under EC law will occur. The ECJ has on several occasions held that

[45] Eg, laid down in the case 222/84, *Johnston* ECR [1986] 1651.
[46] 11/70, *Internationale Handelsgesellschaft*, ECR [1970] 1125, at p 1146.

a right under EC law can only be assessed in the light of the Community legal order itself (and not that of a particular Member State) if the unity of Community law and the cohesion of the Community are not to be jeopardized.[47] A right protected under Community law can, just like most rights in the legal orders of the Member States, be restricted in the general interest. This concept in effect translates into the rights and interests of other individuals articulated through the institutions and legal norms of the public power. The general interest is in this context closely linked to the *res publica* in the sense that a restriction that does not infringe the substance of the right[48] and represents a fair balance between the interests of all parties concerned. The point is that the general interest at issue here is one that embraces the entire EC and not only a part of it. It is thus possible that the general interest in the EC might call for a restriction that would not have been permitted in one part (typically a Member State) or vice versa. By taking the entire EU into consideration the balance between competing claims will ideally be based on more universalistic principles than if they were to be decided within a single Member State thereby connecting to Ciceros ideal that the law ought to be universal for all mankind rather than divided by different states.

It is certainly true that the institutional framework for the EU has not caught up with its judge-made development with its *exodus* from the origins in public international law to a constitutional supra-national legal order. The institutions still reflect a Community where the states have a powerful position between the individuals and the institutions of the EU. On balance, however, the interplay between national courts and the ECJ has developed in such a way as to qualify as a constitutional legal order with individuals as well as states (and it should be recalled that according to the republican ideal the state has no moral standing besides that of its individuals). The EU seems to accord well with the republican ideal as far as the judicial empowerment and rule of law is concerned. Freedom understood as non-domination can reasonably be said to be considerably strengthened by introducing a constitutional bond, ultimately subject to one common judge, between the European individuals.

8 THE PROBLEM OF IDENTIFICATION OF THE *RES PUBLICA* AND THE LEGISLATIVE DEFICIT

The moral dialogue of EC law through courts, as required by the republican ideal, to some degree fulfils Ciceros idea of law as *recta ratio*. However, the other part of the moral dialogue, the one conducted in legislative assemblies, is underdeveloped at the European level. This condition is aggravated

[47] 44/79, *Hauer*, ECR [1979] 3727, § 14.
[48] 44/79, *Hauer*, ECR [1979] 3727, § 30.

by the fact that the members of the European Parliament are elected on national lists with the concomitant effect that there is rarely any European party politics of the kind that we are used to in the Member States.[49] The democratic deficit of the EU is well known and this is not the place to give a full account of the problem. It is sufficient to point out that the legislature has a pivotal role in conducting public reasoning thereby interpreting the *res publica* and that this is a problematic process within the EU.

There are two dimensions to the problem of the legislative deficit. The first is that the European Parliament plays a rather insignificant role in the legislation taking place at the EU level. The second is that the current emphasis on a system of mutual recognition, rather than legislation at the EU level, risks weakening the degree of public reasoning at the EU level and, as a result, undermining its *res publica.*

Concerning the role of the European Parliament (EP) it is well known that it is the only legislative assembly that remotely meets the republican requirements of an elected assembly and that it wields, at most, a veto power over the actions of the Commission and the Council. Even though this state of affairs could be, and often is, viewed as problematic, in itself it is not incompatible with a republican ideal (which does not require that the legislature can act on its own initiative) as long as legislative measures of significance are subject to the deliberations of the elected assembly that reflects the diverse opinions held in contemporary society. Still, the picture that emerges in the EU is that the EP only intervenes sporadically in the legislative process, particularly in politically charged areas like the second and third pillar.

A closer examination of legislation passed at the EU level also reveals that the amount of legislation in the EU adopted by the Commission alone, without the involvement of the Council (which may or may not include the European Parliament), constitutes the majority of current legislation and it is even in the ascendant.[50] This means that more and more issues which call for public reasoning are in fact decided by the non-elected Commission and its experts. To some degree delegation is inescapable in modern legislation but there is a limit where such delegation becomes incompatible with the Lockean principle that the grant conveyed by the people is to make laws and not legislators. The fact that delegated legislation is steadily increasing in the EU is therefore a point of concern from the point of view of *res publica.*

[49] In 1994 I was myself amused to see Spanish election propaganda for the European Parliament elections where one of the mainstream parties urged the voters to vote for their candidates since these would defend the interests of Spain in the European Parliament. Indicative, one might suspect, of the fact that there was little sense of a European *res publica* present at the party headquarters.

[50] For a fuller account see CF Bergström in SIEPS report 2006:6, Vad hände(r) med den konstitutionella krisen i EU, pp 8–11.

The second problem related to the legislative deficit concerns the tendency towards increasing reliance on mutual recognition rather than legislative measures at the European level. The position was expressed in the conclusions of the Presidency at the summit of the European Council in Tampere (Finland) on 15-16 October 1999 where paragraph 33 of the conclusions contains the following statement:

> The European Council [therefore] endorses the principle of mutual recognition which, in its view, should become the cornerstone of judicial co-operation in both civil and criminal matters within the Union.[51]

The principle of mutual recognition is related to the general principle of loyalty, one of the cornerstones of the Community, laid down in Article 10 ECT. The principle of loyalty applies not only in the relationship between the Member States and the institutions of the EC but also between the Member States themselves.[52]

The basis of the mutual confidence and the horizontal duty of loyalty is a common view concerning the fundamental values on which the different legal orders of the Member States and the Community itself rest (Article 6.1 TEU). An economic and political community presupposes a community of values.

The question of fundamental values concerns the moral foundations of the legal order. The arguments from moral philosophy constitute the contact surface between law and philosophy and are important for the understanding of legal norms since they are expressed in legal argumentation among legal actors. The fundamental values thereby influence the reasoning of both lawyers and politicians and, accordingly, individual judgments, legal norms and legal opinion (the surface level of law). These are both justified and criticised in accordance with the fundamental values. This part of the law can, with the words of the Finnish professor Kaarlo Tuori, be termed the *deep-structure* of the law.[53] The deep-structure is separate from single legal norms and judgments but can change over time as the activities at the surface level sediment downwards and over time the deep-structure may change accordingly.

There is prima facie considerable concurrence between the different legal orders that comprise the EU as regards the fundamental values. This concurrence is, as mentioned earlier, expressed in the Treaties but also in

[51] The conclusions are available at: http://europa.eu.int/council/off/conclu/oct99/oct99_en.htm.

[52] J Temple Lang, Constitutional Law: Article 5 EEC Treaty, *Common Market Law Review* [1990] pp 645–81 at p 671 and J Nergelius, *Amsterdamfördraget och EU:s institutionella maktbalans* (Norstedts Juridik, 1998), p 103.

[53] K Tuori, 'Towards a Multi-layered View of Modern Law', in A Aarnio, R Alexy & G Bergholtz (eds), *Justice, Morality and Society—A Tribute to Aleksander Peczenik* (Juristförlaget i Lund, 1997), p 432ff.

numerous instruments of international law where all Member States are signatories. Most prominent among these is perhaps the European Convention on Human Rights but, among others, the UN Rights of the Child convention should be mentioned in this category. There is by now a rich stock of case law from the two European Courts, the ECJ and the European Court of Human Rights, which has generated an important interaction between national courts and their European counterparts.[54] This interaction has resulted in a largely common European administrative and procedural law as well as considerable agreement in the field of human rights.[55]

The problem concerning mutual recognition is that common values may be interpreted differently and it is well known that the values referred to in Article 6.1 TEU have historically often been in conflict with each other. The final interpretation of different values has traditionally been performed in the national legal order and thus, directly or indirectly, in the (political) democratic decision making process that ultimately governs the legal order of the state in question.

At the international level the classical principle of sovereignty has meant that states are considered as equals[56] and, consequently, that different legislators (states) interpretations of the same fundamental value may in fact diverge considerably. To give an example, the more precise interpretation of the common value freedom of expression (to take an issue that is particularly important in Swedish constitutional law) will most likely be different in state A than in state B. In such a situation, where all states concerned are based on democracy and the rule of law, it will not be possible (if recourse is not to be had to a model of natural law) to explain one solution as better than the other by other means than referring to the moral values underpinning the legal order in question.[57]

The principle of mutual recognition reflects a position where the (sovereign) Member States retain more power to decide themselves on the proper interpretation of the fundamental values than they would have had in the case of a proper unification at the European level. At the same time the principle of mutual recognition means that a diverging interpretation of a fundamental value may be parachuted into the legal order of another Member State. However, and for this very reason, the principle of mutual recognition is not without exceptions. A mutual recognition may be refused when it would be in conflict with the foundations of the legal order (*ordre*

[54] Cf D Edward, 'National Courts—The Powerhouse of Community Law', *The Cambridge Yearbook of European Legal Studies* [2004], p 1ff.

[55] C J Schwarze, 'Tendencies towards a Common Administrative Law in Europe', *European Law Review* [1991] pp 3–19 at p 4ff.

[56] This principle is expressed in the charter of the United Nations Ch 1 Art 2: The Organization is based on the principle of the sovereign equality of all its Members.

[57] With Tuoris terminology one can say that a shared deep-structure can still result in different results at the surface level.

public). Such foundations may well be certain fundamental rights that are expressed in the constitution of the Member State or that are otherwise recognized as fundamental by the legal actors. No Member State seems prepared to give up the right of invoking *ordre public* understood as the ultimate power to decide on fundamental values, not even in relation to other Member States that are all democracies based on the rule of law.

The possibility to be the ultimate judge on the interpretation of fundamental values entails an important aspect of sovereignty.[58] Even if the scope for resorting to *ordre public* in relation to the areas covered by EC law may be limited, it is most likely the question of ultimate authority, rather than differences of culture or history, that impedes an unconditional acceptance of the principle of mutual recognition. Resorting to the concept of *ordre public* against another Member State therefore also entails, explicitly or implicitly, a rejection of that states interpretation of the common fundamental value.[59]

The current alternative to mutual recognition is unification at the European level—a standard (whether of rights protection or product requirements) simply has to be decided at either Member State or European level. As was pointed out before, however, the decision making at the European level does not involve the European Parliament as the legislative assembly to an extent comparable to what is required within the Member States. This weakness is aggravated by the fact that there is a lack of pan-European debate or civil society.[60] On the contrary, political debate is still predominantly conducted within the Member States separately and there currently seems to be no significant development towards a European market square. The European political process therefore seems to have a slimmer chance of conducting public reasoning on the interpretation of the fundamental values when compared to the process in the Member State.

The problem in Europe is that a common and precise interpretation of the shared fundamental value can hardly be given by the political institutions until there is a functioning representative *European* democracy. Until then it seems inescapable that conflicts will occur between diverging interpretations of the fundamental values in the different Member States. These

[58] Cf E Schmidt-Assman, 'Verwaltungskooperation und Verwaltungskooperationsrecht in der Europäischen Gemeinschaft', *Europarecht* [1996] pp 270–301 at p 297f.

[59] The problem of sharing the same ideal but still disagreeing on its precise content is classical and was formulated by Hobbes in the following terms: [Men] may agree indeed in certain general things, as that *theft*, *adultery*, and the like are *sins*; as if they should say that all men account those things *evil*, to which they have given names which are usually taken in an *evil* sense. But we demand not whether theft be a sin, but what is to be termed theft, T Hobbes, above n 26, p 283, § 17.

[60] J Weiler, 'Europe: The Case Against the Case for Statehood', *European Law Journal* [1998] pp 43–62 at p 57. This view was also expressed in the famous *Maastricht* judgment by the German Constitutional Court: 2BvR 2134/92 & 2159/92 *Brunner v European Union Treaty* [1994] 1 CMLR p 87, § 41 (English translation).

will collide in situations that may involve considerations of *ordre public*. In such a case it will, in the absence of interpretation by the political bodies, fall to the courts (in theory ultimately to the ECJ), to decide which interpretation should be given legal effect.

The principle of mutual recognition seeks its origins in the famous decision by the ECJ in the case *Cassis de Dijon*.[61] The principle of mutual recognition was according to Federico Mancini, a former judge on the ECJ, to a large degree motivated by the fact that the political institutions were unable to agree on harmonization of rules related to the internal market.[62] In the same manner it can be assumed that the ECJ, within the field of its jurisdiction, may once again deem it necessary to intervene if the process of mutual recognition runs into trouble in ways that may endanger the achievement of the objectives of the ECT laid down in Articles 2–4. In other words, if the political institutions grind to a halt, the ECJ may find itself forced to go on the offensive.

It should be observed, however, that not even Mancini considers the judges of the ECJ as particularly suited to resolve what at heart is the striking of balance of fundamental moral values.[63] When fundamental values are resolved primarily in the courts, the political institutions are deprived their possibility to contribute ex ante to the reasoning on the proper interpretation of fundamental values, the only possibility remaining being an intervention ex post. The result of such a state of affairs may not only be a lower degree of legitimacy but also perhaps a sub-optimal quality of the answers.[64] Transparency in the sense of public comprehensibility and accessibility may also suffer if the discussion on the fundamental values is conducted in terms of general principles of law, case law and procedural terminology.[65]

The emphasis on the principle of mutual recognition therefore reduces the possibility of a genuine European legislative reasoning on the more precise content of the fundamental values and accordingly means that the definition of the European *res publica* might actually be conducted in the Member States rather than at the European level. The current stress on the principle of mutual recognition means that the interpretation of fundamental values at the European level will move from the political bodies to a more or less unwilling ECJ while at the same time the risk increases that

[61] 120/78, ECR [1979] 649. The principle of mutual recognition is found in § 14 of the judgment.

[62] F Mancini, 'The Making of a Constitution for Europe', *Common Market Law Review*, [1989] pp 595–614 at p 613f.

[63] *Ibid*, at p 612.

[64] A Gutmann & D Thompson, *Democracy and Disagreement* (Cambridge, Belknap/Harvard University Press, 1996) MA, s 347.

[65] Eg see B Holmström in SOU (Swedish Government Official Report): 1999:76, Maktdelning, s 141.

national courts may let the fundamental values of their own legal order prevail in case of conflict. As the scope of EC law is expanding and now encompasses areas that were previously closely linked to Member State sovereignty (eg criminal law and social security), it can not be ruled out that clashes between Member State constitutional law and EC law may jeopardize what the ECJ has accomplished with 40 years of case law developing a constitutional legal order for the Community.[66]

9 THE CLASH OF FREEDOMS—THE SWEDISH VS THE EUROPEAN CONSTITUTION

The difference between the deep-structures of the various legal orders of the Member States may also shed light on some fundamental issues concerning the relationship between national law and the EU itself. The republican ideal accords fairly well with the European constitution as developed by the ECJ based on the notion of freedom as non-domination and the EC is instrumental in furthering this ideal. Even though the ideals that the ECJ has built its constitutional case law on are prima facie shared among all Member States it is obvious that the notion of the EC as a constitutional entity has gone down better in some Member States than in others. Sweden is among the clubs most reluctant members and is indeed distinguished in the sense that the very membership itself is constantly under debate.

The ambiguous attitude towards the membership of the EU is reflected in the Swedish constitution. The IG (regeringsformen) does not contain any general statement of Swedish membership of the EU or any European dimension in particular (as in the German *Grundgesetz* Article 23). The casual observer of the Instrument of Government (IG) will instead be caught slightly by surprise when the EU is suddenly found in Chapter 10, under the heading Relations with other states and international organizations—hardly indicative of a European constitution. The first part of Article 5 of Chapter 10 deals with the EU in the following manner:

> The Riksdag may transfer a right of decision-making which does not affect the principles of the form of government within the framework of European Union cooperation. Such transfer presupposes that protection for rights and freedoms in the field of cooperation to which the transfer relates corresponds to that afforded under this Instrument of Government and the European Convention for the Protection of Human Rights and Fundamental Freedoms.

The transfer of rights to the EU is (apart from a further requirement that a transfer must have the support of three fourths of those voting) made subject to two material conditions; the first is that the transfer may not

[66] F Mancini, 'Europe: The Case for Statehood', *European Law Journal* [1998] pp 29–42 at p 41.

affect the principles of the form of government, the second is that the rights protection in those areas may not fall below the level proscribed by (Chapter 2) of the IG and the European Convention of Human Rights.[67]

The principles of the form of government are not defined in Article 5 but seem to relate to Chapter 1 of the IG which has the heading basic principles of the form of government. In Chapter 1, it is, among other things, stated that all public power in Sweden proceeds from the people (Article 1), expressing the idea of popular sovereignty, and that the Riksdag is the foremost representative of the people (Article 4). These two provisions were central in the debate that preceded the Swedish membership when the constitutional committee stated that transfer of rights could not be made to an extent that jeopardized the position of the Riksdag as the foremost organ of the Swedish state.[68]

The position of the Riksdag as the principal organ of the Swedish state permeates the Swedish constitution and the constitution is primarily designed to protect its status at the top of the Swedish organs of state. The Riksdag controls the government according to the parliamentarian principle and is not subject to any ordinary judicial review by the Swedish courts. On the contrary, a Swedish court may only abstain from applying a law if it is manifestly in conflict with the IG (IG 11:14). The traditional position in Swedish constitutional law is that courts are not to exercise any political power of significance since such a position is atypical of the Swedish constitution where political power should rest with the Riksdag.[69] The Swedish constitution is thus characterized by the ideal of (popular) sovereignty with the Riksdag representing the sovereign people.

The Swedish constitution is not designed to institute a system of checks and balances of the sort associated with the republican model of non-domination. On the contrary, the Swedish constitution seems to operate more on the Hobbesian principle of freedom as non-interference. The Swedish bill of rights laid down in Chapter 2 of the IG is directed primarily to the Riksdag itself rather than to the Swedish courts. This conclusion is supported by the fact that there is a significant shortage of case law on the Chapter 2 of the IG. The Swedish bill of rights is furthermore according to the provisions thought to be operative only in the relationship between the individual and the public institutions (vertically) and not

[67] The second requirement is probably a theft from the German constitutional courts reasoning in the famous *Solange* judgments where the German court said that it would accept the ECJs doctrine of supremacy only as long as (*solange*) the EC provided a rights protection of the same quality as that provided by the German *Grundgesetz*.

[68] As argued by the Constitutional Committee of the Riksdag in its opinion on the Swedish accession to the EU, betänkande (committee report) 1993/94:KU p 27f

[69] Cf proposition (Government bill to the Riksdag proposing legislation) 1975/76:209, p 91, prop 1978/79:195 p 41, SOU 1987:6, p 255 and B Bengtsson, 'Om domstolarnas lagprövning', *Svensk Juristtidning* [1987] p 234.

between individuals (horizontally) which further indicates that the rights laid down in it are more of a non-interference than a non-domination character. The underlying ethos of the IG is thus to preserve the liberty of the Riksdag rather than the individual citizens. This is not to say that Swedish government in its day to day life is characterized by despotical features, only that the institutional design seems to be less preoccupied with the possibility of power concentration than the danger that courts and other organs may impede the smooth will formulation and execution of the decisions of the Riksdag.

The fundamental features of the IG condition the Swedish membership in the EU and the activities of the European institutions. Some of theses fundamental aspects were dealt with by legal council (lagrådet) in its opinion on Treaty Establishing a Constitution for Europe. There can be no question that from the Swedish point of view the exercise of power of the European institutions is seen as borrowed from the Riksdag, a subordination further underlined by the fact that it can, according to the legal council (lagrådet) revoke the transfer of rights to the EU with simple majority.[70] The legal council also cautioned that the transfer laid down in the Treaty Establishing a Constitution for Europe impinged seriously on the core of state sovereignty[71] and that the overall effect of the Treaty entailed a serious weakening of the position of the Riksdag.[72] Surprisingly, the legal council concluded that the Treaty was compatible with the IG. The opinion can be seen as a shot over the bow in the sense that further transfer of rights to the EU would be incompatible with the basic principles of the IG and thus with the democratic principle as it is laid down in the Swedish constitution.

The second requirement of Article 5 of Chapter 10 IG concerns the standard of rights protection and judicial remedies offered by the EU. This requirement, which is at the heart of the republican model, seems to preoccupy the legal council to a significantly smaller degree. The legal council found that the level of rights protection was consistent with both the Swedish IG and with the European Convention of Human Rights and indeed that rights protection would be stronger with the new Treaty.[73]

The reality though is that the requirement concerning rights protection has never been as significant as the requirement concerning the central role of the Riksdag. The EU has, as mentioned earlier, signified something of a rights revolution for European citizens providing them with a new constitutional parameter for judicial review of state action. In Sweden this introduction has truly been of a revolutionary kind and has constituted, at least in

[70] Opinion of the legal council on the Treaty Establishing a Constitution for Europe, 28 Jun 2005, p 2.

[71] *Ibid*, p 7.

[72] *Ibid*, p 7.

[73] Ibid, p 9.

theory, a break with the past tradition of judicial deference to the Riksdag. It can thus reasonably be said that the EU has strengthened the judicial protection of the individual by providing mechanisms for non-domination that were practically unavailable before the accession to the EU. On the issue of rights protection, Sweden sings out of tune.[74]

The apparent difficulties of compatibility between Swedish constitutional law and EC law are no coincidence. They are the result of a conflict in the deep-structure between the republican notion of constitutional law on one hand and the sovereignty oriented model on the other. The membership in the EU has meant that these two diverging constitutions now co-habitat in the same Member State. Moreover, this conflict is liable to generate further tensions in the future. It cannot be ruled out that the Swedish constitution, under the influence of European law, may over time change towards a more republican one where judicial review and a strengthened position of the rights conferred by the IG may come to be less controversial than they are today. The more probable scenario though is that a serious constitutional conflict is more likely in Sweden than in other Member States that have more rights oriented constitutions.

10 THE MISSING LINK: A EUROPEAN REPUBLIC?

From a republican point of view it is clear that the EU has advanced the ideal of freedom as non-domination and strengthened the rule of law in important areas. Enough to merit the consideration of a European *res publica* separate from those in the Member States and one that is not simply the result of cumulating the *res publica* of the various Member States (an analogy to Rousseaus distinction of the general will and the will of all). The EU does not, on a republican view, take away the political freedom of national parliaments as much as it provides freedom to challenge arbitrary action both by states and other individuals. To reconnect to Harringtons distinction; it is one thing to be free *from* the jurisdiction of the EC and quite another to be free *by* it. If law is assessed against the republican measure of non-domination it is no exaggeration to state that the EC has indeed provided justiciable freedom that individuals previously could only hope for as concession.

There are, on the other hand, significant shortcomings when it comes to the political institutions involvement in the interpretation of the European *res publica*. The Member States still operate as a powerful obstacle to a politicisation (much more than they have been an obstacle to legalisation) of the EU. This means that the republican ideal of law as reason is largely

[74] Cf U Bernitz, 'Det europeiska konstitutionsprojektet och den svenska grundlagen', *Europarättslig Tidskrift* [2006] pp 66–78.

forced to operate with only one of the two wings of reasoning institutions, namely the courts. Put in Ciceros spirit: *recta ratio* in the law is better achieved through interaction between both political and judicial bodies than through only one of them.

The call for politicising the EU should not be confounded with the call for a European state. The republican ideal would be outright hostile to the idea of creating a sovereign European Parliament since this would represent a potential dominator of continental proportions. The creation of a European state would fit very well with the Hobbesian notion of sovereignty (if such a European democracy was the objective) but has no such implications for a republican theory of government. The question to be asked then is not if the EU is fully democratic according to a Hobbesian understanding of sovereign power but whether it is adequately democratic from a republican point of view.[75] To this it could be added that, according to a republican model based on the principle of subsidiarity and embracing several different levels of government, a holistic view where consideration is given to democratic elements both at the European level and at Member State (conceivably also at local) level there is a plurality of public fora for European citizens to exercise their civic rights without holding that one particular of these must be the foremost one.

The EU has signified an important challenge to our constitutional conceptions of state, law and democracy. However, much of the debate has focused on the constitutional models rather than on the moral values that underpin these models. Therefore this article has focused on the reasons, ie the moral values, for the existence of law and political society according to the republican constitution rather than on the models themselves since such an approach runs the risk of confusing the model with the underlying values that the model was supposed to safeguard.

The EU is not a state but it is a form of government that secures important values that have been the focus of state power ever since the Roman republic. If a republican view is taken where law and government are designed to secure freedom as non domination and law as a coherent *recta ratio* we could move beyond the monolithic Swedish conception of democracy and welcome the fact that we have become members of a European republic, with a European *res publica*.

BIBLIOGRAPHY

Bengtsson, B, 'Om domstolarnas lagprövning', *Svensk Juristtidning* [1987] p 234.

Bernitz, U, 'Det europeiska konstitutionsprojektet och den svenska grundlagen', *Europarättslig Tidskrift* [2006] pp 66–78.

[75] As argued by N MacCormick, *Questioning Sovereignty—Law, State and Practical Reason* (Oxford, Oxford University Press, 1999), p 145ff.

Cicero, 'The Republic', in *The Republic and The Laws* (Oxford, Oxford University Press, 1998).
Denza, E, 'The Relationship between international and national law', in Evans, MD (ed), *International Law* (Oxford, Oxford University Press, 2006).
Dworkin, R, *Laws Empire* (Cambridge, MA, Harvard University Press, 1986).
Edwards, D, 'National Courts—The Powerhouse of Community Law', *The Cambridge Yearbook of European Legal Studies* [2004].
Hare, R, *Freedom and Reason* (Oxford, Oxford University Press 1963).
Harrington, J, 'The Commonwealth of Oceana', *The Commonwealth of Oceana and A System of Politics* (Cambridge, Cambridge University Press [1656] 1992).
Hart Ely, J, *Democracy and Distrust—A Theory of Judicial Review* (Cambridge, MA, Harvard University Press, 1980).
Hobbes, T, 'The Citizen', in *Man and Citizen* (Indianapolis, Hackett Publishing [1642] 1991).
——, *Leviathan* (Cambridge, Cambridge University Press [1651] 1991).
Locke, J, *An Essay Concerning Human Understanding* (Oxford, Oxford University Press [1690] 1975).
——, *Two Treatises of Government* (Cambridge, Cambridge University Press [1689] 1988).
MacCormick, N, *Questioning Sovereignty—Law, State and Practical Reason* (Oxford, Oxford University Press, 1999).
Madison, J, 'The Federalist no 48 and The Federalist no 55', in Hamilton, A, Madison J, & Jay, J, *The Federalist* (Everymans Library [1787] 1992).
Mancini, F, 'The Making of a Constitution for Europe', *Common Market Law Review* [1989] pp 595–614.
——, 'Europe: The Case for Statehood', *European Law Journal* [1998] pp 29–42.
Mancini, F, & Keeling, D, 'Democracy and the European Court of Justice', *The Modern Law Review* [1994] pp 175–90.
Nergelius, J, *Amsterdamfördraget och EU:s institutionella maktbalans* (Stockholm, Norstedts Juridik, 1998).
Pettit, P, *Republicanism—A Theory of Freedom and Government* (Oxford, Oxford University Press, 1997).
Pocock, JGA, *The Machiavellian Moment—Florentine Political Thought and the Atlantic Republican Tradition* (Princeton, Princeton University Press, 1975).
Priestly, J, *Political Writings* (Cambridge, Cambridge University Press [1769] 1993), p 140.
Rousseau, JJ, 'The Social Contract' in *The Social Contract and other later political writings* (Cambridge University Press [1762] 1997).
Schmidt-Assman, E, 'Verwaltungskooperation und Verwaltungskooperationsrecht' in der Europäischen Gemeinschaft, *Europarecht* [1996] pp 270–301.
Schwarze, J, 'Tendencies towards a Common Administrative Law in Europe', *European Law Review* [1991] pp 3–19.
Skinner, Q, *The Foundations of Modern Political Thought* (Cambridge, Cambridge University Press, 78).
Temple Lang, J, 'Constitutional Law: Article 5 EEC Treaty', *Common Market Law Review* [1990] pp 645–81.
Tridimas, T, *The General Principles of EC Law* (Oxford, Oxford University Press, 1999).

Tuori, K, 'Towards a Multi-layered View of Modern Law', in Aarnio, A, Alexy R, & Bergholtz, G (eds), *Justice, Morality and Society—A Tribute to Aleksander Peczenik* (Lund, Juristförlaget i Lund, 1997).
Waldron, J, *The Dignity of Legislation* (Cambridge, Cambridge University Press, 1999).
Weiler, J, 'Europe: The Case Against the Case for Statehood', *European Law Journal* [1998] pp 43–62.

5

Inter-Institutional Bargaining in the EU: Comitology and Financial Services

JOSEFIN ALMER*

1 INTRODUCTION

1.1 Background

ON 17 JULY 2006 the Council adopted a decision amending the so called comitology decision and introducing a new comitology procedure; *the regulatory procedure with scrutiny*, This new procedure will put the European Parliament on an 'equal footing' with the Council regarding the supervision and control of delegated legislation to the Commission in the field of co-decision. According to Richard Corbett, the rapporteur of the European Parliament, the deal is 'a significant step forward for the European Parliament'.[1]

Until now, the European Parliament has not had the same right as the Council to supervise delegated legislation, not even when the European Parliament has co-legislated and made decisions together with the Council on what to delegate to the Commission. This situation has been the source of discontent for the European Parliament for a long time and resulted in inter-institutional conflicts regarding delegation to the Commission between the European Parliament and the Council when adopting framework legislation. The European Parliament has argued that since it is a co-legislator it should have the same possibility of controlling the delegated legislation as the Council. The long-term solution that would satisfy the Parliament would be an amendment of Article 202 of the EC Treaty. In the

* Research Assistant and Doctoral Candidate in European Law at the Swedish Institute for European Policy Studies and Stockholm University.

[1] See Mr Corbett during a debate on 21 June 2006 in the Legal Affairs Committee of the European Parliament.

short-term the European Parliament has argued for an amendment of the so-called comitology decision.

The purpose of this article is to try and answer the following questions. What circumstances made the new deal on comitology possible? What were the incentives for the Council? In this article it is argued that it was the parallel development in the field of financial services, the so-called 'Lamfalussy deal', which gave the European Parliament the 'weapon' it needed to make the Council accept an agreement on comitology.

1.2 Outline

In order to set a common frame of reference for the rest of the text the article will begin with a short background on comitology in general and the stand of the European Parliament on comitology in particular (part 2). Thereafter, in part 3, there will be a more detailed description of the development in the field of financial services focusing on the so-called Lamfalussy report on the securities market. In this article it is argued that it was the 'Lamfalussy deal' that made the 'comitology deal' possible and some extra attention will therefore be given to how the 'Lamfalussy deal' came about. In part 4 of the article, a brief account is given of the reform of comitology and the debate on the future of the Union that led to the signing of the Constitutional Treaty. Finally, in part 5, some conclusions will be drawn on why and how the comitology deal came about seen in the light of developments in the area of financial services.

2 BACKGROUND

2.1 Comitology

Article 202 of the Treaty establishing the European Community (ECT) states that the Council shall confer on the Commission, in the acts which the Council adopts, powers for the implementation of the rules which the Council lays down. Furthermore, according to Article 202 ECT, the Council may impose certain requirements in respect of the exercise of these powers. The requirements that the Council has imposed on the Commission are in the form of a decision (in the strict sense set out in Article 249 ECT), according to which the Commission, when implementing basic legislation must co-operate with committees consisting of representatives from national authorities. The cooperation between the Commission and the committees was first formalised in a Council Decision from 1987.[2] On 28 June 1999, the decision was replaced by Council Decision 1999/468, the

[2] 1987/373/EEC: Council Decision of 13 July 1987 laying down the procedures for the exercise of implementing powers conferred on the Commission.

so-called comitology decision.[3] The comitology decision regulates the different types of comitology procedures. The procedures are distinguished by the extent to which their opinions are binding for the Commission. There are three types of comitology procedures: the advisory procedure, the management procedure, and the regulatory procedure.

According to the least binding procedure, the advisory procedure, the Commission shall take utmost account of the opinion delivered by the committee, and it shall inform the committee of the manner in which its opinion has been taken into account. According to the management procedure, the Commission shall adopt the implementing legislation which shall apply immediately. However, if the implementing legislation is not in accordance with the opinion of the committee, the Commission shall inform the Council, where a different measure can be adopted. According to the regulatory procedure, the Commission shall adopt the implementing legislation if it is in accordance with the opinion of the committee. If that is not the case, the Commission shall submit the proposal to the Council and inform the European Parliament.[4]

Three declarations are attached to the comitology decision. According to the first one the Commission states that under the management procedure the Commission recalls that its constant practice is to secure a satisfactory decision which will gain the widest possible support in the comitology committee. Furthermore, the Commission will take account of the position of the members of the committee and act in such a way 'as to avoid going against any predominant position which might emerge against the appropriateness of an implementing measure'. The second statement is from the Council and the Commission and regulates how to align the old comitology procedures with the new one. According to the third declaration the Commission states that it will avoid going against any predominant position in the Council against the appropriateness of an implementing measure in the review of proposals for implementing measures concerning particularly sensitive sectors.[5]

The choice between the different comitology procedures is governed by the principles set out in the decision, for example, that the management procedure should be applied where the common agricultural policy is concerned; the regulatory procedure should be applied when the implementing measures concern 'measures of general scope designed to apply essential provisions of basic instruments'. It should be noted, though, that the criteria for the choice of the different procedures are non-binding.[6]

[3] 1999/468/EC: Council Decision of 28 June 1999 laying down the procedures for the exercise of implementing powers conferred on the Commission.

[4] See Arts 3, 4 and 5 of Council Decision 1999/468, *ibid.*

[5] See the declarations attached to Council Decision 1999/468, *ibid.*

[6] See P Craig, *EU Administrative Law* (Oxford, Oxford University Press, 2006) pp 99–142, on comitology in general.

2.2 The European Parliament and Comitology

The European Parliament has always seen comitology as a threat to its own role; both as a legislator but also as a political supervisor of the Commission. Since the 1960s, the European Parliament has demanded that it obtain influence over the process by a so-called *droit de regard*: which would include a right to be kept informed and a right to state its opinion. In the first comitology decision from 1987, the European Parliament was not even mentioned; comitology was a matter for the Council and the Commission only. When the co-decision procedure was introduced, the European Parliament had a stronger case and in the second comitology decision, the European Parliament was given some influence at least.[7]

According to the preamble of the decision, the purpose of the new decision was, inter alia, to 'improve the involvement of the European Parliament in those cases where the basic instrument conferring implementation powers on the Commission was adopted in accordance with the procedure laid down in Article 251 of the Treaty' and 'to give the European Parliament an opportunity to have its views taken into consideration' when it considers that a measure adopted under the regulatory procedure exceeds the scope provided for in the basic legal act. Furthermore, the purpose was to improve information to the European Parliament by providing that the Commission should inform it on a regular basis of committee proceedings, transmit to it documents related to activities of committees and inform it whenever the Commission transmits to the Council measures or proposals for measures to be taken.[8]

According to Article 8 of the comitology decision, in the field of co-decision the European Parliament has the right to adopt a resolution if it considers that a draft implementing measure goes beyond the scope of the delegation. If that is the case, the Commission shall take the resolution into account and may submit a new draft measure, continue with the procedure or submit a proposal to the legislators on the basis of the Treaty. Furthermore, according to Article 7, the European Parliament shall be informed by the Commission of committee proceedings on a regular basis.[9]

The tactic of the European Parliament has been to use the powers at its disposal to try and influence other areas. The European Parliament may, in the field of co-decision for example, refuse delegation or delay the adoption of important legislation in order to get its way in some other area.[10] One successful example of this tactic can be found in the field of financial services.

[7] See CF Bergström, *Comitology—Delegation of Powers in the European Union and the Committee System* (Oxford, Oxford University Press, 2005), pp 313–5.

[8] See Council Decision 1999/468, above n 3.

[9] See Art 8 of Council Decision 1999/468, above n 3.

[10] See CF Bergström, above n 7.

3 THE FINANCIAL MARKET AND COMITOLOGY

3.1 Background

The financial market consists of the activities of banks, insurance companies, stock brokers and securities managers. According to the Treaty, the market should have been harmonised by 31 December 1992.[11] During the 1990s several actions have been taken in order to achieve the goal of an integrated financial market without succeeding.[12]

Between 1993 and 1999[13] negotiations between the Council and the European Parliament in the conciliation committee have failed to lead to the adoption of the legislative act in question on three occasions alone.[14] One of these occasions concerned amendments of Council Directive 93/6/EEC on the capital adequacy of investment firms and credit institutions and Council Directive 93/22/EEC on investment in securities.[15] These directives constitute the cornerstone of the regulation of the securities market. The original directives were adopted by the Council before the co-decision procedure came into force. The Commission's original proposal included a proposal for the setting up of a securities committee, which would act as a regulatory comitology committee.[16] When the Council adopted the directive, the issues were divided and the Council chose to keep the implementing power to itself for the time being.[17] Thus, the Commission's proposal to set up a securities committee was postponed, which indicates that the governments considered the field too politically sensitive to delegate to the Commission the power to implement the legislation. Even though a securities committee was suggested in order to secure the interests of the governments, they

[11] See Art 14 of the EC Treaty.

[12] See COM (1999) 232, 11.05.99, Financial Services: implementing the framework for financial markets: Action Plan Communication from the Commission. See also the Commission General Report on the Activities of the European Union, 1998 p 25.

[13] Co-decision was introduced 1993 and the new comitology decision was adopted in 1999.

[14] See T Dahlman, 'Förlikningsinstitutet—från Maastricht till Amsterdam', *ERT*, 2000, p 55. One case concerned a directive on voice telephony, the other a proposal for a directive on biotechnology, and the third the amendment of two directives concerning the securities market.

[15] Council Dir 93/6/EEC of the 15 Mar 1993 on capital adequacy of investment firms and credit institutions Official Journal L 141/93 pp 1–26 and Council Dir 93/22/EEC of the 10 May 1993 on investment services in the securities field Official Journal L 141/93 pp 27–46.

[16] See Proposal on a Council Directive on capital adequacy of investment firms and credit institutions Official Journal C 152/90 p 6. Amended proposal for a Council Directive on capital adequacy of investment firms and credit institutions Official Journal C 50/92 p 5. Proposal for a Council Directive on investment services in the securities field Official Journal C 43/89 p 7. Amended proposal for a Council Directive on investment services in the securities field Official Journal C 42/90 p 7.

[17] According to Art 202 of the EC Treaty the Council may reserve the right, in specific cases, to exercise directly implementing powers itself instead of delegating the implementation to the Commission.

apparently wanted to keep full control of the legislation. This was, however, intended to be only a temporary solution.[18]

On 17 July 1995 the Commission proposed a number of changes to the new directives in order to set up a securities comitology committee.[19] At that time the field was subordinate to the co-decision procedure. The European Parliament suggested four amendments to the Commission's proposal following the first reading, which all concerned the committee procedure and delegation to the Commission.[20] The Commission presented an amended proposal on 20 June 1996 which took one of the amendments suggested by the European Parliament into account. However, the European Parliament had proposed to change the comitology procedure into a less restrictive one and the suggestion was not taken into consideration.[21] On 16 December 1996 the Council adopted a common position,[22] according to which the purpose of the amendment of the directives was to establish a comitology committee for securities and to give the Commission the authority to update and adapt the directives in question.[23] On 9 April 1997 the European Parliament proposed further amendments on the committee procedure following its second reading.[24]

The Commission presented a draft opinion on 10 July 1997, after having considered the common position of the Council as well as the European Parliament's proposal, in which the Parliament's proposal concerning the

[18] See Explanatory Memorandum COM (1995) 360. Proposal for a European Parliament and Council Directive amending Council Dir 93/6/EEC of 15 Mar 1993 on the capital adequacy of investment firms and credit institutions and Council Dir 93/22/EEC of 10 May 1993 on investment services in the securities field, Official Journal C 253/95 p 19.

[19] See COM (1995) 360 final. Proposal for a European Parliament and Council Directive amending Council Dir 93/6/EEC of 15 Mar 1993 on the capital adequacy of investment firms and credit institutions and Council Dir 93/22/EEC of 10 May 1993 on investment services in the securities field, Official Journal C 253/95 p 19.

[20] A4-0034/96, first reading resolution of Proposal for a European Parliament and Council Directive amending Council Dir 93/6/EEC of 15 Mar 1993 on the capital adequacy of investment firms and credit institutions and Council Dir 93/22/EEC of 10 May 1993 on investment services in the securities field (COM(95)0360-C4-0305/95-95/0188(COD)), Official Journal C 152/96 p 18.

[21] COM (1996) 292 final. Amended proposal for a European Parliament and Council Directive amending Council Dir 93/6/EEC of 15 Mar 1993 on the capital adequacy of investment firms and credit institutions and Council Dir 93/22/EEC of 10 May 1993 on investment services in the securities field, Official Journal C 221/96 p 31.

[22] C4-0005/97-95/0188(COD), Council Common Position. Common position (EC) No 8/97 of 16 Dec 1996 adopted by the Council with a view to adopting a European Parliament and Council Directive amending Dir 93/6/EEC on the capital adequacy of investment firms and credit institutions and Dir 93/22/EEC on investment services in the securities field, Official Journal C 69/97 p 1.

[23] See Bulletin EU 12-1996, internal market (22/29), point 1.3.38.

[24] A4-0093/97, Decision on the common position adopted by the Council with a view to adopting a European Parliament and Council Directive on amending Council Dir 93/6/EEC on the capital adequacy of investment firms and credit institutions and Dir 93/22/EEC on investment services in the securities field (C4-0005/97-95/0188(COD)) (Co-decision procedure-second reading), Official Journal C 132/97 p 83.

committee procedure was still not accepted.[25] A conciliation committee was set up on 10 February 1998 in order to bring the different opinions of the Council and the European Parliament in line with each other, but they could not agree on a common proposal and the legal act was therefore not adopted.[26] The Commission's proposal to set up a comitology securities committee was rejected this time as well. The failure on the first occasion was due to the fact that the governments did not want to transfer the implementing authority to the Commission, and on the second occasion the European Parliament could not accept the proposed regulatory comitology procedure.

This case illustrates both the difficulties for the institutions to agree on a system for the adoption of legal acts in the securities market, as well as the general conflicts of interest between the institutions regarding comitology. When the governments finally agreed to delegate to the Commission the power to implement the directives in question, the condition was that a more binding comitology procedure would be used. The governments were prepared to delegate legislative powers, even though the field was politically sensitive, since that was a necessary step in order to be able to adapt the legislation rapidly enough to the fast-changing securities market. The European Parliament maintained its view that a less binding procedure should be applied since many political issues would be discussed implying the importance of democratic control. It was agreed in general terms that a delegation would take place. The discussion concerned which committee procedure should be applied.

The two directives were amended a number of times, but the original articles on implementing authorities were kept unchanged. Thus, the initial temporary solution became permanent for more than 10 years, due to institutional disputes regarding comitology.[27]

Thus, there was a deadlock on the securities market. The Council and the European Parliament could not agree on a system of delegation in this field. For the time being the Council kept the implementing power to itself concerning the application of the directive on investment services and all

[25] See also COM (1997) 355 final. Opinion of the Commission pursuant to Art 189b(2)(d) of the EC Treaty, on the European Parliament's amendment to the Council's common position regarding the proposal for an amendment of the European Parliament and Council Dir 93/6/EEC on the capital adequacy of investment firms and credit institutions and Council Dir 93/22/EEC on investment services in the securities field.

[26] See Bulletin EU 4-1998, internal market (16/21), point 1.2.34.

[27] Dir 93/22 has been amended by 95/26, 97/09, 00/64 and 02/87, Dir 93/6 has been amended by 98/31, 98/33, 02/87, 04/39 and 05/01. Arts 29 and 10 of the directives read: '*Pending the adoption of a further Directive* laying down provisions adapting this Directive to technical progress in the areas specified below, *the Council shall*, in accordance with Decision 87/373/EEC, acting by a qualified majority on a proposal from the Commission, *adopt any adaptations which may be necessary*' (emphasis added). The directives were repealed by 04/39 and 06/46.

legislation had to be passed through the time-consuming co-decision procedure. This was not acceptable since it meant that the legislation could not be adapted rapidly enough to new developments on the securities market.

According to the European Parliament, the delay of the reform of the European financial market was due to the fact that there was a lack of political will for reform in the Council. In a resolution on 4 May 1999, the European Parliament stated its view on comitology in general and the financial market in particular. The European Parliament stated in the resolution that it was sceptical to a piece of legislation which only dealt with essential principles and left the details to the Commission. Legal rights could not be guaranteed in this way. The European Parliament referred to its attitude towards comitology in general that had been expressed by the European Parliament many times before and to promises from the Commission to diminish the democratic deficit.[28]

In order to find a solution for the problems regarding the lack of integration of the European Securities Market the Council decided to set up a Committee of Wise Men that had as its mandate to address this issue.[29] The chairman of the Wise Men Committee was Baron Alexandre Lamfalussy, the former president of the European Monetary Institute, and the committee is therefore commonly referred to as the Lamfalussy committee. The mandate of the committee was to address the procedural aspects of the market and not the substance.[30]

3.2 The Implementation of the Lamfalussy Model

The final report of the Lamfalussy committee was presented on 15 February 2001. The main conclusion drawn by the group was that the most pressing problem was that the regulatory framework was too rigid, too slow and in general not very well adapted to the needs of the fast changing and

[28] Resolution on the communication from the Commission on Financial Services: Building a Framework for Action (COM(98) 0625 C4-0688/98), OJ C 279 1999 p 97.

[29] See http://www.europa.eu.int/comm/internal_market/en/finances/general/pogroup.htm. On 8 Feb 2000, the Financial Services policy group met to discuss the securities market. The group stated that it was necessary to improve the financial market and on 17 Jul 2000 the EcoFin Council decided to set up a Committee of Wise Men. See also www.europa.eu.int/comm/internal_market/en/finances/general, 2002-08-15, Financial Services policy group discusses securities markets. 10328/00 (Presse 263), ECOFIN, Brussels 17 Jul 2000.

[30] See also Communication from the Commission entitled 'Financial Services: Building a Framework for Action' presented on 28 Oct 1998. In this Communication the Commission concluded that 'compared to the situation in other industrialised countries, the EU financial services sector is still lagging behind.' In the Communication the Commission presented a number of 'action points', inter alia, that 'the Council and the European Parliament are invited to work together with the Commission to explore a possible inter-institutional agreement enshrining the modalities for *stream-lined, flexible and speedier legislation* in the single financial services market [and] should be committed to exercise a degree of *self-restraint in the legislative process to avoid over-complex legislation*.' See p 8 of the communication.

developing securities market.[31] The proposed remedy for this was to introduce a four-level system for adoption, implementation, transposition, and monitoring of the legislation. The four-level system, now implemented and in force, is based on an extensive use of comitology and consultation with market practitioners and end-users. The basic idea of the system is that the legislators, the Council and the European Parliament, should focus on the essential elements of the legislation leaving the details and technical measures needed to be implemented to the Commission.

Very briefly the four-level system can be described as follows; at level one, the adoption phase, the Commission adopts a proposal for a directive or a regulation after a full consultation process. The proposal is subsequently sent to the European Parliament and the Council, that together adopt the legislative act and reach an agreement on framework principles and definitions of implementing powers according to the co-decision procedure.

At level two, the implementing phase, the Commission adopts the implementing measures in cooperation with two committees, the European Securities Committee (ESC), and the Committee of European Securities Regulators (CESR). The Commission first consults the ESC and after that requests advice from the CESR on the implementing measures. The CESR prepares the advice in consultation with market practitioners, end-users and consumers and submits its advice to the Commission. On the basis of the advice from the CESR, the Commission then makes a proposal to the ESC. The Commission adopts the implementing measures after an approving vote from the ESC.

At level three, the transposition phase, the CESR works to ensure consistent implementation and application of EU legislation in all Member States, for example by adopting guidelines and common standards.

At level four, the monitoring phase, the Commission fulfils its function as guardian of the treaty by checking compliance with EU legislation in Member States and, if necessary, by taking legal action if a breach is suspected.[32]

In 1998 the Council and the European Parliament were not able to agree on the establishment of a securities committee or on formalising delegation to the Commission. Was there any reason to believe that the Council and the European Parliament were prepared to carry out the Lamfalussy reform of 2001, only three years later, based on an even wider use of comitology?

One important event that had happened after the negotiations in the conciliation committee broke down in 1998 was that the new comitology

[31] See Final Report of the Committee of Wise Men on the Regulation of European Securities Markets, Brussel, 15 Feb 2001, pp 13–14.

[32] See Final Report of the Committee of Wise Men, above n 31, p 6. For an assessment on how the Lamfalussy model works in practice, see L Afrell, and K Back, 'Lamfalussymodellen—en ny lagstiftningsprocess inom EU', *ERT* 2005 p 434.

decision had entered into force. This decision met some of the European Parliament's demands. However, the Lamfalussy report was meant to be applicable not only on two directives but on the whole of the securities market and the negotiations proved to be difficult.

The Member States were able to welcome the proposals in the Lamfalussy report only after the Commission had promised *not to go against the dominant view of the governments when passing secondary legislation.*[33] At a summit meeting in Stockholm 23–24 March 2001 the Member States adopted a resolution on a more effective securities market. In the resolution they stressed that a dynamic securities market was an important part of the implementation of the Commission's action plan for the financial market. The legislative procedure had to be speeded up. The governments welcomed the Lamfalussy report and the proposed four-level system. In the resolution the Commission was encouraged to inform the Council and the European Parliament about legislative proposals at an early stage. The division of the legislation into basic legislation on the one hand and secondary legislation adopted by the Commission on the other should be decided on a case-by-case basis, according to the resolution. The European Parliament should always be informed of comitology measures. If the European Parliament were to be of the opinion that the Commission exceeds its powers, the Commission must take this into consideration and reconsider the matter and state the reasons for the proposal.[34]

On 15 March 2001, before the summit in Stockholm, the European Parliament passed a resolution which welcomed the Lamfalussy report.[35] However, the European Parliament considered that negotiations were needed with the Council and the Commission about certain inter-institutional problems still remaining. Among other things, the European Parliament considered that openness was important and that the new committees should be democratically responsible. The Commission was obliged to send proposals for the committees to the European Parliament at the same time as they were sent to the Council. The European Parliament concluded that it could control the new regulatory committee in two ways: by deciding the scope of the delegated powers to the Commission and by *refusing delegation the following time.* Another resolution was adopted only a few weeks later in which the European Parliament emphasized the importance of an effective democratic control of secondary legislation. The European Parliament stressed the importance of receiving all the documents that are sent to the new committees. The Commission was not allowed

[33] 'Power struggle over financial services?' www.EurActiv.com. Agreement on Lamfalussy proposals' www.EurActiv.com. Compare with the declarations attached to the comitology decision, see above part 2.1.

[34] See Stockholm European Council (23–4 Mar 2001): Presidency conclusions.

[35] See European Parliament resolution on the final report of the Committee of Wise Men on the regulation of European securities markets, B5-0173/2001.

to oppose a resolution of the European Parliament but was obliged to start a legislative procedure according to the co-decision procedure if the Commission had exceeded its powers of implementation in the European Parliament's opinion. The European Parliament emphasized that *it would use its powers according to the co-decision procedure* to make sure that the Commission did not exceed its powers.[36]

Almost one year later, in January 2002 the Parliament issued a report on the reform of the legislative procedure on the securities market and a resolution was adopted on 5 February 2002. This was possible after the Commission had given the European Parliament certain promises on how to apply the new system, inter alia, that the time limit for the European Parliament was extended to three months instead of one in which to examine draft implementing measures, that the Commission would take utmost account of the European Parliament's position, and, most relevant for present purposes, the inclusion of so-called sunset clauses in all basic legislation in this field, see below.[37]

3.3 The Institutional and Legal Framework of the European Securities Market

Thus, the proposed four-level system of the Lamfalussy committee was implemented and approved by the institutions on 5 February 2002 and the new institutional framework was also in place.

The ESC, was established by a Commission Decision in June 2001.[38] The decision established the advisory capacity of the ESC. According to Article 2 of the decision, 'the role of the Committee shall be to advise the Commission on policy issues as well as on draft legislative proposals the Commission might adopt in the field of securities'. This means that the Committee shall advise the Commission in level one initiatives during the initiation phase. At level two, the implementing phase, the Committee functions as a regulatory comitology committee. ESC is composed of representatives of the Member States and chaired by a representative of the

[36] See European Parliament resolution on the Stockholm European Council on 23/24 Mar 2001, B5-0244/2001.

[37] See European Parliament resolution on the implementation of financial services legislation, Committee on Constitutional Affairs, Rapporteur: Karl von Wogau, A5-0011/2002. SPEECH/02/44 Romano Prodi, 'Implementation of financial services legislation in the context of the Lamfalussy Report' Intervention by President Romano Prodi to the plenary session of the European Parliament in Strasbourg, 5 Feb 2002.

[38] See Commission Decision 2001/528/EC of 6 Jun 2001 establishing the ESC (OJ 2001 L 191/45). In Nov 2003 Art 2 of the Decision was amended by Commission Decision 2004/8/EC of 5 Nov 2003 amending Decision 2001/528/EC establishing the ESC (OJ 2004 L 3/33) extending the role of the Committee to advise the Commission not only in the field of securities but also on undertakings for collective investment in transferable securities (UCITS).

Commission.[39] Summary records of all meetings are made available on the ESC website.[40]

The CESR, was also established by a Commission Decision in June 2001.[41] The CESR is an independent advisory group and its two main tasks are to:

advise the Commission on level two measures, and
co-ordinate national implementation at level three.[42]

The CESR is composed 'of high-level representatives from the national public authorities competent in the field of securities'.[43] The Committee shall consult extensively with market actors, consumers and end-users at an early stage before giving its advice to the Commission. The CESR shall also submit an annual report to the Commission. The Committee meets at least four times a year and a member of the Commission is entitled to participate at all meetings. The CESR produces guidelines, recommendations and standards. The work is prepared by expert groups established on a non-permanent basis.[44] In 2003 the Lamfalussy model was extended to the rest of the financial market and the institutional framework was extended to the area of banking and insurance.

The first directive that was adopted according to the new procedure was a directive on market abuse that was adopted in 2003. In total four 'Lamfalussy level 1 Directives' have been adopted; a directive on markets in financial instruments, a prospectus directive, a transparency directive and a directive on market abuse.[45] A 'sunset clause' was included in all these directives in accordance with the inter-institutional compromise:

> Without prejudice to the implementing measures already adopted, on the expiry of a four-year period following the entry into force of this Directive, the application of its provisions requiring the adoption of technical rules and decisions in accordance with paragraph 2 shall be suspended. On a proposal from the Commission, the European Parliament and the Council may renew the provisions concerned in accordance with the procedure laid down in Article 251 of the Treaty and, to that end, they shall review them prior to the expiry of the period referred to above.[46]

[39] See Art 3 of Decision 2001/528/EC, *ibid.*

[40] See http://www.europa.eu.int/comm/internal_market/en/finances/mobil/esc_en.htm.

[41] See Commission Decision 2001/527/EC of 6 June 2001 establishing the CESR (OJ 2001 L 191/43).

[42] See http://www.cesr.eu/.

[43] See Art 3 of Commission Decision 2001/527/EC above n 41.

[44] See Arts 5 and 6 of Commission Decision 2001/527/EC, above n 41, and the CESR website http://www.cesr.eu/.

[45] See the Commission website on financial services, http://ec.europa.eu/internal_market/top_layer/index_24_en.htm.

[46] See Art 17 of the Market Abuse Directive. See also Proposal for a Directive of the European Parliament and of the Council Amending Dir 2003/6/EC on insider dealing and market manipulation (market abuse), as regards the implementing powers conferred on the Commission, COM (2006) 913.

These clauses were used by the European Parliament in the inter-institutional bargaining over new legislation and in the discussions leading to the introduction of the new comitology procedure. In the next part a brief explanation of the discussion on the future of comitology will be given in the lead up to the introduction of the new regulatory procedure with scrutiny but first a short account will be given on the debate on the reform of Article 202 ECT that primarily took place in the Convention on the Future of Europe.

4 THE DEBATE ON THE FUTURE OF THE UNION AND COMITOLOGY

4.1 Amendment of Article 202 of the EC Treaty

Article 202 of the EC Treaty was amended at the latest Intergovernmental Conference (IGC) that was concluded by the signing of the Constitutional Treaty by the Heads of States and Government of the Union on 29 October 2004.[47] However, the Treaty will probably not enter into force in its present form due to difficulties that have arisen in the ratification process. Despite this it is relevant for our present purposes since the European Parliament uses the final text of the Treaty as a reference on how it envisages the regulation of the supervision of delegated legislation in the future.

On 3 December 2002 the European Parliament presented a report on the typology of acts and the hierarchy of legislation in the European Union to the Convention. The European Parliament made references to resolutions adopted before dealing with the same issues and also to its resolution on financial services from 5 February 2002. According to the report, enlargement together with the confirmation that the Union has two legislators would make a restructuring of implementing competences necessary: Article 202 of the Treaty in particular should follow two principles; the implementing powers must be the competence of the Commission or the Member States and not the Council; and the implementing powers should be exercised within the framework of the conditions and limitations set out and supervised by the two institutions that are the legislators of the Union.[48]

The Commission's vision of a long-term based solution for amending the current comitology system was also expressed in a communication presented in December 2002 suggesting that the powers to implement European legislation in the future should be entrusted exclusively to the Commission. It proposed a classification of legislative norms of three levels: *institutional laws*, *laws* adopted under the co-decision procedure and *regulations*, adopted by the Commission, for the purposes of implementing laws. At the second level, the laws could make provision for the power of

[47] See Treaty establishing a Constitution for Europe OJ 2004 C 310/1.

[48] See European Parliament resolution on the typology of acts and the hierarchy of legislation in the European Union, A5-0425/2002.

legislation to be delegated to the Commission for the purpose of amending legal instruments adopted by the legislator. The Commission should only be able to exercise this power within the limits and subject to the conditions of its legislative delegation. Instead of the current control of the Council set out in Article 202 of the EC Treaty, the European Parliament and the Council would exercise ex-ante control, for example through a call-back system.[49]

The hierarchy of legal acts presented in the final text of the Constitutional Treaty does to a large extent realise the Commission's vision:[50]

Article I-36 of the Constitutional Treaty
Delegated European regulations

1. European laws and framework laws may delegate to the Commission the power to adopt delegated European regulations to supplement or amend certain non-essential elements of the law or framework law.
   The objectives, content, scope and duration of the delegation of power shall be explicitly defined in the European laws and framework laws. The essential elements of an area shall be reserved for the European law or framework law and accordingly shall not be the subject of a delegation of power.
2. European laws and framework laws shall explicitly lay down the conditions to which the delegation is subject; these conditions may be as follows:
   (a) the European Parliament or the Council may decide to revoke the delegation;
   (b) the delegated European regulation may enter into force only if no objection has been expressed by the European Parliament or the Council within a period set by the European law or framework law.
   For the purposes of (a) and (b), the European Parliament shall act by a majority of its component members, and the Council by a qualified majority.[51]

The European Parliament adopted a report on the draft Treaty establishing a Constitution for Europe and its opinion on the convening of the IGC.[52] The European Parliament welcomed the hierarchy of legal acts

[49] See COM (2002) 728 final/2, p 7. See also Working Document of 7 Nov 2002 to the Working Group IX on Simplification, Proposal to distinguish legislative and executive functions in the institutional system of the European Union, paper by Mr Ponzano, member of the Convention and the Commission's representative in the Group, WD 16.

[50] See, in general, CF Bergström, and M Rotkirch, *Simply Simplification? The Proposal for a Hierarchy of Legal Acts*, SIEPS 2003:8.

[51] See also declaration no 8 on Art I-36 attached to the Treaty establishing a Constitution for Europe, 'The Conference takes note of the Commission's intention to continue to consult experts appointed by the Member States in the preparation of draft delegated European regulations in the financial services area, in accordance with its established practice.'

[52] See European Parliament resolution on the draft Treaty establishing a Constitution for Europe and the European Parliament's opinion on the convening of the IGC, A5-0299/2003.

that was introduced in the Treaty and wanted to call attention to the fact that it put up a number of conditions for the implementation of the Lamfalussy model and was therefore pleased to see them incorporated into the Constitutional Treaty but considered it to be necessary to have an inter-institutional agreement in place before the Treaty entered into force in order to make sure that level two legislation in the Lamfalussy model was considered as 'delegated regulations' according to the system introduced in the Constitutional Treaty. Even though the Constitutional Treaty probably not will enter into force it is used as a point of reference by the European Parliament and one example can be found in the discussion on the re-casting of two directives in the field of financial services.

On 14 July 2004 a proposal was presented for a re-casting of the Directives of the European Parliament and of the Council 2000/12/EC relating to the taking up and pursuit of the business of credit institutions and Council Directive 93/6/EEC on the capital adequacy of investments firms and credit institutions. According to the proposal the delegating competences would, inter alia, be amended.[53] The European Parliament wanted, inter alia, to include the following:

> The adoption of the necessary implementing measures and the use of the powers delegated to the Commission under this Directive should be subject to the full respect by all European institutions of the existing political agreement based on the European Parliament resolution of 5 February 2002 on the implementation of financial services legislation, on the solemn declaration made before Parliament on the same day by the Commission and on Mr Bolkenstein's letter of 2 October 2001 with regard to the safeguards for Parliament's role in this process. It is important to ensure the rights of Parliament as provided for in Article I-36 of the Treaty establishing a Constitution for Europe. Therefore the provisions conferring implementing powers on the Commission should not enter into force until an inter-institutional agreement codifies the existing agreement.[54]

Furthermore, the European Parliament proposed to introduce a new article in the directives:

> Article 42 [delegation] shall not be applied until the conditions to which the powers of the Parliament, the Commission and the Council of the European Union are subject under Decision 1999/468/EC are modified along the lines of Article I—36 of the Treaty establishing a Constitution for Europe.[55]

The European Parliament also wanted a sunset clause to be inserted in the directives although they were not strict Lamfalussy directives.[56]

[53] See Proposal for a Directive of the European Parliament and of the Council relating to the taking up and pursuit of the business of credit institutions (recast), COM (2004) 486.

[54] See Committee on Economic and Monetary Affairs, Capital adequacy of investment firms and credit institutions, A6-0257/2005, amendment 14.

[55] See Committee on Economic and Monetary Affairs, Capital adequacy of investment firms and credit institutions, A6-0257/2005, amendment 490.

[56] Both Dirs 1993/6 and 2000/12 have been repealed by 2006/48.

The Commission and the European Parliament both support a reform of the comitology system. But is a reform of the system also in the interest of the Council? The present system seems to work well in the interest of the Member States and of the Council as an institution. Well, there may be several reasons for the Council to amend the comitology decision but one of the reasons, at least, is that the European Parliament has made a reform of the comitology system a condition for the approval and adoption of the legislation in the field of financial services.

In a report from 23 January 2002 on the implementation of financial services legislation the Parliament stated that: 'the European Parliament is being increasingly confronted with situations where it feels that its powers are likely to be eroded by the comitology procedure as laid down in the Council Decision. This is true in particular of the framework of directives following the Lamfalussy report, where too much room is left to the Commission'.[57]

In November 2002 the European Parliament adopted a resolution on the extension of the Lamfalussy process to include the entire financial services sector. In this resolution the Parliament: 'recalls its position that the current institutional framework governing the powers to adopt implementing measures is inadequate, unbalanced and lacking transparency, and that there must be a clear Council commitment to reform in order to guarantee a proper institutional balance before the European Parliament could agree to the proposed extension of the Lamfalussy process' and the Parliament: 'underlines that implementing measures adopted on the basis of a legal act adopted under the co-decision procedure should also be subject to equal control by the two co-legislators.'[58]

The temporary solution has been the inclusion of sunset clauses in the basic legislation as well as commitments made by the Council to reform the comitology system.

4.2 Amendment of the Comitology Decision

The Commission presented a proposal to amend the comitology decision on 11 December 2002 although the Commission, as the European Parliament, would have preferred an amendment of Article 202 and the Commission stressed that the proposal to amend the comitology decision should only be seen as a temporary measure.[59] According to the Commission, the

[57] See Report from 23 Jan 2002 on the implementation of financial services legislation, Committee on Constitutional Affairs, Rapporteur: Karl von Wogau, A5-0011/2002.

[58] See European Parliament resolution on financial regulation, supervision and stability, Extension of the Lamfalussy process to the entire financial services sector (for Copenhagen Summit), P5_TA(2002)0565.

[59] See Proposal for a Council Decision amending Decision 1999/468/EC laying down the procedures for the exercise of implementing powers conferred on the Commission COM (2002) 719.

primary purpose of the proposal was to enhance the role of the European Parliament as regards the supervision of the implementation of legislation decided by co-decision. The Commission also saw the reform as a way of clarifying the exercise of executive functions. The proposal was later amended on 22 April 2004 with regard to some of the objections raised by the European Parliament. It entailed three major changes. First, it tried to place the European Parliament and the Council on an equal footing during the supervisory phase of the comitology process by granting the European Parliament co-decision status with the Council when supervising the implementing powers conferred upon the Commission.[60]

Secondly, the Commission proposed to reduce the number of committees from three to two. It abolished the management committee procedure and made the least restrictive advisory committee procedure the standard one.[61]

Thirdly, the proposal envisaged the choice of the two remaining procedures, in relation to measures adopted under co-decision, to be prescribed and no longer left to the discretion of the legislating institution. The existing regulatory procedure, *ie* the most restrictive one, was revised for implementing measures under co-decision by introducing two distinct phases. In the initial phase, the Commission would be responsible for drawing up implementing measures. The committee could influence the substance of the measure by delivering an unfavourable opinion. However, it was ultimately the Commission that would be responsible for the substance of the draft. In the second phase, both the European Parliament and the Council would oversee the executive role of the Commission by expressing opposition to the Commission's draft implementing measure. In such a case, the Commission would have four choices. Taking the objections into account, it could present a legislative proposal, make a modification of its draft, adopt the original draft without changes, or, finally, withdraw its draft.[62]

An amended proposal was transmitted to the Council and the European Parliament in April 2004. The main substantive changes in the amended proposal, compared to the original proposal, were that the Council would always have to react to any European Parliament position that the Commission proposal was ultra vires, that the deadline for the legislators to raise objections had been extended by one month, that the Commission was obliged to ensure that all relevant documents were available on the Internet and that all relevant information had to be at the disposal of the European Parliament. Furthermore, the amended proposal included a paragraph in

[60] See Art 2 of the proposal, COM (2002) 719.

[61] See Art 1 of the proposal, COM (2002) 719.

[62] See Art 1 of the proposal, COM (2002) 719, and amended proposal for a Council Decision amending Decision 1999/468/EC laying down the procedures for the exercise of implementing powers conferred on the Commission, COM (2004) 324 final. See also House of Commons, European Scrutiny Committee, Thirty-seventh report of session 2002–03, published 26 Nov 2003.

the recital stating that the decision should not affect the Lamfalussy structure in the field of financial services.[63]

This was all taking place at a time when the Constitutional Treaty preparations were still underway and the proposal was not discussed in the Council until, as the European Parliament puts it, 'the introduction of clauses conferring implementing powers on the Commission became again contentious and Parliament started to introduce so-called sunset clauses into the texts, especially in the financial market sector, limiting the delegation of powers in time.'[64]

An inter-institutional agreement on comitology was reached in June 2006 and includes, inter alia, a new regulatory procedure with scrutiny that shall be used for measures of general scope that will amend non-essential elements of a basic instrument adopted in accordance with co-decision. The essential elements of an act can only be amended by the legislators.[65]

According to a statement annexed to the agreement the European Parliament, the Council and the Commission 'emphasise that, in the context of the existing Treaty, the Decision provides a horizontal and satisfactory solution to the European Parliament's wish to scrutinise the implementation of instruments adopted under the co-decision procedure.'[66]

5 CONCLUDING COMMENTS

In this article it is has been argued that it is difficult to assess the reasons behind the new deal on comitology without taking into account the parallel development in the field of financial services in general and in particular the way in which the European Parliament has used powers gained in that field to get a reform of comitology.

Comitology has been the source of inter-institutional conflicts ever since its introduction but it was not until the co-decision procedure was introduced in 1993 that the European Parliament obtained both a better bargaining position as a co-legislator and co-delegator as well as a significantly improved

[63] See COM (2004) 324 final. See also, House of Commons, European Scrutiny Committee, Twenty-third report of session 2003–04, published 1 Jul 2004. See European Parliament Second Report of 11 Jul 2003 on the proposal for a Council Decision on amending Decision 1999/468/EC laying down the procedures for the exercise of implementing powers conferred on the Commission, A5-0266/2003 final; and European Parliament legislative resolution of 2 Sep 2003 on the proposal for a Council Decision on amending Decision 1999/468/EC laying down the procedures for the exercise of implementing powers conferred on the Commission, P5_TA-PROV 0352/2003.

[64] See Report from 3 Jul 2006 on the draft Council Decision amending Decision 1999/468/EC laying down the procedures for the exercice of implementing powers conferred on the Commission, Committee on Constitutional Affairs, A6-0236/2006, p 7.

[65] See CK Bradley St, *Delegated Legislation and Parliamentary Supervision in the European Community*, forthcoming article, on the new regulatory procedure with scrutiny.

[66] See CK Bradley St, *Delegated Legislation and Parliamentary Supervision in the European Community*, forthcoming article.

case. The European Parliament's struggle with comitology was intensive in the 1990s and one example of this can be found in the field of financial services and has been described above. In 1999 the Council adopted a new comitology decision that gave the European Parliament more influence.

When the Lamfalussy model was going to be implemented in the field of securities it was clear, however, that the European Parliament had no intention of letting go of its basic concerns regarding comitology. It took almost one year before the European Parliament could accept the new legislative model in this field that was based, inter alia, on an extensive use of comitology and delegation to the Commission. The European Parliament agreed to implement the model after it had received a promise from the Commission to include, inter alia, so-called sunset clauses in all basic legislation.

At the same time the debate on the Future of Europe was taking place leading to the signing of the Constitutional Treaty on 29 October 2004. The Constitutional Treaty included an amendment of Article 202, the legal basis for the comitology system. The Commission had also presented a proposal for an amendment of the comitology decision. When it was clear that the Constitutional Treaty would not enter into force, the Council started negotiating a new or amended comitology decision. A deal on comitology was finally reached in the summer of 2006. Does this mean that the European Parliament is satisfied with the solution on comitology and that the ongoing inter-institutional conflict over comitology is over?

The European Parliament states that 'the Constitutional Treaty [...]grants Parliament the right to revoke the delegation of powers (Article I-36). The final compromise text for a new regulatory procedure with scrutiny does not provide for such a right for the Parliament. The right to revoke a delegation of powers will therefore remain one of the key demands of the European Parliament, something which could be achieved notably by the Constitutional Treaty'.[67]

The reform treaty will include the equivalent to Article I-36, which would mean that the on-going conflict between the institutions regarding comitology might finally come to an end when and if the reform treaty enters into force.[68]

BIBLIOGRAPHY

Legislation

Council Decision 1987/373/EEC of 13 July 1987 laying down the procedures for the exercise of implementing powers conferred on the Commission.

[67] See Report on the conclusion of an inter-institutional agreement taking the form of a joint statement concerning the draft for a Council Decision amending Decision 1999/468, Committee on Constitutional Affairs, Rapporteur: Richard Corbett, A6-237/2006.

[68] See Presidency Conclusions, Brussels European Council, 21 and 22 June 2007.

Council Directive 93/6/EEC of the 15 March 1993 on capital adequacy of investment firms and credit institutions (OJ 1993 L 141/1-26).
Council Directive 93/22/EEC of the 10 May 1993 on investment services in the securities field (OJ 1993 L 141/27-46).
Council Decision 1999/468/EC of 28 June 1999 laying down the procedures for the exercise of implementing powers conferred on the Commission.
Commission Decision 2001/527/EC of 6 June 2001 establishing the Committee of European Securities Regulators (OJ 2001 L 191/43).
Commission Decision 2001/528/EC of 6 June 2001 establishing the European Securities Committee (OJ 2001 L 191/45).
European Parliament and Council Directive 2003/6/EC of 28 January 2003 on insider dealing and market manipulation (market abuse) (OJ 2003 L 96/16–25).
Commission Decision 2004/8/EC of 5 November 2003 amending Decision 2001/528/EC establishing the European Securities Committee (OJ 2004 L 3/33).

Articles and Literature

Afrell, L, and Back K, Lamfalussymodellen—en ny lagstiftningsprocess inom EU, *ERT* 2005 p 434.
Bergström, CF, *Comitology—Delegation of Powers in the European Union and the Committee System* (Oxford, Oxford University Press, 2005).
Bergström, CF and Rotkirch, M, *Simply Simplification? The Proposal for a Hierarchy of Legal Acts*, SIEPS 2003:8.
Bradley, St CK, *Delegated Legislation and Parliamentary Supervision in the European Community*, forthcoming article.
Craig, P, *EU Administrative Law* (Oxford, Oxford University Press, 2006).
Dahlman, T, Förlikningsinstitutet—från Maastricht till Amsterdam, *ERT*, 2000.

Documents from the Commission

Proposal for a Council Directive on investment services in the securities field (OJ 1989 C 43/7).
Amended proposal for a Council Directive on investment services in the securities field (OJ 1990 C 42/7).
Proposal on a Council Directive on capital adequacy of investment firms and credit institutions (OJ 1990 C 152/6).
Amended proposal for a Council Directive on capital adequacy of investment firms and credit institutions (OJ 1992 C 50/5).
Proposal for a European Parliament and Council Directive amending Council Directive 93/6/EEC of 15 March 1993 on the capital adequacy of investment firms and credit institutions and Council Directive 93/22/EEC of 10 May 1993 on investment services in the securities field (OJ 1995 C 253/19).
Amended proposal for a European Parliament and Council Directive amending Council Directive 93/6/EEC of 15 March 1993 on the capital adequacy of investment firms and credit institutions and Council Directive 93/22/EEC of 10 May 1993 on investment services in the securities field (OJ 1996 C 221/31).

Opinion of the Commission pursuant to Article 189b(2)(d) of the EC Treaty, on the European Parliament's amendment to the Council's common position regarding the proposal for an amendment of the European Parliament and Council Directive 93/6/EEC on the capital adequacy of investment firms and credit institutions and Council Directive 93/22/EEC on investment services in the securities field, COM (1997) 355.
Commission General Report on the Activities of the European Union, 1998.
Communication from the Commission entitled "Financial Services: Building a Framework for Action" presented on 28 October 1998.
Financial Services: implementing the framework for financial markets: Action Plan Communication from the Commission, COM (1999) 232.
Proposal for a Council Decision amending Decision 1999/468/EC laying down the procedures for the exercise of implementing powers conferred on the Commission COM (2002) 719.
For the European Union: peace, freedom, solidarity—Communication of the Commission on the institutional architecture, COM (2002) 728.
Amended proposal for a Council Decision amending Decision 1999/468/EC laying down the procedures for the exercise of implementing powers conferred on the Commission, COM (2004) 324 final.
Proposal for a Directive of the European Parliament and of the Council relating to the taking up and pursuit of the business of credit institutions (recast), COM (2004) 486.
Proposal for a Directive of the European Parliament and of the Council Amending Directive 2003/6/EC on insider dealing and market manipulation (market abuse), as regards the implementing powers conferred on the Commission, COM (2006) 913.

Documents from the European Parliament

First reading resolution of Proposal for a European Parliament and Council Directive amending Council Directive 93/6/EEC of 15 March 1993 on the capital adequacy of investment firms and credit institutions and Council Directive 93/22/EEC of 10 May 1993 on investment services in the securities field, A4-0034/96.
Decision on the common position adopted by the Council with a view to adopting a European Parliament and Council Directive on amending Council Directive 93/6/EEC on the capital adequacy of investment firms and credit institutions and Directive 93/22/EEC on investment services in the securities field, A4-0093/97.
European Parliament resolution on the final report of the Committee of Wise Men on the regulation of European securities markets, B5-0173/2001.
European Parliament resolution on the Stockholm European Council on 23/24 March 2001, B5-0244/2001.
Report from 23 January 2002 on the implementation of financial services legislation, Committee on Constitutional Affairs, Rapporteur: Karl von Wogau, A5-0011/2002.
European Parliament resolution on the typology of acts and the hierarchy of legislation in the European Union, A5-0425/2002.

European Parliament resolution on financial regulation, supervision and stability, Extension of the Lamfalussy process to the entire financial services sector (for Copenhagen Summit), P5_TA(2002)0565.

European Parliament Second Report of 11 July 2003 on the proposal for a Council Decision on amending Decision 1999/468/EC laying down the procedures for the exercise of implementing powers conferred on the Commission, A5-0266/2003.

European Parliament resolution on the draft Treaty establishing a Constitution for Europe and the European Parliament's opinion on the convening of the Intergovernmental Conference (IGC), A5-0299/2003.

European Parliament legislative Resolution of 2 September 2003 on the proposal for a Council Decision on amending Decision 1999/468/EC laying down the procedures for the exercise of implementing powers conferred on the Commission, P5_TA-PROV 0352/2003.

Capital adequacy of investment firms and credit institutions, Committee on Economic and Monetary Affairs, A6-0257/2005.

European Parliament Report from 3 July 2006 on the draft Council Decision amending Decision 1999/468/EC laying down the procedures for the exercise of implementing powers conferred on the Commission, Committee on Constitutional Affairs, A6-0236/2006.

Report on the conclusion of an inter-institutional agreement taking the form of a joint statement concerning the draft for a Council Decision amending Decision 1999/468, Committee on Constitutional Affairs, Rapporteur: Richard Corbett, A6-237/2006.

Miscellaneous

Council Common position (EC) No 8/97 of 16 December 1996 adopted by the Council with a view to adopting a European Parliament and Council Directive amending Directive 93/6/EEC on the capital adequacy of investment firms and credit institutions and Directive 93/22/EEC on investment services in the securities field, C4-0005/97-95/0188(COD).

Bulletin EU 12-1996.

Bulletin EU 4-1998.

Final Report of the Committee of Wise Men on the Regulation of European Securities Markets, Brussel, 15 February 2001.

Stockholm European Council (23–24 March 2001): Presidency conclusions.

'Implementation of financial services legislation in the context of the Lamfalussy Report' Intervention by President Romano Prodi to the plenary session of the European Parliament in Strasbourg, 5th February 2002, SPEECH/02/44.

Working document of 7 November 2002 to the Working Group IX on Simplification, Proposal to distinguish legislative and executive functions in the institutional system of the European Union, paper by Mr Ponzano, member of the Convention and the Commission's representative in the Group, WD 16.

House of Commons, European Scrutiny Committee, Thirty-seventh report of session 2002–03, published 26 November 2003.

House of Commons, European Scrutiny Committee, Twenty-third report of session 2003–04, published 1 July 2004.

Treaty establishing a Constitution for Europe (OJ 2004 C 310/1).
Debate on 21 June 2006 in the Legal Affairs Committee of the European Parliament.

Websites

www.europa.eu.int/comm/internal_market/en/finances/general
'Power struggle over financial services?' www.EurActiv.com.
'Agreement on Lamfalussy proposals' www.EurActiv.com.
http://www.cesr.eu/

6

Articles 235/288, Section 2, EC Treaty: Still of Constitutional Importance, if There Ever Were Any?

GÖRAN LYSÉN*

1 SOME STARTING POINTS[1]

IT MUST, OF course, be born in mind that the European Communities (EC) are creations in public international law, ie they are international organisations regardless of their sophistication and far-reaching purposes.[2] However, these two factors have undoubtedly affected their modes of operation and caused the EC to appear federal in nature, ie a sort of *functional federalism*. This state of affairs calls for a fully-fledged democratic structure, transparency and effective legal remedies within the structure. The Courts are nevertheless international courts, set to interpret and apply international treaties. Consequently, it is not the matter of national courts concerned here. International organizations such as the EC may be held internationally responsible for breaches of their obligations under international law relative to other subjects in that law.[3] The responsibility

* Professor emeritus in public international law, Uppsala University.

[1] It should be noted that there is an abundance of literature on Art 288, s 2. Suffice it to mention the most recent and comprehensive treatise by J Wakefield, *Judicial Protection through the Use of Article 288(2) EC* (Kluwer International, 2002).

[2] The present EU as per the EU Treaty obviously lacks legal personality. It is noted that other writers hold the opposite opinion, however, without launching any convincing arguments for their case, see further G Lysén, *Framework decision. Who is liable to pay compensation for violations of the rights of the individual? A public international law approach* (SIFIR No 18, Iustus, 2006). The issue of responsibility of the EU will, thus, not arise. Instead the Member States are responsible under international law for their actions according to the EU Treaty in violating their international obligations elsewhere, and according to national law, as far as such laws so permit, by means of actions for compensation.

[3] See G Lysén, *Folkrättsligt ansvar. En studie av EG/EU och dess medlemsstater* (*International responsibility. A Study of the EC/EU and its Member States*) (SIFIR No 14, Iustus, 2002).

of the EC in relation to individuals for breaching their rights under the Treaties does not derive from international responsibility but is set out in the Treaties in accordance with specific provisions. The responsibility of the Member States when they breach EC Law under the *Francovich*-doctrine is based upon their international responsibility,[4] however, re-modelled by the EC Court (ECJ or the Court) under the so-called loyalty clause in Article 10 in the EC Treaty.[5] Or, rather, it is more appropriate to call the phenomena an institutionalisation of international responsibility within Community law.[6] Article 10 alone will not explain this responsibility of the Member States.

The Coal and Steel Community (CECA) was dissolved as per a Protocol annexed to the Amsterdam Treaty in 1997; the CECA was quite special in that the subjects addressed by the Treaty were the coal and steel producers in the Community. Under the present EC Treaties all individuals may be concerned by actions or omissions on the part of the EC. These producers mentioned had a special relationship to the Community, and they were administered by it, meaning that the CECA to a certain extent belonged to the category of administrative unions created in the 19th and 20th centuries for specific purposes such as the World Postal Union in 1874 and later creations, for example, the specialised international organisations connected to the UN such as the ICAO. The special position of these undertakings was reflected, for example, in their standing to challenge before the Court decisions adopted by the Community represented by the High Authority as was expressed in Articles 33 and 34 as well as to claim damages from the Community according to Article 40 on the grounds of *faute de service* and *faute de personnelle* committed by the administration or civil servants. These notions were based on French administrative law. An action for damages directed against the state has not always been, and still is not, the normally accepted state of affairs, but rather that '[t]he King can do no wrong' has prevailed. In some countries, however, such an action has been allowed since a long time ago, for example, in France.

The CECA Treaty was different on many points from the EC Treaties of Rome 1957. The wording in the EC Treaties is entirely different with regard to the possibility to claim compensation for wrongs committed by

[4] In Case C-224/01, *Köbler* [2003] I-10239, recital 32, the Court noted that in international law, for the purpose of breach of legal duty, a state is considered as a single entity, thus including its courts.

[5] See, in particular, Cases C-6 & 9/90, *Francovich/Italy* [1990] ECR I-5357, and Cases C-46/93 and C-48/93, *Brasserie du Pêcheur and Factortame* [1996] ECR I-1029.

[6] See ILC's 2001 *Articles on Responsibility of States for internationally wrongful acts*, Official Records of the General Assembly, Fifty-sixth session, Supplement No 10 (A/56/10), ch IV.E.1).

the institutions of the EC. It is worthwhile to quote the second section in Article 288 of the EC Treaty:

> In the case of non-contractual liability, the Community shall, in accordance with the general principles common to the laws of the Member States, make good any damage caused by its institutions or by its servants in the performance of their duties.

From the wording it is completely clear that the notions from the French administrative system were not overtly transferred to the EC Treaties. In the EC Treaties there are a number of legal remedies established, and one of them is the action for indemnity in Article 235, to which the substantive provisions in Article 288 adhere. The important question was once upon a time whether the EC Treaties, nevertheless, had taken over the system from the CECA Treaty. As it turned out by subsequent case law from the Court, this was not the case, but a rather different system. There were, of course, many reasons for such a determination, one of which was that the EC Treaty is not limited to the administration of two categories of undertakings but envisage the institutions to be engaged in true legislative activities as if it were a federation. Evidently, these activities are an important difference relative to the CECA Treaty, causing clear repercussions on the indemnity action. Having said this, it must be recognized as well that the systems are associated, since the EC action for indemnity involves both the responsibility of the administration for being insufficient and the legislator acting in violation of the constitution (the Treaties). In the former case the influences from the CECA Treaty are still obvious.

2 THE INDEPENDENCE OF THE ACTION FOR INDEMNITY

According to Article 230 the possibility for individuals to challenge legal acts from the EC institutions are very limited. They may only challenge acts addressed to them, ie. rather administrative decisions in various forms as to substance. In fact, they have also few possibilities to directly influence the legislative activities pursued by the EC institutions. An indirect way to attack general legislation (normative acts) exists when it is executed on the national level by national authorities. The implementing decisions addressed to individuals may be attacked in the national courts of the Member States on the basis that the underlying regulation is invalid, and a national court may make a reference to the Court for a preliminary ruling according to Article 234. In this way a regulation, for example, may be found invalid.

Article 235 does itself not state any real limitations for those who want to sue the Community for damages. In the very early case of *Plaumann* the Court found that '[a]n administrative measure which has not been annulled cannot of itself constitute a wrongful act on the part of the administration inflicting damage on those whom it affects'.[7] The plaintiff lacked locus

[7] Case 25/62, *Plaumann/Commission* [1963] ECR 95 at p 108.

standi as far as an action for annulment was concerned but had a right to institute an action for indemnity according to Article 235. The ruling was very severally criticised. It was said, that it was not based on general principles of law common to the laws of the Member States, and it did not comply with the Treaty structure. This very narrow interpretation of the indemnity action was thought to have its basis in the fact that the Court wanted to prevent individuals from circumventing the very limited rights in Articles 230 and 232 to attack normative acts.

Eight years later, in the *Lütticke* case,[8] the Commission held that an action for indemnity based on a non-censured omission to act should be declared inadmissible, because in reality it was a matter of a disguised action to establish an omission as illegal under Article 232. By using the indemnity action in this way, the Commission considered that the plaintiff would achieve the same thing or a similar result as if he had been allowed to start an action in this case under Article 232. The Court disallowed this theory in stating:

> The action for damages provided for by Article 178 [235] and the second paragraph of Article 215 [288] was established by the Treaty as an independent form of action with a particular purpose to fulfil within the system of actions and subject to conditions for its use, conceived with a view to its specific purpose.

Accordingly, an action for indemnity is always admissible, regardless of whether the alleged illegal action or omission has been established or not in a direct action before the Court or by a preliminary ruling before the institution of the indemnity action is made. The indemnity action is thus separate from an action for annulment. The Commission and the Council made this objection during a number of years, not only in the *Schöppenstedt* case[9] and as late as in the *Ludwigshafener Walzmühle* case in 1980.[10] The Court has always rejected this objection, and the Court of First Instance (CFI) has most recently confirmed the independence of the action for indemnity.[11] It should be noted that if an illegality is recognized on the part of the EC in an action for indemnity, there is no formal requirement imposed by the Treaty on the institutions to take any measures. However, in a legal order based on the rule of law, measures will nevertheless be undertaken, because such acts cannot be sustained. This standing taken by the Court provided the procedural requirements for a constitutional review of community legislation by indirect means in the form of the indemnity action. The first tool was in place, but the next had to come, namely the substantive requirements for a successful indemnity action as an *effective remedy* (see the ECHR, Article 13) under the Treaty.

[8] Case 4/69, *Lütticke/Commission* [1971] ECR 325.
[9] Case 5/71, *Schöppenstedt/Council* [1971] ECR 975.
[10] Cases 197 to 200, 243, 245 and 247/80, *Ludwigshafener Walzmühle/Council and Commission* [1981] ECR 3211.
[11] See, eg, T-170/00, *Förde-Reederei/Council and Commission* [2002] ECR II-515, recital 35.

3 SUBSTANTIVE REQUIREMENTS OF THE INDEMNITY ACTION

Already in the *Lütticke* case,[12] the Court established that the responsibility of the EC required 'the existence of a set of circumstances comprising actual damage, a causal link between the damage claimed and conduct alleged against the institution, and the illegality of such conduct' which echoes the requirements from the CECA as to administrative wrongs and also generally accepted criteria. The criteria for legislative wrongs were still to be formulated.

The *Schöppenstedt* case is the most important single case in this context.[13] It should be noted that the Court had already held the EEC responsible on the basis of *faute de service* in administrative matters,[14] but concerning legislative measures of a normative character it formulated the so-called *Schöppenstedt*-formula:

> Where legislative action involving measures of economic policy is concerned, the Community does not incur non-contractual liability for damage suffered by individuals as a consequence of that action, by virtue of the provisions contained in Article 215 second paragraph, of the Treaty, unless *a sufficiently flagrant violation of a superior rule of law for the protection of the individual* has occurred (emphasis added).

Advocate General Roemer focused in this case on whether according to the laws of the Member States it was permitted to make good damage caused by a normative act. He answered this question in the affirmative, because at least some of them did. It was not a matter of seeking the lowest denominator. He also thought that one should take into account the treaty structure and the remedies available to individuals, for example, that damages could be paid under the CECA Treaty when normative acts were the cause of the damage. One of his arguments is, of course, of special interest in going beyond the technical legal reasoning, namely the mentioning of the *insufficient parliamentary control* in the Community, which required a stronger judicial control than normally thought required. At that point in time the present Parliament was called the Assembly, and was composed of members from the national parliaments in the Member States. The powers of the Assembly were consultative only. As to whether the normative act accused to be illegal should have been annulled or declared invalid before the institution of an indemnity action, he found, referring to the *Lütticke* case and to the massive criticism launched by legal writers against the *Plaumann* case, that this should not be the case. Consequently, by the Court's finding, the scene was set for an indirect constitutional review on special grounds (indemnity action) by others

[12] Case 4/69, *Lütticke/Commission* [1971] ECR 325, recital 10.
[13] Case 5/71, *Schöppenstedt/Council* [1971] ECR 975.
[14] See eg, Cases 5, 7 & 132-24/66, *Kampffmeyer/Commission* [1967] 245.

than the privileged in Article 230, thus remedying to some extent the deficit of parliamentary powers.

From the *Schöppenstedt*-formula it was clear that the *mere* illegality of a normative act, which would do in an action for annulment or for invalidity, was not sufficient to render the Community liable to pay damages.[15] This suggested that the formula only applied to illegal acts coming within its ambit, and in other cases the mere illegality would do.[16] The question was how the Court would apply the extra elements in the established formula. The idea of 'a superior rule of law for the protection of the individual' came from the German legal system, and had there been given a rather broad interpretation. Article 34 EC Treaty protects market operators,[17] while 'the system of the division of powers between the various Community institutions' does not do so.[18] Superior rules of law are determined according to the hierarchy of norms as of the Community legal order. It is noted that the misuse of power is a superior rule of law protecting the individual the existence of which would render the Community liable.[19] The majority of claims for indemnity are found within the realms of the common agricultural policy where heavy market interventions take place.

The real difficulty and stumbling block, as it turned out to be, was how a 'sufficiently flagrant violation' should be measured, later rephrased into 'a sufficiently serious breach'. This expression has also been explained with regard to the nature of the violation/breach in terms of power exercise, that an institution must have acted in such a way that it 'manifestly and gravely disregarded the limits on the exercise of its powers'.[20] This was the case when 'exceptional and special circumstances existed'.[21] This expression echoes the German concept of *Sonderopferung* and the French of *egalité devant les charges publiques* which may provide compensation when there is no illegality on the part of legislator, evidently, something which does not fit into the *Schöppenstedt*-formula dealing with breaches of higher norms protecting the individual. The expressions 'a sufficiently serious breach' and 'manifestly and gravely disregarded the limits on the exercise of its powers' have sometimes been seen to operate as two separate concepts but been declared by the Court to be cumulative,[22] and the

[15] Case 143/77, *Koninklijke Scholten-Honig NV/Council and Commission* [1979] 3583, recital 10.

[16] See on proper conduct, eg, Case 358/88, *Briantex and Di Domenico/EEC and Commission* [1989] ECR 3623, recital 8.

[17] See, eg, Cases 83 and 94/76 & 4, 15 &40/77, *Bayerische HNL and Others/Council and Commission* [1978] ECR 1209, recital 5.

[18] Case C-282/90, *Vreugdenhil/Commission* [1992] ECR I-1937, recitals 19–24.

[19] Case T-489/93, *Unifruit Hellas/Commission* [1994] ECR II-1201, recital 40.

[20] Cases 83 and 94/76 & 4, 15 & 40/77, *Bayerische HNL and Others/Council and Commission* [1978] ECR 1209, recital 6.

[21] Case 194-206/83, *Asteris/Commission* [1985] ECR 2815, recital 21.

[22] Case C-390/95P, *Antillean Rice Mills and Others/Commission* [199] ECR I-769, recital 68.

existence of either is sufficient to render the Community liable. The Court has never tried to define or refine these expressions to give them proper contents, but has used them on a case-by-case basis, rendering the case law somewhat inconsistent.

The Court went even further into confusion of concepts when stating that the exercise of power must verge on the arbitrary in order to incur liability.[23] Almost 15 years later the Court said, that:[24]

> the concept of arbitrary conduct ... does not provide a basis for holding that a finding of conduct verging on the arbitrary represents a necessary condition or formulation for the Community to be rendered liable within the framework of the EEC Treaty according to the abovementioned case-law of the Court of Justice.

A few more old cases should be mentioned in order to complete the picture. In the *CNTA* case the plaintiff was successful but could not show he had suffered any harm. The Court explained:[25]

> In the absence of an overriding matter of public interest, the Commission has violated a superior rule of law, thus rendering the Community liable by failing to include in Regulation No. 189/72 transitional measures for the protection of the confidence which a trader might legitimately have had in the Community rules.

Furthermore, in the *Ireks-Arkady* case where the plaintiffs also were successful, it appears that the requirement for a sufficiently serious breach was met by reference to the following circumstances:[26]

1) the principle of equality, embodied in particular in the second subparagraph of Article 40(3) of the EEC Treaty ... occupies a particularly important place among the rules of Community law intended to protect the interest of the individual;
2) the disregard of that principle in this case affected a limited and clearly defined group of commercial operators;
3) the damage ... goes beyond the border of the economic risks inherent in the activities in the sector concerned;[27]
4) equality of treatment was ended by the Council in 1974 without sufficient justification.

The reasons set forth by the Court deal with a number of different issues of which only one relates to a sufficiently serious breach. The first relates to

[23] Cases 116 and 124/77, *Amylum/Council and Commission* [1979] ECR 3497, recital 19, and Case 143/77, *Koninklijke Scholten-Honig NV/Council and Commission* [1979] 3583, recital 16.

[24] Case C-220/91P, *Commission/Stahlwerke Peine-Salzgitter* [1993] ECR I-2393, recital 51.

[25] Case 74/74, *CNTA/Commission* [1975] ECR 533, recital 44.

[26] Case 238/78, *Ireks-Arkady/Council and Commission* [1979] ECR 2955.

[27] This requirement with regard to the nature of damage was set out for the first time in Cases 83 and 94/76 & 4, 15 & 40/77, *Bayerische HNL and Others/Council and Commission* [1978] ECR 1209.

the requirement of a superior rule of law being breached which protects the individual. The second relates to the causal link as expressed per a limited number of victims. It seems that this requirement was breached and became irrelevant already in this case, because the number of victims turned out to be more numerous than it first appeared. It was certainly quashed by the milk quota cases where the Council had to provide for general compensation to all those milk producers, who had suffered harm.[28] The third concerns the nature of the recoverable damage, and only the fourth approaches the nature of the breach, implying that if there had been sufficient justification in the public interest, there had been no liability on the Community part, *ie* the same reasoning as found also in the *CNTA* case. This, evidently, begs the question as to how the public interest, on principle, should be more precisely determined.

It is well understood that an indemnity system cannot be constructed so as to cripple the legislator in always risking massive claims for compensation. The protection offered to the institutions by the Court has, however, gone too far, because in a society based on the rule of law, it is expected as a general rule that the legislator adopts a lawful conduct, and is penalized for those illegalities that it produces; the search for justifications for illegality is the wrong way. The attitude of the Court is explained in a sort of policy statement in the *Balkan Import/Export* case:[29]

> As the evolution of a complex economic situation is involved, the Commission and the Management Committee enjoy, in this respect, a wide measure of discretion. In reviewing the legality of the exercise of such discretion, the court must confine itself to examining whether it contains a manifest error or constitutes a misuse of power or whether the authority did not clearly exceed the bounds of its discretion.

It is clear that the Court here abdicated from its role as the guardian of the Treaties, when it stated that certain conduct on the part of the institutions was not subject to legal review on the grounds stated in Article 230. Certainly the institutions may enjoy discretion in economic policy matters and in other kinds of policies, but this being so does not mean that they may act illegally and not to have to answer for it. From the statement that followed, as far as the action for indemnity was concerned, the Court said, that 'individuals may be required, in sectors coming within the economic policy of the Community, to accept within reasonable limits certain harmful effects on their economic interests as a result of a legislative measures without being able to obtain compensation from public funds even if the measure has been declared null and void'. This was clearly applied in the

[28] Case C-104/89 and C-37/90, *Mulder and Others/Council and Commission* [1992] ECR I-3061.

[29] Case 55/75, *Balkan Import/Export GmbH/HZA Berlin-Packhof* [1976] ECR 19.

Bayerische HNL case in that 'the public authorities can only exceptionally and in special circumstances incur liability for legislative measures which are the result of choices of economic policy'.[30] The Court has here left the Community legislator almost unfettered freedom to decide both policy and the public interest. The general defence on the part of the Community institutions has been to invoke 'overriding public interest', when having acted illegally. That interest must by defined and checked. Wakefield makes the observation that the Strasbourg Court's approach under the ECHR to the public interest is similar to what the Court showed in the second *Mulder* case,[31] namely not to questioning the perceived public interest as expressed by 'democratically accountable regimes in which the legislative bodies will be required to redefine the public interest every few year in election contests'.[32] These conditions do not exist with regard to the EC Council. She also notes that '[t]he Courts have never required the Community Institutions to explain how the policy on which the claims is founded serves the public interests'.[33] Evidently, both policy and public interest viewed from this perspective bring to the fore the constitutional conditions prevailing in the EC, which are not the same compared to those in any of the Member States. Consequently, it appears wrong by the Court to have adopted the Strasbourg attitude.

A slight shift may perhaps be detected in cases handed down by the Court in more recent years, despite the imprecise concepts with which the Court has operated. This shift appears to coincide largely with the formulation of the *Francovich*-doctrine in 1990. The case of *Sofrimport*, which also was adjudicated in 1990, concerned import of apples in transit from Chile; the public interest was of importance. The plaintiff was successful in that there was no 'overriding public interest' with regard to the measures applicable to goods in transit why the breach was sufficiently serious. Nor was the damage below the level of the normal risk involved in the commercial activity concerned. The first *Mulder* case[34] and connecting cases show a piece of legislation on the part of the Community that has traits from a nightmare brought from Kafka. In the second *Mulder* case the Court had no difficulty to find that the Community had incurred liability according to the *Schöppenstedt*-formula.

The *Schöppenstedt*-formula applies to legislative measures involving choices of economic policy as it itself states, and one would have thought that the formula was limited in application to choices of economic policy

[30] Cases 83 and 94/76 & 4, 15 & 40/77, *Bayerische HNL and Others/Council and Commission* [1978] ECR 1209, recital 5.

[31] Case C-104/89 and C-37/90, *Mulder and Others/Council and Commission* [1992] ECR I-3061.

[32] *Ibid*, p 131.

[33] *Ibid*, p 132.

[34] Case 120/86, *Mulder/Minister van Landbouw en Visserij* [1988] ECR 2321.

and not to extend to other areas of legislative activities. From some cases of the CFI, in particular the *Pharos* case,[35] it seems that the formula would apply to any legislative act. Evidently, such a development of the case law will even further diminish the judicial protection offered to the individual. So will also the case law in including decisions and other acts other than 'ordinary administrative measures' into the concept of legislative acts.[36]

In conclusion at this point, it is clear that the Courts had failed, according to the EC Treaty system, in over-ambitiously protecting the institutions (see in particular the *Amylum* case, or the 'isoglucose cases') at the expense of the individuals, to provide for an effective remedy against legislative wrongs under the indemnity action, and also to secure a constitutional review brought about by the EU citizens, and not only by those privileged in Article 230. It should be kept in mind that the indemnity action is no *actio popularis*, because only those individuals that may present a bona fide case may be successful in any respect. If the Court had been more demanding on the institutions in asking questions on policy and the public interest under the Treaty, the Court would have been able to set higher legal standards to be met by the Community legislator. Evidently, here is a missed opportunity by the Court.

4 THE THEORY OF THE MERGER OF THE *SCHÖPPENSTEDT*- AND *FRANCOVICH*-DOCTRINES—A FATAL MISCONCEPTION OR A GENIUS MOVE?

The criteria stated in the *Francovich* case echoed those for holding states internationally responsible for breaches of legal duty under international law, that '[m]ember States are obliged to make good loss and damage caused to individuals by breaches of Community law for which they can be held responsible'.[37] The innovative feature here was, of course, to let the international responsibility of the Member States to be invoked before their own courts. The criteria were generally applicable, and encompass all possible breaches of legal duty committed by the Member States. In this case it was the failure to implement a directive in proper time. The liability to pay compensation was dependent upon the nature of the breach. The further three requirements were:

> The first of those conditions is that the result prescribed by the directive should entail the grant of rights to individuals. The second condition is that it should be possible to identify the content of those rights on the basis of the provisions of

[35] Case T-105/96, *Pharos SA/Commission* [1998] ECR II-285, recital 62.

[36] Case C-282/90, *Vreugdenhil/Commission* [1992] ECR I-1937, Opinion of Advocate General Darmon at para 41.

[37] C-6 & 9/90, *Francovich/Italy* [1990] ECR I-5357, recital 37.

> the directive. Finally, the third condition is the existence of a causal link between the breach of the State' s obligation and the loss and damage suffered by the injured parties.

International responsibility may come before the Court under Article 227, should one Member State sue another Member State for breach of legal duty of the EC Treaty and claim reparation for sustained damage as a result of the breach. In such a case the defending Member State would be entitled under international law to invoke 'excuses and justifications' for having acted in breach of the Treaty, and the question is, of course, if the Court would allow the normal defences according to international law or modify them to fit into the Community legal order established under the Treaties. The issue of defences is important because the Court did not mention any in the *Francovich* case. Under all circumstances it seems unlikely, for many reasons, that defences under the *Francovich*-doctrine would be the same as those in an action based on Article 227. If a state claims compensation for its injured citizens, the damage suffered by a state is never identical to the sum of the individuals' claims.

In the *Brasserie du Pêcheur* case, the Court supplied the defences, since they were obviously required, considering the fact there may be a number of different kinds of breaches of Community law and not limited to the simple omission to implement a directive on time. The moderating elements of the responsibility were:

1) the rule of law infringed must be intended to confer rights on the individuals
2) the breach must be sufficiently serious, and,
3) there must be a direct causal link between the breach of the obligation resting on the State and the damage sustained by the injured parties.

The Court arrived at these three criteria after having considered that Member States normally do not have any wide discretionary powers when implementing Community law, even if the national legislator has to take measures. However, the Court added:

> In contrast, where a Member State acts in a field where it has a wide discretion, comparable to that of the Community institutions in implementing Community policies, the conditions under which it may incur liability must, in principle, be the same as those under which the Community institutions incur liability in a comparable situation.

The only new element in the *Brasserie du Pêcheur* case was that the breach must be sufficiently serious a language, which is borrowed from the *Schöppenstedt*-formula, and the Court said that:

> the decisive test for finding that a breach of Community law is sufficiently serious is whether the Member State or the Community institution concerned manifestly and gravely disregarded the limits on its discretion (recital 55).

To find out whether this was the case regard should be had to (recital 56):

> the clarity and precision of the rule breached, the measure of discretion left by that rule to the national or Community authorities, whether the infringement and the damage caused was intentional or involuntary, whether any error of law was excusable or inexcusable, the fact that the position taken by a Community institution may have contributed towards the omission, and the adoption or retention of national measures or practices contrary to Community law.

Compared to the defences under the *Schöppenstedt*-formula, it is obvious that the justification of having acted illegally in the public interest does not and cannot exist here, since the Member States do not create policy but only implement those already established by the Community. It may have been a necessary statement of policy by the Court to equate the liability of the Community and the responsibility of the Member States. From a legal point of view this seems wrong, both because of the different functions of the Community (legislator) and the Member States (executor) and because of the different legal bases for liability and responsibility. It should be noted that the Court has consolidated the reasoning behind the *Francovich* and the *Brasserie du Pêcher* cases into one single formula in making 'a sufficiently serious breach' a general condition for responsibility on the part of the Member States, although there are per se cases such as the non-implementation of a directive.[38]

Until the *Bergaderm* case of 4 July 2000, no attempt had been made to harmonise or merge the conditions for the Community liability and the responsibility of the Member States.[39] The plaintiff argued in this case that a directive was not a legislative act but an administrative since it in fact, at that time, only concerned him. In the former case the *Schöppenstedt*-formula would apply, and in the latter case the *Lütticke* case. The CFI had held that it was a legislative act. The Court on appeal referred, however, to the *Brasserie de Pecheur* case in recitals 40–44, and did not mention at all the *Schöppenstadt*-formula or any case connected to it. This was quite an unexpected turn by the Court. The result of this approach seemed to be that all acts, whether legislative or administrative would be subject to the test of whether the administration/legislator had manifestly and gravely disregarded the limits on its discretion, however, moderated by '[w]here the Member State or the institution in question has only considerably reduced, or even no, discretion, the mere infringement of Community law may be sufficient to establish the existence of a sufficiently serious breach' (recital 44). The appeal was partly found inadmissible, partly unfounded. In the cases of *Camar and Tico* of 8 June 2000, the CFI noted, 'in the

[38] Case C-178/94, C-179/94, C-188/94, C 189/94 and C-194/94, *Erich Dillenkofer/Germany* [1996] ECR I-4845.

[39] Case C-352/98P, *Bergaderm and Goupil/Commission* [2000] ECR I-5291.

field of administrative action, any infringement of law constitutes illegality which may give rise to liability on the part of the Community'.[40] In the *Fresh Marine Company* case of 24 October 2000, the CFI did not apply the merged concepts but talked about negligence and degrees of fault on the part of the Commission, and found the Community liable to pay damages.[41] The CFI introduced the merged concepts in March 2001 in referring to the *Bergaderm* case.[42] Both judgments were delivered on the same day by the same judges. Since then there are a number of cases in which the merged concepts has been applied. Another chamber of the CFI, however, found liability of the Community caused by the Commission in referring to the *Schöppenstedt*-formula as late as February 2003 a judgment,[43] which was set aside by the Court with reference the merged formula in so far as there was no inaction, in a sufficiently serious way, on the part of the Commission.[44] It does not seem that the difference between the two Courts had anything to do with the formula applied but rather with the concrete appreciation of whether the Commission had been slow or not (discretion).[45] It seems that Court was right in not blaming the Commission here considering the factual circumstances.

There are some distinctive changes in the merged concepts-approach relative to the *Schöppenstedt*-formula. The case of *Agraz*, for example, gives a clear picture of the new state of affairs.[46] The normal basic criteria apply, that is unlawful conduct, and actual damage and a causal link between the two elements. The unlawful conduct must represent a sufficiently serious breach of a rule of law intended to confer rights on the individual. The test for the existence of such a breach is that the Community institution concerned has manifestly and seriously disregarded the limits on its discretion. However, if the institution has only a considerably reduced discretion, or

[40] Cases T-79/96, T-260/97 and T-117/98, *Camar Srl and Tico srl/Commission of the European Communities and Council of the European Union*, [2000] ECR II-2193, recital 205. The plaintiffs were successful.

[41] Case T-178/98, *Fresh Marine Company AS/Commission* [2000] ECR II-3331. The plaintiff was successful. The appeal from the Commission was dismissed in Case C-472/00P, [2003] ECR I-4167.

[42] Case T-52/99, *T Port/Commission* [2001] ECR II-981, and Case T-30/99, *Bocchi Food Trade International/Commission* [2001] ECR II-943.

[43] Cases T-344/00 and T-345/00, *CEVA and Pharmacia/Commission* [2003] ECR II-229, recitals 95–96. The plaintiffs were successful.

[44] Case C-198/03P, *Commission/CEVA and Pfizer* [2005] ECR I-6357, recitals 62–65.

[45] Case C-243/05P, *Agraz and others/Commission* (nyr), the Court said in recital 32: 'Recognition that the institution concerned has discretion has not, moreover, prevented the Court, in a number of cases, from finding the existence of damage capable of compensation (see, inter alia, Case 74/74 *CNTA* v *Commission* [1975] ECR 533 and Case 238/78 *Ireks-Arkady* v *Council and Commission* [1979] ECR 2955)'.

[46] Case T-285/03, *Agraz and Others/Commission* [2005] ECR II-1063, recitals 38-41. On appeal, in Case C-243/05P (nyr), the Court set aside the CFI's judgment in so far as the loss had been found not to be certain.

even none, the mere infringement may be sufficient to find that there is a sufficiently serious breach.

Three comments must directly be made. *First*, the violation of a 'superior rule of law for the protection of the individual' has been substituted by a breach of a rule of law intended to confer rights on the individual. On the surface it would seem, that the *protection* offered by superior rules of law would be more extensive than *finding rights* on the part of the individual. However, it also seems that the outcome will depend very much on interpretation and the construing of rights of the individual. *Secondly*, there are no references to an 'overriding public interest' but focus is set on the limits of discretion, where there may exist complex situations, implying 'difficulties in the application or interpretation of the legislation' as envisaged in the *Brasserie du Pêcheur case*,[47] which in the final end seems to include what may be expected from a normally prudent and diligent administration.[48] The public interest may, of course, be included in the complexity of a situation but it has disappeared as a general defence. So seems also the requirement of a small group of injured individuals, as a consequence to relate to their rights instead of general protective rules. The limited or non-existent discretion seems to include all administrative and legislative acts. The procedure to apply would look like the following in employing these criteria: breach of a rule of law intended to create rights on the individual, if so the breach must be sufficiently serious. The affirmative would almost always be the case, if there would be a limited or no discretion at all for the Community institution. If this is not the case, one must show that the boundaries were clearly exceeded, also in very complex situations. Accordingly, the rules for holding the Community liable have become more complex and less square-shaped allowing for sophisticated reasoning in balancing different interests. By the second *Mulder* case it seems that the *Schöppenstedt*-formula had come to the end of the road, because the Court had since long failed to develop and define the elements in this formula.

5 CONSTITUTIONAL DEVELOPMENTS

On several occasions above, references have been made to the constitutional structure of the EC, in particular, the statement made by Advocate General Roemer about the weak parliamentary control, comes to the fore. There may also be other defects that warrant strong judicial control of the Community legislator.

[47] See Case T-364/03, *Medici Grimm/Council* [2006] ECR II-79, recital 80.
[48] Case T-285/03, *Agraz and Others/Commission* [2005] ECR II-1063, recital 40.

The starting point is the fact, of course, that the Community is an international organisation, and it may be doubted because of this fact, whether the Community in that state of affairs ever will be equipped with a structure politically and legally comparable to a well-equipped state. Still, the meetings of the ministers from the Member States in the EC Council are a diplomatic conference of states, where a kind of veto still exists. Such a finding would make the statement by Advocate General Roemer eternally true. Evidently, the assumption is that the national political and legal structures, whose institutions act on the basis of the ECHR and under surveillance of the Strasbourg Court, are superior to the constitutional edifice of the Communities. However, it would be incorrect not to consider the constitutional changes/improvements made since the creations of the Communities.

The Assembly, now the Parliament, had only advisory powers originally. The development of the Assembly/Parliament started with the establishment of the Communities' own resources under the Budgetary Treaties in the beginning of the 1970s. Under these Treaties, constantly having been amended in various ways since then, the Parliament got the final say over the free part of the Community budget, enabling the Parliament to wage power on the EC Council. The members of the Parliament are since 1979 directly elected by the EU citizens, although not according to the same electoral system. By later Treaties (Single European Act, Amsterdam and Nice), it may now be said that the Community legislator has become a true bicameral legislator, where the powers of the Parliament roughly have been transferred from the EC Council, consequently at the expense of the national governments. The legislative process is a most complicated one, which to a great extent lacks transparency, where only the big lobbying groups may fully catch up with different pieces of legislation. The distance between the ordinary citizen and the Community institutions is considerable in view of the fact that political influence is strongly diluted in the staircase of the present power structure, such as in the case of the national parliament, from which springs the national government, which in its turn acts in the EC Council. Although there is an Ombudsman, this person is not considered as a legal remedy under the ECHR.

In conclusion it is difficult to find, however, the slightest suggestion of any arguments to the effect that the constitutional structure of the EC would have changed, so as to have justified, in any way, or that the protection has become obsolete, a diminished legal protection of the individuals. There is still a need for a strong indemnity action to rectify legislative wrongs; the indemnity action is the last resort to the individual. Since the indemnity action has (in its own right) existed since the inception of the EC Treaties, this action must be taken seriously as a constitutional device and let to become an *effective* remedy. The responsibility devolves on the Courts to see to that.

6 SOME CONCLUDING REMARKS

The questions put in the title of this article should both be answered in the affirmative. The important argument put forward by the Advocate General Roemer, to make the Community responsible for legislative wrongs at all, was the insufficient powers of the Assembly/Parliament, a deficit which necessarily was to be counterbalanced by strong judicial control. Certain sacrifices by individuals during the pioneering period when the Common Market/Internal Market was constructed and completed by the end of 1992 may perhaps have been warranted. Such reasoning does not seem to have any justification at all any longer. This is so, also in view of the fact that the Council and Commission would have gained experience in regulating market-interventions, in particular in the agricultural sector so as to avoid previous mistakes of a gross magnitude. Furthermore, the Community has become even more complex than at the time when the *Schöppenstedt*-formula was created, even if the powers of the Parliament have become more extensive. The number of Member States has not only increased by more than four times its original size but the Community has also got more extensive powers, because of repeated amendments to the original Treaty; besides that, there are a great number of Community Agencies, the Monetary Union and other bodies, having their own legal personality. To this also adds the Union Treaty. In conclusion, one can only say that the need for a constitutional review by means of the indemnity action remains even stronger today. The recent case law, properly developed, can meet this need. It goes without saying, that a strong protection of the individuals is all the more needed in the complex EU Treaty on a Constitution for Europe.

7

2005—The Year when European Law and its Supremacy was Finally Acknowledged by Swedish Courts

JOAKIM NERGELIUS*

1 INTRODUCTION

THOUGH THE SUPREMACY of European law in general and EU law in particular in relation to Swedish national law should of course have been a clear and generally recognised fact ever since Sweden joined the European Union in 1995, it is nevertheless a fact that Swedish courts reacted slowly to the possible implications of European law in Swedish national law, taking much time to fully recognise and acknowledge that accession to the European Union meant, among other things, clear limitations for the powers of the sovereign legislator, also in politically highly sensitive matters. This was evident in some cases where the highest courts, the Supreme Court (*Högsta Domstolen*) as well as the Supreme Administrative Court (*Regeringsrätten*) simply made a few clear mistakes by misinterpreting preliminary rulings from ECJ[1] or not asking for such judgments from ECJ in cases where it would have been highly justified and even required.[2] Also a clearly contestable interpretation of the European Convention of

* Joakim Nergelius is Professor of Law at the University of Örebro, Sweden and Associate Professor in European and Comparative Law at Åbo Academy (Turku), Finland.

[1] In particular the so-called *Data Delecta* case, NJA (*Nytt Juridiskt Arkiv*) 1996 p 668. Also the so-called *Volvo Service* case, NJA 1998 p 474, where the Supreme Court refused to await the outcome in a similar case pending before the ECJ before rendering its own judgment (and then deciding in favour of Volvo, against the interest of a small car repair service, contrary to the conclusion to which ECJ a few months later arrived in the case C-63/97, *BMW v Deenik*, ECR 1999 I p 905) may be mentioned here.

[2] Apart from the *Volvo Service* case, in particular the rather well-known *Barsebäck* case concerning the closure of a nuclear reactor comes to mind here; see *RÅ* (*Regeringsrättens Årsbok*) 1999 ref 76 (criticised most recently by the ECJ référendaire Martin Johansson, in *Sveinbjörnsdottir* confirmed by *Högsta Domstolen*—but reluctance to apply Community law seems to persist, 'Europarättslig tidskrift' (*ERT*) 2005 pp 507–19).

Human Rights, contrary to the interpretation made afterwards by the Strasbourg court in a similar case, should be mentioned here.[3]

Those issues, and the general attitudes of Swedish courts in view of the new situation in particular, have been heavily debated in Swedish legal doctrine[4], which has however also observed the 'positive' tendencies, in terms of increased judicial review and even a kind of judicial activism, that this 'Europeanisation' of Swedish law in the late 1990s brought about.[5] To summarise this discussion, I think it is fair to say that the 'sub-ordination', more or less, of Swedish law in some respects to European law represents the most important constitutional change in modern Swedish constitutional history, which has indeed transformed the constitutional perspective also in other ways. More than anything else, it has meant that above the traditionally so important and very rarely contested legislation, there is now in Sweden and some other Nordic countries not only some rather old and very rarely invoked constitutions, but also the European Convention of Human Rights[6] and the whole body or mass of EU law (*'l'acquis communautaire'*). This has meant, firstly, that conflicts between the traditionally highly respected and hardly contested laws and norms of a higher dignity have become much more frequent than before and, secondly, that it is no longer considered as strange to invoke the constitution itself in legal proceedings—a fact that is undoubtedly important at least in Sweden. In general, the courts have not been wholly unwilling to face up to this new challenge, though some

[3] *NJA* 1998 p 817, concerning the fate of a journalist protesting against Norwegian seal-hunting, which ran contrary to the judgment of the EctHR in *Bladet Tromsö* and *Stensaas v Norway*, 20 May 1999 in case 21980/93.

[4] In the vast literature on the topic, see eg Nergelius, *Förvaltningsprocess, normprövning och Europarätt* (Stockholm 2000), U Bernitz, *Sverige och Europarätten* (Stockholm 2002) (also published in English, Sweden and European law) and I Cameron, 'The Swedish Experience of the European Convention of Human Rights since Incorporation', *International Comparative Law Quarterly* 1999 pp 20–56. More detailed analysis of case-law from Swedish courts in this respect may be found in K Karlsson/F Hägglund, 'En kartläggning av Sveriges första fem år med EG-rätt', *ERT* 1999 pp 437–519 and in a special addendum to no 3 of that journal in 1999 (concerning EC law), as well as in J Södergren, 'Axplock', *ERT* 2002 p 664 ss and 2005 p 33 ss (concerning ECHR).

[5] See eg O Wiklund, 'EG-rättens inflytande over svensk rätt—En konstitutionell omvandling', in U Bernitz/O Wiklund (eds), *Nordiskt lagstiftningssamarbete i det nya Europa* (Stockholm 1996) p 59 as well as Nergelius, The Impact of EC Law in Swedish National Law—A Cultural Revolution, in I Cameron/A Simoni (ed), *Dealing with Integration—Vol 2*, (Uppsala 1998) pp 165–82 and *Maktdelning och politikens judikalisering in SOU 1999:58 (Löser juridiken demokratins problem?)* pp 55–84. Perhaps the clearest expression of an awareness from Swedish courts of the supremacy of EU law is the so-called *Lassagård* case from 1997 (RÅ 1997 ref 65), where the Supreme Administrative Court set aside a rather crucial law concerning legal remedies in administrative law because it was found to be contrary to the general principles of EU law.

[6] During the 1990s, the Convention was incorporated into the national law of all the Nordic states, which was necessary in order to give it a legally binding force in those countries that are traditionally dualistic in the way they consider the relationship between national and international law. The incorporation was not done at exactly the same time or in exactly the same way in all the 5 states, but that is a detail that will not be dealt with here.

clear errors have been made by different Swedish courts in this respect (not least by the Supreme Courts), as mentioned above. Still, given the reactions and reflexes also of courts like eg the Labour court (*Arbetsdomstolen*[7]), it could in fact be justified to state that the full, total extent of the impact of European law in general and EU law in particular had not really dawned on the Swedish courts during the first then years of EU membership. In other words, though things have in fact improved a lot in the last 10 years in this respect, they could still be a whole lot better.

A clear sign or indication of this fact also came when the EU Commission in the fall of 2004 adressed the Swedish government with a request for an explanation of the fact that Swedish courts had so rarely, since 1995, asked for preliminary rulings from the ECJ.[8] Having faced this criticism, Sweden decided to enact a new law by the 1 July 2006, which states that if leave for appeal (*prövningstillstånd*) is not granted by any of the two highest courts in cases where matters of EU law are invoked, those two courts have to state the reasons for such an omission or decision.[9] Undoubtedly, also this 'move under pressure' from the Swedish legislator—which proved that previous critics of the exaggerated cautiousness in this respect from the highest courts were not entirely wrong—has contributed to a sharpened and heightened awareness concerning the importance and relevance of European law among Swedish lawyers.

Still, it was only in 2005 that the Supreme Court, in particular, showed that it was finally willing to grasp and comply with the full effect not only of the supremacy of EU law, but also of the European Convention of Human Rights. In two judgments during that year (as well as in one request for a preliminary ruling), the Supreme Court arrived at conclusions that may in light of its previous case-law in this area only be described as sensational, through the use of arguments that were also highly unusual and unexpected in a historical context.

[7] As far as that court is concerned, it could even be said that until it asked for a preliminary ruling in the highly contested *Laval* case in 2005 (C-341/05), it hardly showed any awareness at all of that particular aspect of EU law.

[8] The official name or reference of the letter from the Commission is 2003/2161, C (2004) 3899. The cases that led the Commission to initiate this action was partly the above-mentioned *Barsebäck* case (RÅ 1999 ref 76), which led to a vivid debate, but also the *Lyckeskog* case, C-99/00, ECR I 2002 p 4839, where the Court of Appeal in Gothenburg asked whether it was to be considered as the highest instance in a petty criminal case. During the proceedings in that case, it seems to have occurred to the EU Commission that when the two highest courts in Sweden decide *not* to grant a leave for appeal, they are not obliged to justify their decisions, which means that they could in fact 'ignore' Art 234 s 3 of the EC Treaty without there being any real possibility to control their actions. The Commission, hardly surprising, found this possibility in combination with the generally low frequency of demands for preliminary rulings from Swedish courts unsatisfactory and thus decided to take action against it.

[9] The new law is called lag (2006:502), med vissa bestämmelser om förhandsavgörande från EG-domstolen.

2 THE EVENTS OF 2005—TWO SPECTACULAR JUDGMENTS AND ONE STRETCHED HAND TO THE COURT OF JUSTICE

The two important judgments that were delivered by the Supreme Court thus both concerned the European Convention of Human Rights, the status of which in Swedish domestic law has in fact been disputed ever since 1 January 1995, when Sweden joined the European Union. At the same time, a decision was made by the Swedish Parliament to finally incorporate the ECHR into Swedish national law, which was necessary in order to make it legally binding in Sweden, given the country's traditionally dualistic view on the relationship between international and national law. This was a logical move, given that ECHR is also a part of EU law and that the Convention was already being used by Swedish courts as a means of interpretation,[10] but at the same time it was not done by clearly stating that the Convention was now superior to Swedish law. Instead, an article was invoked in chapter 2 of the Swedish constitution (*Regeringsformen*, Instrument of Government, IG), according to which laws may not be enacted which are contrary to the Convention. This article (chapter 2, Article 23) does however not reveal what would actually happen should a law that is contrary to the European Convention in fact be passed by the Swedish Parliament, which is the result of a legally not so fortunate political compromise from 1993.[11] One of the results of this solution is that a certain basic right is better protected if it may be invoked under EC law than if it is 'only' part of and protected by the ECHR, as shown by the *Lassagård* case from 1997, where the fact that a right to a legal hearing and a fair trial could be deduced not only from ECHR but also from EC law, was decisive for the outcome.[12]

In other words, the ECHR, despite being referred to in IG chapter 2, Article 23, was not given constitutional status, but is as such incorporated through an ordinary law.[13] IG 2:23 simply states that 'No act of law or other provision may be adopted' which contravenes Sweden's undertakings under the ECHR. Thus, this may be seen as a rule directed to the legislator rather than the courts,[14] an impression that is strengthened by the fact that since ECHR is incorporated as an ordinary law, the restrictions and limitations on judicial review imposed by IG 11:14 (the so called criteria of manifest lack

[10] See eg the Supreme Court cases NJA 1988 p 572 and 1991 p 512 (I).

[11] The *travaux préparatoires* where some not so convincing explanations for the compromise sought are presented may be found in SOU 1993:40, prop 1993/94:117 and the report from the Constitutional Committee of the Parliament (*Konstitutionsutskottet*) 1993/94:24. For critical discussions in the doctrine, see Bernitz, ch 5 *The Incorporation of the European Human Rights Convention into Swedish Law—A half Measure* and *Nergelius*, (Svensk statsrätt, Lund 2006) p 153 ss.

[12] RÅ 1997 ref 65.

[13] The number of which is 1994:1500.

[14] Cameron, *An Introduction to the European Convention on Human Rights*, 5th edn (Uppsala 2006) p 155 ss, as well as Bernitz, *European Law in Sweden*, p 81 ss.

of constitutionality, *uppenbarhetskravet*, in order for a law to be set aside) apply with even greater force in relation to ECHR than in relation to the national constitution(s).[15] The situation, should a law passed either before or after 1 January 1995 be in conflict with the ECHR, was in the *travaux préparatoires* handed to the courts to deal with by the use of ordinary means of interpretation (eg rules on *lex posterior* and *lex specialis*).

What does this mean in practice, then? It could of course be seen to indicate that when a conflict, which is not manifest, will arise between the ECHR and a Swedish law or ordinance, the law or ordinance shall be applied.[16] But on the other hand, it must be noted that in the travaux préparatoires, both from the government and the Constitutional Committee of the Parliament, mention is made of the 'special character' and status of ECHR, which ought to give it a certain weight of its own in future conflicts with domestic laws (or ordinances).[17] On the basis of those remarks, Swedish courts ought to be able to find at least some room for manoeuvering if they want to secure the respect (or even supremacy) of the ECHR.

Still, which is perhaps not entirely surprising against this background, the Swedish courts have so far been reluctant to use the ECHR, at least when this would mean setting aside a national law. In one case from 1998,[18] the Supreme Court as mentioned above even refused to uphold the Convention (as well as the Freedom of Speech Act, *Yttrandefrihetsgrundlagen*) against a demand from Swedish and Norwegian authorities to execute a penal judgment from a Norwegian court (which was all the more embarrassing since Norway was six months later condemned by EctHR for violating the ECHR concerning the same issue).[19] At the same time, both the highest

[15] For some recent remarks on this issue, taking new jurisprudence into account, see A Bohlin/W Warnling-Nerep, *Förvaltningsrättens grunder* (Stockholm 2004) p 334 s.

[16] Of course, it shall also be noted that the similarities between ECHR and ch 2 IG, which contains a rights catalogue, are striking. The main difference is that the protection of personal integrity and family life (Art 8 ECHR) is definitely weaker in the Swedish constitution(s), given not least the wide right to access to documents in Sweden.

[17] Prop 1993/94:117 p 37 s as well as KU 1993/94:24 p 19 s.

[18] NJA 1998 p 817.

[19] *Bladet Tromsö* and *Stensaas v Norway*, Case 21980/93, Reports 1999 p. The case concerned Norwegian fishermen who had publicly criticised methods used in the hunting of seal. For this, they were condemned to penalties by Norwegian courts, which in the case before EctHR was considered to be a violation of their freedom of speech (art 10 ECHR). The Swedish case concerned a fisherman, Odd Lindberg, who had made such critical comments in a TV program which was later broadcasted in Sweden (and thus also seen in Norway, where almost everyone is able to watch Swedish TV). He was therefore also sentenced to a fine by a Norwegian court. The Norwegian authorities then chased him, after he had taken refuge to Sweden, eager to have the penalty imposed. They were then helped by the Swedish authorities and the Supreme Court could not find that the ECHR prevented those from executing the fine in Sweden (despite the fact that under the Freedom of Speech Act, the editor of the TV program and not Lindberg himself was legally responsible for any comments made in the program). From at least two points of view (and maybe also considering so-called *ordre public* in private international law), therefore, this judgment must be considered as a clear error.

courts have been very clear in terms of acknowledging eg the impact of the principle of proportionality, flowing from ECHR.[20]

In the last few years, questions related to administrative tax sanctions (or penalties) and the possibility for Swedish courts to impose damages when the Convention has been violated have been in the focus of the discussion.[21] In both areas, it seems clear that while EctHR has found that certain violations of ECHR had taken place in Sweden, Swedish courts were slow or even reluctant to take the full consequences of those judgments and come to the same conclusions as the EctHR did in almost identical cases.[22] As far as economic compensation for violations of the convention is concerned, Swedish courts tended to view this as an exclusive competence of the EctHR, though this is not quite in line with the case-law of that court, nor with ECHR itself (see not least its Article 13).[23]

The importance of the so-called *Lundgren* case[24] should thus be seen in this light. In that case, which must be seen as a breakthrough for the direct applicability of the ECHR in Swedish law, a man had been informed that he was suspected of economic crimes in 1991. Since then, he had difficulties supporting himself; his company went bankrupt and after that it was hard for him to find any other job. A criminal charge was raised against him in 1993, but the trial did not take place until 1997 and the aquitting sentence from the court of first instance did not win its full legal force and effect (*laga kraft*) before the fall of 1998. This time-extension of the procedure was considered as unacceptable and contrary to Article 6 of ECHR by the Supreme Court, which granted Lundgren, the formerly accused man who was now the claimant in the tort case, financial compensation due to the fact that Swedish public authorities had not complied with the ECHR. As indicated above, the judgment followed after some previous cases where

[20] See eg, besides some of the cases referred to above, the case NJA 2001 p 439.

[21] For an overview of this discussion, see J Södergren in Europarättslig tidskrift 2002 pp 659–82.

[22] The procedure for imposing administrative tax sanctions (skattetillägg) has eg, been found by EctHR to be contrary to Art 6 ECHR in the cases *Janosevic* and *Västberga Taxi/ Vulic v Sweden*, 34619 and 36985/97, judgment 23 Jul 2002, Reports 2002 p.

[23] At the same time, however, ECHR is regularly being invoked and applied in a number of criminal law cases, not least in relation to the procedures applied. Thus, the picture is mixed and it seems to early to make a full evaluation of how ECHR is being dealt with by Swedish courts. While waiting for that, it may be noted that a number of new monographies on the topic reveal a considerable interest in it from law scholars; see apart from the highly respected standard comment by H Danelius, *Mänskliga rättigheter i europeisk praxis: en kommentar till Europakonventionen om de mänskliga rättigheterna* (Stockholm 2002); also 2 dissertations on the right to property from recent years; K Åhman, *Egendomsskyddet—Äganderätten enligt artikel 1 första tilläggsprotokollet till den Europeiska konventionen om de mänskliga fri- och rättigheterna* (Uppsala 2000) and G Gauksdottir, *The Right to Property and the European Convention on Human Rights—A Nordic Approach*, (Lund 2004). Judge Danelius also contributes regular comments on the case-law of EctHR to the periodical *Svensk Juristtidning*.

[24] NJA 2005 p 462.

lower courts had totally refused to grant financial compensation due to the fact that the ECHR had been violated by public authorities. Still, the Supreme Court in 2003, in the so-called *Holm* case[25], had indicated that such financial compensation could after all occur, had the Convention really been violated, which was thus found to be the case here. Lundgren was consequently awarded compensation from the state firstly for his financial losses, based on his loss of income during a number of years, formally according to the rules in the Swedish Tort law (*Skadeståndslagen*) but in reality because Swedish authorities had violated Article 6 of ECHR, with the sum of 700.000 SEK. On top of that, he was also granted compensation for that violation as such, in itself so to speak (so called *ideell skada* or immaterial damage) with 100.000 SEK. In that latter respect, the right to compensation, interestingly enough, was considered as a part of the obligation that Sweden owns within its national law, according to Article 13 of ECHR, to provide efficient remedies in order to prevent or compensate violations of the Convention within due time.

One effect of the judgment is, in my view, that Article 13 of ECHR may now be considered as a general rule on financial compensation, which is henceforth to be applied by national courts when it has been clearly established that violations of the Convention have really taken place. So far, there has been fairly little debate in the Swedish doctrine concerning the implications of the judgment[26], but such a conclusion can hardly be too far-reaching. Apart from that, it seems likely that the judgment will have far-reaching implications also concerning future situations where individuals rightly or wrongly feel that they have been badly treated by public authorities.[27] The judgment in the Lundgren case is therefore likely to increase the rule of law and the legal certainty in Sweden in the future.

The circumstances in the other remarkable case from 2005, the internationally well-known and observed *Reverend Åke Green* case[28] which has merited considerable attention worldwide, were perhaps even more peculiar. As may be well-known to the reader, the case concerned a reverend (not in the official, formerly state church (*Svenska kyrkan*) but in a

[25] NJA 2003 p 217.

[26] See however Åhman in *Juridisk Tidskrift (JT)* 2005/06 pp 424–430, as well as Södergren in that same journal 2004/05 pp 762–75.

[27] It may be noted that a similar, interesting case, where the basis for a claim to compensation is however the Swedish constitution and not ECHR (in particular ch 2, Art 18 and ch 10, Art 5 IG) is currently pending before the Supreme Court; see T-3772/06, *Innala v the state*, which concerns restrictions in fishing rights in the north of Sweden and is a sequel to the previous cases NJA 1996 p 370 and 2001 p 210. Already through those 2 cases, it has in fact been established that the state has here made a clear mistake and violated the IG, and the question now is thus which kind of financial compensation that the affected fishermen may be entitled to.

[28] NJA 2005 p 805.

smaller religious community), who during a sermon in July 2003 made an unprecedented, unexpected and very brutal or even violent attack against homosexuals as a group. Quoting and referring to the bible he warned, among other things, against an increased spread of aids through legalisation of homosexual relations, called the legislators who had made such official relations possible, legal lunatics, and denounced homosexuals as a 'cancer tumour' in the societal body. He also made it clear that he had been in touch with the media before the speech and had actually been active in trying to spread his views in the general debate; consequently, newspapers and a local TV station were invited to his sermon.

The Swedish law on agitation or incitement against certain minorities or groups of people (*hets mot folkgrupp*) had actually been amended only a few years before, in order to include incitement against persons based on their sexual orientation. Thus, it was fairly clear that Reverend Green had in fact violated this Swedish law and he was sentenced for this (to one month in prison) by the city court in Kalmar in south-east Sweden. Still, the question was of course if this Swedish law was compatible with the Swedish constitution and the European Convention of Human Rights, which do both protect freedom of speech as well as freedom of religion. The Court of Appeal did not think so and found that in particular the freedom of religion, given that the remarks were made during a sermon, outweighed the Swedish legislation (given also that according to the Swedish Constitution, IG chapter 2, Articles 1, 12 and 13, the freedom of religion is as such unrestricted and not possible to limit by law).

The state prosecutor (*Riksåklagaren*) who has an unlimited right to bring cases to the Supreme Court, appealed against this aquitting sentence and claimed that Green should be sentenced to a prison punishment. The argumentation of the Supreme Court in this case was particularly interesting—and at the same time slightly puzzling and confusing—in a European law perspective.

The Supreme Court analysed the new Swedish legislation in some detail and first of all, quite surprisingly or at least unexpectedly rapidly, came to the conclusion that it was not contrary to the protection of freedom of speech and religion in the Swedish constitution. This was done by invoking the requirement of manifest error in IG chapter 11, Article 14, which may have been right or wrong in this case but was here definitely not done in a very convincing way. Above all, it shall be noted that this restriction on judicial review by the courts applies also in relation to the European Convention on Human Rights (ECHR), according to IG chapter 2, Article 23 and its *travaux préparatoires*.[29] Thus, once the Supreme Court had come

[29] But not in relation to EC law, for obvious reasons, as shown eg by the *Lassagård* case (RÅ 1997 ref 65).

to that conclusion, it should in fact have been impossible also to claim that the Swedish law was incompatible with ECHR and, consequently, that Green should be aquitted.

Nevertheless, the Supreme Court managed to arrive at exactly that result, using a quite complicated line of reasoning according to which the case-law of the Strasbourg court clearly shows that the only kind of speech in religious situations which is not protected by the freedoms of religion and speech in Articles 9–10 of the Convention is so called 'hate speech' or, in other words, clear incitements to violent acts or persecution of specific groups of individuals. Once again, this conclusion may be right or wrong as such,[30] but in this specific case, it led to some quite strange and puzzling results.

First of all, the Supreme Court here showed a clear reluctance to really exercise judicial review as such and decide whether the law in question was after all incompatible with ECHR. Instead, it said that if Green was sentenced and then brought the case to the Strasbourg court—which he had in fact publicly declared that he was going to do—it would be likely that the European Court of Human Rights (EctHR) would find that Sweden had violated the ECHR. But as everyone can see, this is actually less of a judgment based on the existing legal rules that the Supreme Court has to apply than a speculation about the future outcome; should a certain individual decide to act in a certain way and should, then, certain judges in Strasbourg decide to settle the case in a certain manner, in some four or five years from now (given the heavy workload of the Strasbourg court). This attitude may of course be seen as very pro-European indeed, but at the same time the Supreme Court may here be criticised for not exercising its true competence to decide a case and, in fact, even for abdicating from its position as the highest court of the country (and conveniently, in a very controversial case, more or less handling over that role to the Strasbourg court).

What actually seems to have been the crucial issue, from the point of view of the Swedish Supreme Court, is to be able to avoid applying the Swedish law without really stating that it is contrary to the ECHR as such, which explains the emphasis and detailed analysis of the jurisprudence of the Strasbourg court in the judgment. Referring to that jurisprudence, the Supreme Court found that it would be impossible to sentence Reverend Green to a punishment, though the new law is still not considered as incompatible with the Convention. Thus, the judgment may be seen as 'pro-European' while still expressing a traditional, cautious attitude to the exercise of judicial review.[31] Time will tell whether it will in the future be

[30] It was in fact based on a heavy amount of quoted case-law, including many old and new cases falling under both those two articles, which must as such be described as solid.

[31] In this latter respect, it is similar to yet another—strictly national—case on judicial review from 2005, NJA 2005 p 33.

considered as a wise and bold judgment or not, but there is no doubt that it reveals a very clear—perhaps even too big - respect from the Supreme Court in relation to the EctHR.[32]

On top of those two judgments, we may then also mention a third interesting case from 2005, where the Supreme Court contrary to its previous positions and not too few plain errors in its handling of EU law asked, quite surprisingly, for a preliminary ruling, namely the so-called *Unibet* case.[33] That request was highly surprising, since it is an established fact within Swedish law that no right to an *abstract* judicial review exists;[34] in other words, the courts will only exercise judicial review—under or within the restrictions imposed by IG chapter 11, Article 14—when there is a concrete case or dispute pending where the law or legal act in question may be applied and not ever *in abstracto*, just because a certain party may believe for one reason or another that a certain legal act is unconstitutional.[35] Against that background, it was highly surprising when the Supreme Court in November 2005 decided to ask the ECJ if this lack of possibilities in the exercise of judicial review or rather, this limitation of the possible ways under which judicial review may be exercised by Swedish courts, was compatible or not with EU law.[36]

If you consider the circumstances of the case, the request is even more surprising, in particular given that ECJ has in fact never demanded any specific details or specific design of any particular model of judicial review within the legal systems of the Member States, as long as a right to an effective remedy may be said to exist (also as far as review of the relationship between EU law and national law is concerned). In this particular case, the gambling company Unibet had been charged by a Swedish prosecutor for violating Swedish gambling and lottery rules. Thus, a criminal case was pending in which Unibet was free to invoke an alleged unconstitutionality or incompatibility with EU law of the Swedish legislation. At the same time, Unibet had sued the Swedish state and asked for financial compensation due to the fact that the company could not freely exercise its trade. And if that was not enough, Unibet had also initiated an administrative procedure

[32] Apart from that, it also seems clear that it puts opinions made during the exercise of religious activities in a somewhat 'preferred position' in relation to other, similar verbal attacks, a fact that became even clearer when the Supreme Court in 2006 came to a totally different conclusion in a similar case where some neo-nazis who had attacked homosexuals in leaflets, using in fact less provocative words than Reverend Green, were found guilty; see NJA 2006 s 467.

[33] The case in question has the number C-432/05.

[34] See in particular NJA 1987 p 198, where this was clearly declared by the Supreme Court. See also RÅ 1994 n 277 and 654.

[35] I do here, in order to simplify, not deal with certain special features of IG ch 11, Art 14, like the fact that not only courts but also other public authorities may exercise judicial review and that such review may also concern the compatibility of a regulation or decree with a superior rule.

in which it was complaining or appealing against not being granted a certain gambling licence. Also in both those two latter proceedings, Unibet was free to invoke any legal arguments it wished, including urging the courts to exercise judicial review.[37] Thus, the likeliness that the ECJ should find that Swedish law is on this particular point contrary to EU law seemed limited, to put it mildly,[38] and the cautious attitude of the Supreme Court when asking for the opinion of the ECJ in this case definitely stands in strong contrast to the attitude(s) previously shown by that court in those kind of cases. When the judgment was given in March 2007, it was also clear that the Swedish Court had somehow overestimated the demands of EU law in this respect, since the judgment clearly shows that there seems to exist no autonomous right to an *abstract* judicial review, independent of a specific case or dispute. This was actually established already in a case in 1987[39] and it was now confirmed by the ECJ that EU law does not impose any specific conditions on the Member States in terms of allowing specific forms of judicial review, as long as effective remedies exist before independent courts of law.[40] It is thus yet another example of a change in the positions recently taken by Swedish courts in relation to European law, the reasons of which we must now analyse a little bit more.

3 CONCLUSIONS AND A VIEW TO THE FUTURE

There is in my view no doubt that the case-law from the Swedish Supreme Court presented and analysed above does indeed represent a true shift in the positions taken by the highest Swedish judicial body in relation to European law, in particular when compared to the attitude(s) shown before by that particular court (and partly also by the Supreme Administrative Court). The two judgments are thus important and significant, in many different ways.

At the same time, the question may be raised if they—and also the preliminary ruling requested by the Supreme Court in the *Unibet* case—do really represent a true, sincere wish from the Supreme Court to deal with European law in a serious way, or if they are rather to be seen as a step back under pressure, under the gun so to speak—given that the EU Commission had in 2004 protested against a limited use of the instrument of preliminary

[36] The request in question was made in the case(s) Ö-4474-04 and 752-05.

[37] In fact, the case which did reach the Supreme Court, and finally the ECJ, was a spin-off effect of one of those procedures, in which Unibet claimed that it had the right to have judicial review exercised independently of the specific dispute taking place before the court. When the court of first instance rejected that claim, Unibet appealed both to the Court of Appeal and later to the Supreme Court, which took an unexpected interest in the arguments raised by the company.

[38] As indicated also by Advocate General Sharpston in his opinion of the 30 Nov 2006.

[39] NJA 1987 p 198.

ruling by Swedish courts (and by the two highest courts in particular) and that there existed by this time a number of voices in the Swedish doctrine that raised criticisms against parts of the jurisprudence from those two courts. Thus, though highly interesting, those two important judgments and the surprising request for a preliminary ruling concerning a very peculiar constitutional matter, are after all not entirely convincing in the sudden pro-european convictions that they reveal. Further substantive proof of a true change of mind from the high Swedish judges is wanted and indeed wished for in this respect, in order for the critical parts of the doctrine to believe that this sudden reversal of opinion is really to be taken seriously.

From another point of view, however, this new, more pro-european or at least cautious attitude from the Swedish Supreme Court may be entirely positive and well in line with the general tendencies within EU law, since it corresponds to the signals from the ECJ, during the whole 21st century, which are consistently saying that national supreme courts shall respect the so-called CILFIT criteria from the well-known case from 1982[41], according to which the highest courts of the Member States are obliged to ask for preliminary rulings from the ECJ in the lack of an *acte clair* or *acte éclairé* situation.[42] This has been a consistent trend in the jurisprudence of ECJ ever since the *Lyckeskog* judgment from 2002[43], continuing via the *Köbler* case from 2003[44], leading finally to the very clear and interesting *Traghetti del Mediterraneo* judgment from 2006.[45] Both those latter cases also reveal that failures from courts of the highest instance in this respect may lead to a non-contractual liability of the Member States. In other words, the CILFIT criteria are 'alive and kickin', also after the EU enlargement, which further, it may be noted, also reveals the relevance of some of the previous criticism raised against the two highest courts of Sweden some 10 years ago.

The only way for the highest national courts to adapt to this now very clear jurisprudence from ECJ is to apply EU law, if necessary before or instead of national law, in any case of possible conflict between the two systems. In a way, that is the direction in which the Supreme Court does now seem to be moving. It shall be very interesting to see if that tendency continues.

[40] Case C-432/05, Judgment 13 Mar 2007.

[41] 283/81, ECR 1982 p 3415.

[42] Ie when the EU act to be applied is either undoubtedly very clear to its meaning or has recently been interpreted by the ECJ.

[43] C-99/00, ECR 2002 I p 4839.

[44] C-224/01, ECR 2003 I p 10239.

8

Interpretation of the Trade Mark Directive

PROFESSOR LARS PEHRSON

DURING THE 1970S and 1980s, it became evident from the case law of the European Court of Justice, the ECJ, that there could be conflicts between national trade mark provisions and community law, especially the provisions on free movement of goods. Owners of trade marks and other intellectual property rights invoked those rights in order to prevent parallel importation. In a number of cases, the ECJ stated the proprietor of an intellectual property right could not rely on its right in order to prevent import into one member state of goods that the proprietor himself had sold in another member state. The same was true if the goods were sold not by the proprietor but with his consent.[1] Another problem was that some kinds of signs were impossible to register as trade marks in certain countries. There were also some conflicts between national trade mark rights on the one side and the right to provide services and the competition rules on the other. Having regard to those conflicts, the council found it necessary to approximate the laws of the member states relating to trade marks and adopted the trade mark directive.[2]

According to the directive, only the provisions that most directly affect the internal market are approximated. Consequently, the directive does not contain

[1] See eg Case 70/70, *Deutsche Grammophon v Metro*, [1971] ECR 487, Case 55 and 57/80, *Musik-Vertrieb Membran and K-tel v GEMA*, [1981] ECR 147, and Case 58/80, *Dansk Supermarked v Imerco*, [1981] ECR 18, as far as copyright and neighbouring rights are concerned, Case 15/74, *Centrafarm v Sterling Drug*, [1974] ECR 1147, as far as patent rights are concerned, Case 144/81, *Keurkoop v Nancy Keen Gifts*, [1982] ECR 2853, as far as design rights are concerned, and Case 16/74, *Centrafarm v Winthrop*, [1974] ECR 1183, as far as trade mark rights are concerned. See concerning the development eg L Pehrson, *EG och immaterialrätten* (*EG and the intellectual property rights*), (Stockholm, 1985) p 30 *et sec;* P Oliver, *Free movement of Goods in the European Community*, 3rd edn (London, Sweet & Maxwell, 1996), p 247 *et sec*; H-H Lidgard, *Parallelhandel. Konsumtion av immaterialrätt i Europa och USA* (*Parallel trade. Exhaustion of rights in Europe and the US*) (Stockholm, Norstedts Juridik, 2002).

[2] Dir 89/104/EEC.

any full-scale approximation. Examples of provisions that are approximated are those which regulate the kind of signs a trade mark may consist of; Article 2, absolute and relative grounds for refusal of a registration; Articles 3 and 4, the rights conferred on the proprietor of a trade mark; Article 5, different limitations of the rights; Articles 6 and 7; and the user requirement, Article 10.[3]

One important limitation is that the directive is solely applicable to registered trade marks. However, the directive does not deprive a member state from protecting trade marks by use[4] and most member states do that either under the trade mark legislation or under unfair competition legislation or, as in Sweden, under both.

Further, the directive contains no provisions relating to the procedure when trade mark applications are granted or refused. Nor does the directive deal with the procedure governing revocation or invalidity. The member states are free to fix such provision of procedure as they see fit.[5]

As far as the extent of discretion enjoyed by the member states when legislating in the area of trade mark law, it follows from the preamble that:

> the objective at which this approximation of laws is aiming requires that the conditions for obtaining and continuing to hold a registered trade mark are, in general, identical in all Member States.[6]

Despite the above-quoted statement, there are some provisions in the directive which the national legislator has a right to derogate from, eg Article 5(3). Nevertheless, the extent of discretion enjoyed by the national legislator must be regarded as very limited.

The implementation of the trade mark directive gave rise to a number of amendments to the Swedish and the other Nordic trade mark acts. However, in my opinion, those amendments did not change the main principles upon which Nordic trade mark law relied before the amendments.

The ECJ has interpreted different articles in the directive in a large number of cases. The purpose of this article is to analyse:

(i) to what extent, if any, the ECJ has accepted differences between the directive and the member states' national legislation, and,
(ii) to what extent the ECJ has interpreted the directive in way that differs from traditional Swedish and other Nordic trade mark law.

Because of the large number of cases decided by the ECJ and the number of different issues involved, it is not possible to deal with all the cases and

[3] All references are to the trade mark directive if not otherwise is stated.
[4] Recital 4.
[5] Recital 5.
[6] Recital 7.

issues. This article is limited to analysing cases dealing with the following matters:

— the signs of which a trade mark may consist,
— distinctiveness,
— confusingly similarity,
— trade marks with a reputation,
— import, and
— the user requirement.

The issues have been chosen because they are essential to trade mark law. Another motive has been to comprehend the most well-known cases.

All the cases in which the ECJ applies the trade mark directive come before the court as a reference for a preliminary ruling under Article 234 of the Treaty. Consequently, the court has only stated how a certain article in the directive should be interpreted. No ruling has been given as to the individual dispute before the national court. Thus, we do not know whether the court was of the opinion that a certain trade mark, eg, lacked distinctiveness or whether a trade mark was confusingly similar to another.

However, almost all the material provisions in the trade mark directive have a counterpart in the Community trade mark regulation.[7] When the ECJ decides a case under the regulation, the court also forms an opinion in the individual dispute. In a number of cases decided under the trade mark regulation, the ECJ has applied principles originally developed in cases decided under the directive.[8] Consequently, in the cases decided under the regulation we get an understanding of the result of the application of the principles the ECJ has developed, eg as regards confusingly similar trade marks. Some such cases will be discussed in the article.

1 THE SIGNS OF WHICH A TRADE MARK MAY CONSIST

A trade mark may consist of any sign capable of being represented graphically and capable of distinguishing the goods or services of one undertaking from those of other undertakings, Article 2. The two requirements fulfil two different aims. The first requirement aims at making the trade mark readily accessible to the competent authorities and to the public, particularly different undertakings. For the authorities, it is necessary to know exactly the nature and appearance of the signs of which the trade marks consist. Otherwise it is not possible for the authorities to examine the applications for registration and to publish and maintain the trade mark registers. The

[7] Reg 40/94/EG.

[8] Eg Case C-361/04 P, *Claude-Ruiz-Picasso m fl v OHIM och DaimlerChysler*, [2006] ECR I-643.

undertakings on the other hand must be able get information on the trade marks registered to avoid committing infringements.

The second aim is to state the kind of signs which may fulfil a trade mark function and therefore, according to the legislator, ought to be possible to register. Whether an individual trade mark is capable of fulfilling the function of distinguishing goods or services from those of other undertakings is dealt with under the headline 'Distinctiveness'. This part of the article focuses on the kind of signs which are capable of being represented graphically and accordingly may be registered as a matter of principle. Examples of such marks are given in Article 2 itself; words, including personal names, designs, letters, numerals, and the shape of goods or of their packaging.

Opening up the possibility of applying for the registration of all different signs which are capable of being represented graphically was quite liberal at the time the trade mark directive was adopted. In many jurisdictions, the shape of the goods in particular was not treated as a sign which could constitute a trade mark. Before the implementation of the directive into Swedish trade mark law, the shape of the good or its packaging could only be registered if the good or its packaging was 'peculiar'. Additionally the possibility of having personal names or letters, ie abbreviations, registered was restricted in different ways.

A trade mark may be capable of being represented graphically although the trade mark cannot be perceived graphically. Sound marks are an example. The first case in which the ECJ decided whether or not a trade mark which is not perceived graphically could nevertheless be registered deals with a mark consisting of the smell of the substance methyl cinnamate.[9] The German Patent and Trade Mark Office had refused to register the mark. The proprietor of the trade mark appealed against the decision and the German Federal Court asked for a preliminary ruling. The ECJ found:

> that a trade mark may consist of a mark which is not in itself capable of being perceived visually, provided that it can be represented graphically.

As examples of what in particular could represent such a trade mark the court mentioned 'images, lines and characters'. However, the representation must be 'clear, precise, self-contained, easily accessible, intelligible, durable and objective'. In respect of olfactory marks, the ECJ further stated that:

> the requirement of graphic representations are not satisfied by a chemical formula, by a description in written words, by the deposit of an odour sample or by a combination of those elements.

[9] Case C-277/00, *Sieckmann*, [2002] ECR I-11737. See, about the Case, E Lunell, Dofter och ljud som föremål för varumärkesrätt—några kommentarer kring Sieckmann-fallet (Scents and sounds as trade mark subject matter—some comments about the 'Sieckmann' case), NIR (*Nordic Intellectual Property Law Review*) 2003 p 124 *et sec.*

In principle, the interpretation of the ECJ is quite liberal in the way that a mark which is not capable of being perceived graphically may nevertheless be registered. However, in practice the legal situation is very different, at least as far as olfactory marks are concerned. It seems very difficult, if not impossible, to represent such a mark in a clear, precise, self-contained, easily accessible, intelligible, durable and objective way by using images, lines or characters. Thus, in practice, it is not possible to register olfactory marks.

Today, sound marks are quite usual, especially for radio and TV-programmes (signature tunes or jingles). Sound marks are also often used for other products and services when they are advertised on radio and television.

In a trade mark dispute involving the melody Für Elise, the question arose as to whether such a melody could be registered as a trade mark under the directive.[10] The ECJ started by referring to its statement in Sieckmann according to which marks which are not capable of being perceived graphically may also be registered if they can be represented graphically. According to the ECJ, this criteria is fulfilled, as far as sound marks are concerned, if the mark is represented by a stave divided into measures and showing, in particular, a clef, musical notes and rests whose form indicates the relative value and, where necessary, accidentals. On the other hand, the requirement is not satisfied when the mark is represented graphically by means of a description using the written language, such as an indication that the mark merely consists of the notes going to make up a musical work, or that it is the cry of an animal, or by means of a simple onomatopoeia, or by means of a sequence of musical notes.

Unlike olfactory marks, sounds marks may be also be registered in practice although the conditions under which a sound mark may be registered are quite strict. Probably only musical works fulfil those conditions. A sound mark like the lion's roar, which is the trade mark of Metro-Goldwyn-Mayer, will probably be very difficult to express in the kind of notes which it is necessary to use according to the ECJ.

The more liberal attitude towards sound marks compared to olfactory marks is easily understandable as sound marks are much more common and therefore represent a larger value. The ECJ might also have been influenced by some national trade mark offices which had accepted registration of such marks before the judgment was passed in the Shield Mark case.[11] However, in the USA olfactory marks have also been protected.

[10] Case 283/01, *Shield Mark v Joost Kist*, REG 2003 p I-14313.

[11] It follows from the judgment that the common Benelux trade mark office had accepted sound marks. This was the case also as far as the Swedish trade mark office is concerned, see eg the case reported in *NIR* (*Nordic Intellectual Property Law Review*) 2000 p 312 and prop (*Parliament Bill*) 1992/93:48 p 71.

From a theoretical point of view it seems obvious that a colour can be represented graphically and, consequently, may be registered. However, another question is what the representation shall consist of. In this context, the ECJ has stated that the colours shall be specified according to an international colour classification system.[12]

Quite often an undertaking wants to register a combination of colours without specifying how the colours will be used on the goods or its packaging or in advertising. The ECJ has been reluctant to accept such applications. According to the ECJ, the application must include a systematic arrangement associating the colours concerned in a predetermined and uniform way.[13]

In a recent case from the ECJ, *Dyson*, the questions put by the national court related to an application for registration of a trade mark consisting of all the conceivable shapes of a transparent bin or collection chamber forming part of the external surface of a vacuum cleaner.[14] Consequently, the mark was capable of taking on a multitude of different appearances. The ECJ found that such a trade mark did not constitute a 'mark' according to Article 2.

The two last judgments are very consistent. Neither colours nor shapes which are not specifically determined can constitute a mark under Article 2. In principle, the situation in those two cases does not differ from an application covering, eg, all different words with the prefix Mac. It seems evident that such an application does not refer to one mark, but an indefinite number of marks.

In *Dyson*, the ECJ did not only base its decision on the fact that the application did not refer to one specific shape. Interestingly enough the court also found that the granting of the registration would give the proprietor of the trade mark an unfair competitive advantage. As we will see when other cases are analysed, the ECJ quite often refer to competition aspects.

Under Article 3(1)(e) certain kinds of marks may not be registered as trade marks. This is true, eg, as far as marks which exclusively consist of 'the shape of goods which is necessary to obtain a technical result'.[15] The shape of the head of certain razors sold by Philips under the trade mark Philishave was registered, eg, in the U.K. as a trade mark for said razors. In a dispute, a competitor of Philips claimed that the registration of the razor head as a trade mark was incompatible with Article 3(1)(e).[16] According to the ECJ, the aim of the provision is to prevent trade mark protection from

[12] Case 49/02, *Heidelberger Bauchemie*, [2004] ECR I-6129.

[13] Case 49/02, *Heidelberger Bauchemie*, [2004] ECR I-5129.

[14] Case C-321/03, *Dyson v Registrar of Trade marks*, not yet reported.

[15] The other to kinds of marks which always shall be refused registration are marks that exclusively consists of the shape which results from the nature of the good itself (eg a ball) or of the shape which gives substantial value to the goods (eg the ornament on knifes and forks).

[16] Case C-299/99, *Philips v Remington*, [2002] ECR I-5475.

granting to the proprietor of a mark a monopoly on technical solutions or functional characteristics of a product.[17] Consequently, it is not possible to register the shape of a product if it is established that the essential functional features of the shape are attributable only to the technical result. Whether there are other shapes which allow the same technical result to be obtained has no impact. In my opinion the ECJ has interpreted Article 3(1)(e) quite broadly. In no other case has competition been protected so clearly and to such an extent, something which is very welcome.

The analysis of the case law from the ECJ shows that that the court has not given the national legislators any discretion when implementing into their national trade mark legislation the provisions of the trade mark directive dealing with what kind of marks a trade mark may consist of.

As already stated, the provisions of the directive constitute an extension of the kind of marks which it is possible to register compared to older Nordic trade mark law. However, the former legislation had been criticized even before the adoption of the directive.[18] The main reason was that all marks, irrespective of their kind, can fulfil the function of a trade mark if the marks have distinctiveness. Therefore, it is possible that the Swedish trade mark legislation would have been amended without the adoption of the directive.

From a Nordic point of view, the ECJ's interpretation of the directive gives no cause for surprise, except perhaps the interpretation of Article 3(1)(e) dealing with functional features.[19] Under the article only 'marks which consists exclusively ... the shape of goods which is necessary to obtain a technical result' may not be registered. According to the ECJ, it is sufficient that 'the essential functional features of shape' are attributable to the technical result. This must be considered as an extension of the marks consisting of the shape of goods that may not be registered. From a competition aspect, the ECJ's interpretation of is, in my view, an advantage.

2 DISTINCTIVENESS

As previously stated, only marks which are capable of distinguishing the goods or services of one undertaking from those of other undertakings may be registered, Article 1. The notion of distinctiveness is further elaborated

[17] Para 78.

[18] See eg L Pehrson, *Varumärken från konsumentsynpunkt (Trade marks from a Consumer's Point of view)* (Helsingborg, Liber Förleg, 1981) p 45 *et sec.*

[19] See eg M Levin, 'Varumärkesrättsligt "designskydd" ur ett svenskt perspective ('Trade mark Law "Design Protection" from a Swedish Perspective', *NIR* (*Nordic Intellectual Property Law Review*) 1996 p 297 *et sec.*; FM Andreasen, 'Varen som sit eget varemærke' ('The product as a trade mark of its own'), NIR (*Nordic Intellectual Property Law Review*) 2001 p 177 *et sec.* (Danish law).

in Article 3, according to which an application for registration of a trade mark shall be refused if the mark:

- is devoid of any distinctive character, Article 3(1)(b), or
- consists exclusively of a mark or indication which may serve, in trade, to designate the kind, quality, quantity, intended purpose, value, geographical origin or the time of production of the good or of rendering of the service, or other characteristics of the good or service, Article 3(1)(c).

The latter provision is taken from Article 6 *quinquies* B (2) of the Paris Convention, which all member states have adhered to.

Should a trade mark have been registered although it lacks distinctiveness, the registration shall be declared invalid in the event that someone brings an action. However, a member state may stipulate that the trade mark which, after it has been registered, has acquired distinctive character by use may not be invalidated, Article 4(3).

The purpose of those provisions is obvious; a mark which cannot fulfil the function of distinguishing the goods or services of one undertaking from those of other undertakings cannot fulfil the function of being a trade mark. The ECJ has also recognised that the Article fulfils a public interest which requires that it should be possible for marks and indications which are descriptive of the characteristics of the goods or services in respect of which registration is sought to be used by all undertakings.[20] If it were possible to register such marks, the proprietors would have an unfair competitive advantage.

The use of a specific mark may give rise to a change in the meaning of the mark. Consequently, if a mark with no inherent distinctiveness is, nevertheless, used as a trade mark it is possible that the relevant part of the public start to perceive the mark as a trade mark. The mark has received a secondary meaning. Therefore, the directive includes a provision stipulating that a trade mark shall not be refused registration if the trade mark, prior to the date of application for registration and following the use which has been made of it, has acquired a distinctive character, Article 3(3).

When deciding whether a trade mark application is to be granted or not, the knowledge of the national trade mark office is limited to the name of the applicant, the trade mark in question and the goods or services in respect of which the application refers. At least that is the case as far as the Swedish trade mark office is concerned. However, the ECJ has stated that the authority must have regard to all relevant facts and circumstances when

[20] Joined Cases C-108/97 och C-109/97, *Windsurfing Chiemsee v Boots- und Segelzubehör Walter Huber and Frans Attenberger*, [1999] ECR I-2779, para 25.

examining the application.[21] Nevertheless, as the member states remain free to decide the provision of the procedure concerning the registration it must be acceptable that the authority only takes such facts and circumstances into account which the applicant has included in its application or has otherwise informed the authority about.

Many different kinds of marks may constitute a trade mark. The ECJ has consistently held that the assessment of whether a trade mark has distinctive character shall be carried out according to the same criteria irrespective of the kind of mark.[22] It is quite another matter that certain kinds of marks more often lack such distinctive character.

Contrary to the practice of the Swedish and other Nordic trade mark offices, the Benelux Merkenbureau stated in the *Postkantoor* case that it only refused to grant registration of trade marks which manifestly lacked distinctiveness.[23] The ECJ stated that such a practice was incompatible with Article 3 of the directive.

When deciding whether a specific trade mark is distinctive or not, the trade mark authority must use some standard test. As far as trade marks which are intended for consumers in general are concerned, the standard measure consists of an average consumer, reasonably well-informed and reasonably observant and circumspect.[24]

Quite often a trade mark for which an application is submitted consists of a neologism produced by a combination of elements of words of which all elements are descriptive. In my view, the trade mark Biomild, intended for, eg, mild-flavoured yoghurt, is an example. The ECJ stated that such a neologism, as a general rule, is descriptive.[25] However, a neologism may be distinctive provided that it creates an impression which is sufficiently far removed from that produced by the simple combination of the elements embodied in it.

This statement should be regarded in connection with the ECJ's judgment in the case dealing with whether the trade mark Baby-Dry was sufficiently distinctive to be able to be registered under the trade mark regulation.[26] Procter & Gamble had applied for registration of the trade mark Baby-Dry in respect of diapers as a community trade mark. The OHIM and the Court

[21] Case C-363/99, *Koninklijke KPN Nederland v Benelux-Merkenbureau*, [2004] ECR I-1619.

[22] Case C-299/99, *Philips v Remington*, [2002] ECJ I-5475, Case C-53/01 to C-55/01, *Linde and Winward Industries v Rado Uhren*, [2003] ECR I- 3161 and Case C-404/02, *Nichols v Registrar of Trade marks*, [2004] ECR I-8499.

[23] Case C-363/99, *Koninklijke KPN Nederland v Benelux-Merkenbureau*, [2004] ECR 1619.

[24] See eg Case C-299/99, *Philips v Remington*, [2002] ECR I-5475 and joined Cases C-53/01 to C-55/01, *Linde and othes*, [2003] ECR I-3161.

[25] Case C-265/00, *Campina Melkunie v Benelux Merkenbureau*, [2004) ECR I-1699.

[26] Case C-383/99 P, *Procter & Gamble v OHIM*, 2001 [ECR] I-6251.

of First Instance had refused to grant the registration because the trade mark was considered to lack distinctiveness. The ECJ, on the other hand, reversed the case. The court stated:

> In order to assess whether a word combination such as BABY-DRY is capable of distinctiveness, it is therefore necessary to put oneself in the shoes of an English-speaking consumer. From that point of view, and given that the goods concerned in this case are babies' nappies, the determination to be made depends on whether the word combination in question may be viewed as a normal way of referring to the goods or of representing their essential characteristics in common parlance.
>
> As it is, that word combination, whilst it does unquestionably allude to the function which the goods are supposed to fulfil, still does not satisfy the disqualifying criteria set forth in paragraphs 39 to 42 of this judgment. Whilst each of the two words in the combination may form part of expressions used in every day speech to designate the function of babies' nappies, their syntactical unusual juxtaposition is not a familiar expression in the English language, either for designating babies' nappies or for describing their essential characteristics.
>
> Word combinations like Baby-Dry cannot therefore be regarded as exhibiting, as a whole, descriptive character; they are lexical inventions bestowing distinctive power on the mark so formed and may not be refused registration under Article 7(1)(c) of Regulation No 40/94.[27]

In my view, it is evident that the word combination Baby-Dry has greater distinctiveness than the combination Biomild. The first combination is more ingenious and odd.

In the *Biomild*-case, the ECJ also laid down another important principle. When deciding whether a word is distinctive or not, it is irrelevant whether or not there are synonyms capable of designating the same characteristics of the goods or services in question.

A third important principle stated in the *Biomild* case is that a trade mark must be refused registration if it may be interpreted in different ways if at least one of the meanings describes the characteristics of the goods or services concerned. The principle was first laid down in a case decided under the trade mark regulation.[28]

In this respect it is worth mentioning that, although the provisions dealing with distinctiveness are in principle the same, in the directive and the trade mark regulation, the interpretations are different. Under the directive it is sufficient that a word is distinctive in the language or languages used in the country in which the application is made. Under the regulation, on the other hand, the word must be distinctive in all languages used in the Union.[29]

In a later case, an undertaking had lodged an application with the Benelux-Merkenbureau for registration of the trade mark Postkantoor in

[27] Paras 42–4.

[28] Case C-191/01, *OHIM v Wrigley*, [2003] ECR I-12447.

[29] Case C-383/99 P, *Procter & Gamble v OHIM*, 2001 [ECR] I-6251, para 41.

respect of a number of different goods and services eg paper, advertising, insurance, postage-stamps, construction, telecommunications and transport.[30] The Dutch court put a number of questions to the ECJ. As answers to some of them, the ECJ repeated a number of the statements in the *Biomild* case. Some of the other questions dealt with the interest in keeping a certain mark free to be used by all undertakings. The ECJ stated that there the existence of more common marks or indications for designating the characteristics of the goods or services for which the trade mark was intended has no bearing on the possibility of registering a trade mark. That is completely consistent with the principle that the existence of synonyms to a trade mark has no impact on the possibility of registering the mark. Further, the number of actual or potential competitors has no impact either.

During the 1960s and 1970s there was a tendency under Swedish trade mark law to find that a trade mark which had no distinctiveness for a certain product also lacked distinctiveness for some related products. The trade mark Boxer was, eg, considered to lack distinctiveness not only is respect of drawers but also in respect of, eg, shirts.[31] However, in the *Postkantoor* case the ECJ stated that it is of no relevance that a trade mark is descriptive of the characteristics of certain goods or services when it comes to assessing whether the trade mark has distinctive character in relation to other goods or services in respect of which registration of the trade mark is also applied for.

Previously at least, it was quite common that an undertaking applying for registration of a trade mark with limited distinctiveness as an argument for granting registration claimed that the trade mark had been registered in another Nordic country. In the *Postkantoor* case, the ECJ stated that a registration in one member state has no bearing on the examination of the trade mark office in another member state.

The assessment as to whether a mark is sufficiently distinctive involves different questions depending on the kind of mark in question. One example concerns marks consisting of geographical names. In the *Windsurfing* case, which is the first case in which the ECJ interpreted Article 3, the undertaking Windsurfing Chiemsee had used a registered pictorial mark including the word Chiemsee.[32] In a dispute with two other undertakings, the question arose as to whether it was possible for Windsurfing Chiemsee to have an exclusive right to its trade mark and especially the Chiemsee part. The ECJ stated in a preliminary ruling that it is in the public interest

[30] Case C-363/99, *Koninklijke KPN Nederland v Belelux-Merkenbureau*, [2004] ECR 1619.

[31] RÅ (Report of cases from the Supreme Administrative Court) 1967 H 16.

[32] Joined Cases C-108/97 and C-109/97, *Windsurfing Chiemsee v Boots- und Segelzubehör Walter Huber and Franz Attenberger*, [1999] ECR I-2779.

that geographical names remain available to be used by all. Consequently, Article 3.1(c) not only prohibits the registration of a geographical name where the name designates a place which is, in the mind of the relevant part of the public, currently associated with the kind of goods in question, but also to a geographical name which, in the future, is liable to be used by undertakings as an indication of the geographical origin. However, there is no general ban on registering a geographical name as a trade mark. Names which are unknown to the relevant part of the public or which are unlikely to indicate the geographical origin of the kind of goods in question may be registered.

Another kind of trade mark is those which consist of a surname. The *Nichols* case seems to indicate that the ECJ is of the opinion that it is particularly difficult to establish that a mark consisting of a surname has distinctive character.[33] Nevertheless, such difficulty cannot justify stricter general criteria on the assessment of distinctive character. Only the burden to show such character is greater.

As previously stated, the shape of the goods itself may, under certain conditions, be registered as a trade mark. Also in respect of such marks, the assessment of the distinctiveness of the marks shall follow the same standard test. However, the ECJ has stated that it may, in practice, be more difficult to establish distinctiveness in relation to a trade mark consisting of the shape of the product than a word or pictorial mark.[34]

As previously stated, a trade mark may acquire distinctive character by use, Article 3(3). In the *Europolis* case, the ECJ stated that the registration of a trade mark with no inherent distinctiveness may only be allowed if it is proven that the trade mark has acquired distinctive character throughout the territory of the member state in question.[35] Further, it is necessary that the relevant part of the public, or at least a significant proportion thereof, considers the mark to be a trade mark. However, the ECJ did not state what 'a significant proportion' means in this respect. Is it a fixed percentage? Is it a percentage at all? Do the perceptions of all persons belonging to 'the relevant part of the public' have the same impact or is the perception of some group of persons more important? There are a number of questions left to be answered.

An inherent descriptive part of a mark may acquire distinctive character as a consequence of the use of complete marks as a trade mark.[36] The question arose when Nestlé, after having used the mark 'Have a break ... Have a Kit Kat' applied for registration of the trade mark, Have a break.

[33] Case C-404/02, *Nichols v Registrar of Trade marks*, [2004] ECR I-8499.

[34] Case C-299/99, *Philips v Remington*, [2002] ECR I-5475, and joined Cases C-53/01 to C-55/01, *Linde and others*, [2003] ECR I-3161.

[35] Case C-108/05, *Bovemij Verzekeringen v Benelux-Merkenbureau*, not yet reported.

[36] Case C-353/03, *Société des produits Nestle v Mars*, [2005]ECR I-6135.

From the summary of the case law of the ECJ it follows that the court has not accepted different ways of interpreting the provisions on distinctiveness. However, this does not mean that the same mark must always be accepted for registration in all member states. Firstly, a mark may be distinctive in one member state but not in another. This is quite common as far as words are concerned, as a word can be distinctive in one language but not in another. The only way to overcome this is to take all different languages represented in the union into account when assessing the distinctiveness of a mark. For various reasons this is not possible. It will make it very difficult to have a trade mark registered and the registration procedure will be difficult for the national trade mark offices to handle. However, in my view this is an argument for taking all the major languages represented in the union into account when assessing whether a certain mark is distinctive or not.

Secondly, the use made of a mark may have a large impact on the distinctiveness of the mark, see Article 3(3). Consequently, if an undertaking has applied for registration in two different member states, but the mark has only been used in one of the states, the mark will most probably be more distinctive in this state.

Thirdly, the global assessment of distinctiveness may turn out differently depending on the authority which is to carry out the assessment.

For a Swedish trade mark lawyer it is evident that the notion of distinctiveness has been given a much more liberal interpretation by the ECJ compared to the interpretation given by the Swedish courts. This is also true as far as all different kinds of trade marks are concerned, perhaps with the exception of pictorial marks. It took some years before the case law of the ECJ started to influence the Swedish courts. However, during recent years the interpretation has changed and is now more in line with the interpretation of the ECJ. Nevertheless, it is my opinion that the ECJ is still somewhat more liberal that the Swedish courts.

3 CONFUSINGLY SIMILAR TRADE MARKS

In all European countries, the proprietor of a trade mark has an exclusive right to his mark. This exclusive right implies that no one but the proprietor may use the trade mark in the course of trade without the proprietor's consent. However, the exclusive right would be of no real value for the proprietor if it were not extended to include a right to prevent the use of confusingly similar trade marks. The assessment of when a trade mark is confusingly similar to another trade mark is one of the most central issues in trade mark law.

The provisions in the directive dealing with confusingly similar trade marks have a rather complex construction when compared to older trade mark legislation in many of the member states. One reason is that the directive distinguishes between the likelihood of confusion in connection with registration matters, Article 4, and in connection with infringements, Article 5. Certainly, the provisions are very similar, but not, however, identical.

The other reason is the wording of the provisions. As previously stated, the proprietor of a registered trade mark has an exclusive right to the mark, Article 5(1). Consequently, the proprietor is entitled to prevent all third parties which do not have his consent from using any mark which is identical with the registered trade mark in relation to goods or services which are identical with those for which the trade mark is registered, Article 5(1)(a), cf Article 4(1)(a). In such a case the proprietor of the trade mark does not have to show any likelihood of confusion. Although Article 5(1)(a) stipulates that both the marks/trade marks and the goods or services shall be 'identical', the ECJ has stated that the Article shall also apply when the later trade mark reproduces, without any modification or alteration, all elements constituting the earlier trade mark or where, viewed as a whole, the later trade mark contains differences so insignificant that they may go unnoticed by an average consumer.[37]

Where there is no identification between both the mark and the trade mark and the goods or services they represent, Article 5(1)(b) is applicable (cf Article 4(1)(b)). Under this provision, the proprietor of a trade mark may prevent the use of a mark which, because of its identification with, or similarity to, the trade mark and the identification with or similarity to the goods or services covered by the trade mark and the mark, there exists a likelihood of confusion on the part of the public, which includes the likelihood of association between the mark and the trade mark. The ECJ has established a number of principles concerning the interpretation of this provision.

The purpose of a trade mark is to distinguish the goods or services of one undertaking from those of another. Consequently, the fact that the relevant part of the public understands that products marketed and sold under two different but similar trade marks are manufactured in different geographical places does not exclude the two trade marks being considered to be confusingly similar.[38] Many undertakings manufacture their products in different places.

Similarity between two trade marks may cause three different conceptions:

- The public may confuse the later trade mark with the earlier mark, direct confusion.
- The public makes a connection between the proprietor of the later trade mark and the proprietor of the earlier trade mark and confuses them, indirect confusion.

[37] Case C-291/00, *LTJ Diffusion v Sadas Vertbaudet*, [2003] ECR I-2199.
[38] Case C-39/97, *Canon Kabushiki Kaisha v Metro Goldwyn-Mayer*, [1998] ECR I-5507.

— The public considers the later trade mark to be similar to the earlier trade mark and the perception of the later trade mark calls to mind the memory of the earlier trade mark although the two marks are not confused, likelihood of association.

According to the ECJ, the first two conceptions include likelihood of confusion, but not the third one.[39] This is perfectly in line with traditional Swedish trade mark law but contrary to older Benelux trade mark law.

When deciding whether two trade marks are confusingly similar, the similarity between the trade marks and the similarity between the goods or services should not be assessed separately. Instead, likelihood of confusion is a product of similarity between the trade marks and similarity between the goods or services. In a number of cases the ECJ has stated that a lesser degree of similarity between the goods or services may be offset by a greater degree of similarity between the marks and vice versa.[40] The principle has long been part of Swedish and other Nordic trade mark law but was previously not accepted under, eg, German law.[41]

The test of whether two trade marks are confusingly similar starts with the impression given by the trade marks to the average consumer of the goods or services concerned. Consequently, the attention of the average consumer may vary depending on the kind of goods or services. This average consumer shall be deemed to be reasonably well-informed and reasonably observant and circumspect. This standard measure is the same as the one used when determining whether a trade mark is sufficiently distinctive. When using this test, the court must observe that an average consumer normally perceives a trade mark as a whole and does not analyse the different details of the mark. Further, the average consumer rarely has a chance to make a direct comparison between the two marks but must place his trust in the imperfect picture of them he has kept in mind.[42]

39 Case C-251/95, *Sabel v Puma*, [1997] ECR I-6191.

40 Case C-39/97, *Canon Kabushiki Kaisha v Metro Goldwyn-Mayer*, [1998] ECR I-5507, Case C-342/97, *Lloyd Schuhfabrik Meyer & Co v Klijsen Handel*, [1999] I-3819 and Case C-425/98, *Marca Mode v Adidas*, [2001] ECR I-4861.

41 SOU (Commission Report) 1958:10 p 251 *et sec*, 256 *et sec*; U Bernitz, G Karnell, L Pehrson, C Sandgren, *Immaterialrätt och otillbörlig konkurrens (Intellectual property and unfair competition)*, 9th edn (Stockholm, 2005) p 225; M Koktvedgaard, M Levin, *Lärobok i immaterialrätt (Textbook on intellectual property)*, 8th edn (Stockholm, 2004) p 406; BS Lassen, *Oversikt over norsk varemerkelov (Norwegian Trade mark Law—a Survey)* 2nd edn (Oslo, 1997) p 268 *et sec.* As far as older German law, see eg L Pehrson, *Varumärken från konsumentsynpunkt (Trade marks from the consumer's point of view)* (Stockholm, 1981) p 208 with further references to German literature.

42 Case C-251/95, *Sabel v Puma*, [1997] ECR I-6191, Case C-210/96, *Gut Springenheide och Tusky*, [1998] ECR I-4657 and Case C-342/97, *Lloyd Schuhfabrik Meyer & Co v Klijsen Handel*, [1999] ECR I-3819.

The likelihood of confusion shall be appreciated globally. In making this assessment, account should be taken, in particular, of the inherent characteristics of the earlier mark, including the fact that it does or does not contain an element descriptive of the goods or services for which it is protected. Also, the distinctiveness created by the use of the earlier mark shall be observed. Of importance in this connection is the market share held by the mark, how intensive, geographically widespread and long-standing the use of the mark has been, the amount invested by the proprietor in promoting the mark, the proportion or the relevant sector of the public which, because of the mark, identifies the goods or services as originating from a particular undertaking and statements from chambers of commerce and industry or other trade and professional associations.[43]

The similarity between two trade marks may consist of visual, aural and/or conceptual similarity. It is possible that mere aural similarity is sufficient to make two trade marks confusingly similar.[44] Most probably mere similarity between visual or conceptual impression is also sufficient for confusingly similarity to be present.

The ECJ has never stated how large a part of the relevant public that must be confused for the use of the later trade mark to constitute an infringement. There is not even a hint in the case law. The reason is probably that the average consumer is treated as one single person and, consequently, only can perceive a trade mark in one way.

In a preliminary ruling, the ECJ never states whether the two trade marks in question are confusingly similar or not. However, in a decision concerning the trade mark Life, the ECJ came quite close.[45] The company Medion was the proprietor of the trade mark Life for leisure electronic devices. The company brought an action against the company Thomson and claimed that Thomson's use of the trade mark Thomson Life for similar trade marks constituted an infringement. In its preliminary ruling the ECJ stated:

> that where the goods or services are identical there may be a likelihood of confusion on the part of the public where the contested mark is composed by juxtaposing the company name of another party and a registered mark which has normal distinctiveness and which, without alone determining the overall impression conveyed by the composite mark, still has an independent distinctive role therein.

The ECJ expressly rejected the principle that the likelihood of confusion should be subject to the condition that the overall impression of the composite mark must be dominated by the part of the mark which is represented by the earlier mark.[46]

[43] Case C-342/97, *Lloyd Schuhfabrik Meyer & Co v Klijsen Handel*, [1999] ECR I-3819.
[44] Case C-342/97, *Lloyd Schuhfabrik Meyer & Co v Klijsen Handel*, [1999] ECR I-3819.
[45] Case C-120/04, *Medion v Thomson Multimedia*, [2005] ECR I-8551.
[46] Para 32.

There is comprehensive case law from the Court of First Instance decided under the trade mark regulation dealing with confusingly similar trade marks. However, as yet only a few of those cases have been appealed to, and decided by, the ECJ. Nevertheless, the existing case law clearly shows that the court applies the same principles when assessing whether two trade marks are confusingly similar under the regulation.

The first of these cases decided by the ECJ involves a composite word and figurative mark consisting of the name Hubert surmounted by a bust of a chef of jovial appearance raising his right arm with upturned thumb. Registration for the mark was sought, e.g., for milk and milk products in class 29.[47] The application was opposed by the proprietor of the trade mark Saint-Hubert, registered for, eg, cheeses and diary products in class 29. Although there was identification between the goods, both the Court of First Instance and the ECJ found that the marks were not confusingly similar depending on their visual, aural and conceptual differences.

Nor has the trade mark Picaro been held to be confusingly similar to the trade mark Picasso, both for motor vehicles.[48] The Court of First instance, and probably also the ECJ found the two trade marks were visually and phonetically similar, although the similarity in the latter respect was low. However, from a conceptual point of view the marks were not similar. The conceptual differences were so great that it removed the visual and aural similarity.

In a quite resent case, the trade mark Zirh was held not to be confusingly similar to the trade mark Sir accompanied by a heraldic figure.[49] The two trade marks were intended for the same kind of goods. The Court of First Instance and the ECJ found that the conceptual and visual differences negated the aural similarity.

However, the trade mark Vitafruit, for which registration was sought in respect of different kinds of beverages, was held to be confusingly similar to the trade mark Vitafrut, registered for the same kinds of goods.[50] The outcome of the case seems self-evident.

When deciding whether two trade marks are confusingly similar or not, the legal situation is very similar to that of assessing if a trade mark is distinctive. The ECJ has developed a number of principles which the national courts have to follow. Nevertheless, when analyzing whether two trade marks are too similar or not, the conclusion may often be different despite the fact that the courts have applied the same principles. This is also well known as far as the case law within one single member stated is concerned and is difficult to do anything about.

[47] Case C-106/03 P, *Vedial v OHIM*, [2004] ECR I-9573.

[48] Case C-361/04 P, *Claude-Ruiz-Picasso et al v OHIM and Daimer Chysler*, [2006] ECR I-643.

[49] Case C-206/04 P, *Mülhens v OHIM and Zirh International*, [2006] ECR p I-2717.

[50] Case 416/04 9, *The Sunrider v OHIM*, [2006] ECR I-4237.

The ECJ has emphasized the importance of the distinctiveness of the earlier mark. This is true both as far as the inherent distinctiveness and the distinctiveness created by the use of the mark. In earlier Swedish trade mark law, distinctiveness did not have such a major importance.[51] One consequence of this new principle is that in infringement cases at least the proprietor of the earlier mark often invokes a market survey showing the percentage of the public who have knowledge of the mark. Such surveys make infringement cases much more expensive.

The case law from the ECJ relating to the trade mark regulation indicates that the court accepts more similar marks than the Swedish and other Nordic courts did prior to the implementation of the trade mark directive. The reasons for the different interpretations are unknown. One might be that it would be very difficult to grant a community trade mark registration if the scope of protection for the earlier trade marks were more extensive.

In this respect, a comparison between the European trade mark system and the European patent system is interesting. Under the latter system, it is possible to have a patent granted covering a European country, eg Sweden, either by applying for a national patent or applying for a European patent designating Sweden. Since that possibility was introduced, the concept of inventive step, which is a precondition for a patent to be granted, has been reduced by quite some extent.[52] Now, when there are two possibilities of protecting a trade mark in a member state, the preconditions for having a trade mark right granted have also been reduced. One reason might be that the registration office applying the strictest preconditions will not have so many applications to handle. Consequently, that office reduces the preconditions. In the end this may lead to 'a race to the bottom'.

4 MARKS WITH A REPUTATION

If the earlier trade mark has a reputation, it is not necessary that an application for registration of another trade mark is made in request of similar goods or services, Article 4(3).[53] Similarity between the goods or services is not necessary for the use of a younger trade mark to constitute an infringement, Article 5(2).[54] Under these articles, a proprietor of a trade mark which has a reputation can oppose the registration or prevent the use of a mark which, without due cause, takes advantage of, or is detrimental to, the distinctive character or the repute of the trade mark.

[51] See in particular R Wessman, *Varumärkeskonflikter (Trade mark Conflicts)* (Stockholm, 2002).

[52] U Bernitz, G Karnell, L Pehrson & C Sandgren, see above, n 41 p 146.

[53] A member state does not have to include such a provision in its national legislation in favour of earlier national protected marks, only in favour of earlier community trade marks.

[54] This provision is optional for the member states.

At the time of the implementation of the directive into Swedish law, both the government and legal scholars assumed that those articles were only were applicable if the goods or services in question were dissimilar.[55] However, the ECJ does not share this opinion. Articles 4(3) and 5(2) may be applicable irrespective of whether the trade marks represent similar or dissimilar goods or services.[56] The reason was that a trade mark with a reputation could not be afforded a more limited protection than a trade mark with no reputation.[57] Nor is it necessary that the trade marks in question are confusingly similar for Articles 4(3) and 5(2) to be applicable.[58]

The main issue when applying Article 4(3) or 5(2) is of course what constitutes reputation. This issue was addressed in the *Chevy* case.[59] In this case, the ECJ stated that the earlier 'trade mark must be known by a significant part of the public concerned by the products or services which it covers.' Consequently, it is the degree of knowledge within a specific part of the public that is decisive, namely the part of the public that is 'concerned by that trade mark'.[60] It follows from the decision that this part may be very large and consist of most adults or be very small and only comprise of a small number of persons. It seems very likely that a trade mark 'concerns' not only the persons who have actually bought the product in question, but also persons who may consider buying the product. Probably, a trade mark also 'concerns' the persons who had bought a competing product or is considering buying such a product. From an economic point of view, knowledge among such persons surely contributes to a trade mark's reputation.

To have a reputation, the trade mark must be known to a significant part of the public. This means that a percentage of the public must know of the mark. However, the ECJ has found that no given percentage of the public can be stated.[61] One reason might be that a smaller percentage is sufficient when the part of the public concerned by the trade mark is large and vice versa. The problem is that the ECJ has not in any way indicated what 'significant' means in this connection. What the court has said is that the assessment shall take all relevant facts into consideration, in particular

[55] Prop (Parliament Bill) 1992/93:48 p 81 *et sec.*

[56] Case C-292/00, *Davidoff v Gofkid,* [2003] ECR I-389.

[57] Paras 25 and 26.

[58] C-408/01, *Adidas v Fitnessworld*, [2003] ECR I-12537. See further M Bruus, 'Beskyttelse af renommerede varemærker—en streg i sandet?' (Protection of marks with reputation—a line drawn in the sand?, *NIR (Nordic Intellectual Property Law Review)* 2004 p 23 *et sec.*

[59] Case C-375/97, *General Motors v Yplon*, [1999] ECR I-5421. The case is commented by L Pehrson in *JT (The Legal Journal)* 1999–2000 p 421 *et sec.* See in general about marks with a reputation J Rosén, 'Känneteckens goodwillskydd' ('Protection of the goodwill of marks') in *Festskrift till Mogens Koktvedgaard (Essays in honor of Mogens Koktvedgaard)* p 473 *et sec.*

[60] Para 24.

[61] Para 25.

the market share held by the trade mark, the intensity, geographical extent and the duration of its use, and the size of the investment made by the proprietor in promoting the mark.

Under Articles 4(3) and 5(2) the earlier trade mark must have a reputation in the member state in question. According to the ECJ it is sufficient that a reputation exists 'in a substantial part' of the member state.[62] As far as the interpretation of the expression 'a substantial part', the judgment gives some further guidance. As the trade mark Chevy was registered in the Benelux-countries, those three countries should be regarded as equivalent to a member state. The ECJ stated that in such a case it was sufficient that the trade mark had reputation in a part of one of the Benelux countries. Consequently, reputation in, eg, the southern part of Sweden seems to be sufficient for an undertaking to be able to rely on Article 4(3) or 5(2).

The case law of the ECJ shows that there is just one acceptable interpretation of Articles 4(3) and 5(2). However, as long as the court does not indicate anything about the percentage of the public that have to know about the trade mark for the mark having a reputation, it is possible that national courts will come to very different solutions on that issue. It will not be a surprise if the percentage ranges from 25 per cent to 75 per cent.

5 IMPORT

As previously stated, the different ways of treating parallel import under national law was one of the main reasons for adopting the trade mark directive. The ECJ had, in number of decisions, found that it was incompatible with the provisions on the free movement of goods in Articles 28 and 30 of the Treaty if the proprietor of a trade mark in one member state could prevent the import of products which the owner himself, or someone who had his consent, had sold in another member state.[63] However, parallel import from a non-member state to a member state was not, and is not covered by the provisions on the free movement of goods.[64]

Based on the case law from the ECJ, the trade mark directive includes a provision stating that a trade mark right does not entitle the proprietor to prohibit its use in relation to goods which have been put on the market in the community under that trade mark by the proprietor or with his consent,

[62] Para 28.

[63] The legal situation is the same as far as the other intellectual property rights are concerned. The first two trade mark cases are 16/74, *Centrafarm v Winthop*, [1974] ECR 1183. See L Pehrson, *EG och immaterialrätten (EG and the intellectual property rights)* (Stockholm, 1985) p *59 et sec;* H-H Lidgard, *Parallellhandel. Konsumtion av immaterialrätt i Europa och USA (Parallel trade. Exhaustion of rights in Europe and the US)* (Stockhom, 2002).

[64] See eg Case 51/75, *EMI Records v CBS*, [1976] ECR 811.

Article 7(1).[65] However, the directive does not include any explicit provision concerning import from a non-member state to a member state. Such a situation was decided by the ECJ in the well- known *Silhouette* case.[66]

The company Silhouette produces highly priced spectacles which are sold under the trade mark Silhouette. In 1995, Silhouette sold a large number of out-of-fashion spectacle frames to a Bulgarian company, Union Trading. The frames where delivered to Union Trading's office in Bulgaria's capital Sofia. Subsequently, Hartlauer bought the frames and imported them back to Austria. Silhouette brought an action for trade mark infringement. The Austrian Supreme Court referred the following question for a preliminary ruling.

> Is Article 7(1) ......to be interpreted as meaning that the trade mark entitles its proprietor to prohibit a third party from using the mark for goods which have been put on the market under that trade mark in a State which is not a Contracting State.

The court gave the following answer to the question posed:

> National rules providing for exhaustion of trade mark rights in respect of products put on the market outside the EEA under that mark by the proprietor or with his consent are contrary to Article 7(1).

The court stated that this followed from the wording and the scheme of the directive. The rights conferred by a trade mark are stated in Article 5. One of the rights is that the proprietor should have an exclusive right to import goods under the proprietor's trade mark, Article 5(3)(c). In Articles 6 and 7 different limitations as to the right of a trade mark are enumerated. None of these enumerations covers a situation where the proprietor of a trade mark has sold product outside the EU and those products are subsequently imported back to a member state. Consequently, the proprietor of a trade mark right can rely on his trade mark right in such a situation.

In the *Silhouette* case, the Swedish government maintained that Article 7 of the directive did not regulate the situation in question. Consequently, according to the opinion of the Swedish government, the member states were free to regulate this situation as they liked.[67] As is evident from what has already been stated, the ECJ did not share this opinion. On the contrary, the ECJ stated that Articles 5 to 7 of the directive were to be construed as embodying a complete harmonisation of the rules relating to the

[65] Art 7 also includes a second paragraph under which the provision in art 7(1) shall not apply where there exist legitimate reasons to oppose further commercialization of the goods, especially where the condition of the goods is changed or impaired after they have been put on the market. Whether the ECJ is of the same opinion is still an open question.

[66] Case C-355/96, *Silhouette International Schmied GmbH & Co KG v Hartlauer Handelsgesellschaft mbH*, [1998] ECR I-4799.

[67] Para 20.

rights conferred by a trade mark.[68] Such an interpretation was supported by recitals 1 and 9. The conclusion was that the directive contains a full-scale harmonisation of the scope of protection of a trade mark.

In my opinion, the ECJ cannot be criticized for its interpretation of Article 7(1) of the directive. However, it is quite astonishing that parallel and other kinds of import are allowed between member states whereas the opposite is the case as far as import from a non-member state to a member state is concerned. If a right to import products that have been sold in another member state is considered to be advantageous for the public and competition,[69] how come this is not the case when the products are imported from a non-member state? Is import from Sweden to Germany in any way better than import from, e.g., Switzerland to Germany? It seems evident that the purpose of the right to prevent parallel import of products from a non-member state is protectionism.

Of course, import from a non-member state to a member state is allowed if the proprietor of the trade mark consents to the importation. This follows from Article 5 of the directive and implicitly from the fact that a proprietor of a trade mark is not forced to bring an action if a third party imports to a member state goods which were originally marketed in a non-member state. The *Sebago* case[70] mainly deals with what kind of measures that may constitute such consent. By way of introduction, the ECJ confirmed the answer given in the *Silhouette* case. As far as what may constitute consent, the court stated that the text of Article 7(1) gave no direct answer. Nevertheless, the court found that consent within the meaning of Article 7(1) must relate to each individual item of the products in respect of which exhaustion is pleaded. The main reason for this interpretation was that it was already adopted by the court in other cases dealing with exhaustion of rights under Articles 28 and 30 of the treaty and Articles 7(1) of the directive.[71]

The wording of the ECJ's answer in the *Sebago* case seems to indicate that consent had to be explicit. However, the ECJ have not been prepared to go that far. In the *Davidoff* case[72] the ECJ found that consent may implied but only where it is to be inferred from the facts and circumstances prior to, simultaneous with or subsequent to the placing of the goods on the market in a non-member state in a way which unequivocally demonstrates

[68] Para 25. See also joined Cases C- 414/99 to C-416/99, *Zino Davidoff v A & G Imports, Levi Strauss v Tesco Stores and Levin Strauss v Costco Wholesale*, [2001] ECR I-8691, ground 39.

[69] See eg, the Ceccini report from 1988.

[70] Case C-173/98, *Sebago In. And Ancienne Dubois et Fils SA v GB-Unic SA*, [1999] ECR I-4103.

[71] Case C-33/95, *Parfums Christian Dior v Evora*, [1997] ECR 6013 and Case C-63/97, *BMW v Deenik*, [1999 ECR I-869 respectively.

[72] Joined Cases C-414/99 to C-416/99, *Zino Davidoff v A & G Imports, Levi Strauss v Tesco Stores and Levin Strauss v Costco Wholesale*, [2001] ECR I-8691.

that the proprietor has renounced his right to oppose the placing the goods on the market within the community.[73] According to the ECJ, it is a task for the national court to decide whether this precondition is fulfilled or not.

The reason why the ECJ thought it necessary to define the concept of consent was that otherwise the right for a proprietor of a trade mark to oppose import into the community of goods being first marketed in a non-member state would vary depending on the legal system applicable.[74] Such a consequence was unacceptable to the court. Thus, the concept of consent had to be interpreted uniformly throughout the community legal order.[75] The reasons for the specific interpretation made by the ECJ seem to be based on that the court, from a more general point of view, found that situations could not be ruled out where it would reasonable that implicit consent must be accepted. However, the court also enumerated a number of situations were implied consent cannot be inferred.

In a later case, the ECJ has to a certain extent modified its earlier case law.[76]

The American company Stussy was the proprietor of the trade mark Stussy registered in respect of different kinds of clothes in, eg, Germany. Van Doren was Stussy's exclusive distributor in Germany. When van Doren discovered that another undertaking, Lifestyle, was marketing clothes from Stussy in Germany, van Doren brought an action for trade mark infringement. Van Doren claimed that Lifestyle had bought the clothes outside the union and imported then to Germany without Stussy's or van Doren's consent. Lifestyle on the other hand claimed that it had bought the products from Stussy's distributors in other member states. When van Doren claimed that Sportswear should disclose its suppliers Sportswear refused with the motivation that the suppliers would then be forced to stop selling product to Sportswear.

In its preliminary ruling the ECJ stated that:

> the requirements deriving from the protection of the free movement of goods enshrined, *inter alia*, in Article 28 EC and Article 30 EC may mean that this rule of evidence (the rule referred to above, author's comment) needs to be qualified. Accordingly, where a third party succeeds in establishing that there is a real risk of partitioning of national markets if he himself bears the burden of proof, particularly where the trade mark proprietor markets his products in the European Economic Area using an exclusive distribution system, it is a matter for the proprietor of the trade mark to establish that the products were initially placed on the market outside the European Economic Area by him or with his consent. If such

[73] Para 47.
[74] Ground 42.
[75] Ground 37.
[76] Case 244/00, *van Doren + Q v Lifestyle sports + sportswear*, [2003] ECR I-3051. The case is commented by L Pehrson in *JT (The Legal Journal)* 2004–05 p 151 *et sec.*

evidence is adduced, it is a matter for the third party to prove the consent of the trade mark proprietor to subsequent marketing of the products in the European Economic Area.

Parallel import seems to be particularly common as far as the kind of products which are marketed and sold though exclusive distribution systems. Therefore, the exemption rule of evidence laid down in van Doren is very important. As soon as a product is sold via an exclusive distribution system, or, for other reasons, there is a real risk of partitioning the national markets within the EEA, the trade mark owner has to prove that the products subsequently imported were initially placed on the market outside EEA. Only if the proprietor of the trade mark can fulfil this burden of proof, must the importer show that the import is made with the proprietor's consent.

The provision in Article 7 cannot be set aside by a purchasing contract. Assume that such a contract includes a clause stipulating that the purchaser may not resell the products within certain countries belonging to the EEA. If the purchaser nevertheless sells the product in one of the forbidden countries, and thus violates the contract, this does not include any trade mark infringement.[77]

The case law dealing with import from a non-member state into a member state is the case law that most evidently shows that the ECJ does not accept any national deviations from the provisions in the directive.

6 THE USER REQUIREMENT

The directive contains in Articles 10 and 11 quite a strict user requirement. If a trade mark has not been in genuine use during an uninterrupted period of five years in connection with the goods and services in respect of which the trade mark is registered, it may be declared invalid. If the trade mark has only been used in connection with certain of the products for which the trade mark is registered, the registration may be declared invalid in respect of the other products. A general exemption is that a trade mark may not be invalidated if the proprietor has proper reasons for the non-use. The user requirement aims at reducing the number of protected trade marks and thus at reducing the number of conflicts.[78]

The ECJ has delivered two judgments relating to the user requirement. The first judgment involves the undertaking Anzul which was the proprietor of the trade mark Minimax.[79] The trade mark was registered in respect of fire extinguishers and associated products. During 1989 Ansul ceased marketing fire extinguishers but the company continued to sell spare

[77] C-16/03, *Peak Holding v Axolin-Elinor*, [2004] ECR I-11313.

[78] Recital 8.

[79] Case C-40/01, *Ansul v Ajax Brandbeveiliging*, [2003] ECR I-2439.

parts and extinguishing substances, both under the trade mark Minimax. In 1995, a competitor brought an action for cancellation of Ansul's trade mark, based on the understanding that Ansul's use of its trade mark only for spare parts and extinguishing substances did not constitute any genuine use. In its preliminary ruling, the ECJ stated that the fact that a trade mark is not used for a certain product but only for spare parts and other products necessary to have to be able to use the first product does not imply that the use of the trade mark cannot be genuine. This part of the judgment did not come as a surprise. However, the ECJ also made some statements of a more principal nature, inter alia:

> Article 12(1) .... must be interpreted as meaning that there is genuine use of a trade mark where the mark is used in accordance with its essential function, which is to guarantee the identity of the origin of the goods or services for which it is registered, in order to create or preserve an outlet for those goods or services; genuine goods does not include token use for the sole purpose of preserving the rights conferred by the mark. When assessing whether use of the trade mark is genuine, regard must be had to all facts and circumstances relevant to establishing whether the commercial exploitation of the mark is real, particularly whether such use is viewed as warranted in the economic sector concerned to maintain or create a share in the market for the goods or services protected by the mark, the nature of the goods or services at issue, the characteristics of the market and the scale and frequency of use of the mark.

The statement is interesting in three different respects. Firstly, it is the proprietor's intention with the use which decides whether the use is genuine or token. It follows from the judgment that it is up to the national court to decide the proprietor's intention. In this respect, the ECJ does not give any guidelines as to the burden of proof. Consequently, it unclear whether the burden of proof rests with the proprietor of the trade mark or the party which claims that the trade mark is to be declared invalid.

Secondly, when assessing whether the use of a trade mark is genuine or not, regard shall be given to all relevant facts and circumstances. Although the ECJ enumerates different facts and circumstances that are particularly relevant, such a statement can always be interpreted in different ways by the national courts, thus motivating a conclusion that the court, for other reasons, wants to reach.

The third aspect, which is probably the most interesting, is that it follows from the judgment that the user requirement is not necessarily fulfilled as soon as a trade mark has been used genuinely. For the user requirement to be fulfilled, the trade mark must be used to such an extent that is sufficient to maintain, or create, a share in the market for the goods or services protected by the mark. Consequently, it seems as if the use must be so great that it may have an impact on the demand of the product or service. If the market for the product or service in question is large, each single use of the trade mark is not sufficient to fulfil the user requirement. On the other hand, if the market is very small even minimal use may be sufficient. This interpretation is confirmed by the second case decided by the ECJ and involving the user requirement.[80]

In this respect, the case involves a change in Swedish trade mark law. Before the ECJ's judgment in Ansul, minimal use of a trade mark was always sufficient to fulfil the user requirement, provided that the use was genuine. However, the case law has now changed.[81]

7 SOME CONCLUDING REMARKS

The summary and analyses of the ECJ's case law concerning the trade mark directive carried out above shows that the court has never accepted any differences as to the implementation of the directive, except those explicitly allowed. Further, the court has consistently held that the different provisions are to be interpreted in the same way by all national courts and other authorities.

On the other hand, the ECJ has often stated that a certain issue must be assessed taking into account all relevant facts; a global assessment must be carried out. This is the case as far as, eg, distinctiveness, confusing similarity and the user requirement is concerned. Such global assessments may give rise to different results, depending on which national court or other authority that is to carry out the assessment.

When making a global assessment, uncertainty will sometimes occur. Therefore, there will always be new questions for national courts to put to the ECJ. On the other hand, courts in some countries will probably find the guidance already given by the ECJ sufficient to be able to cope with most issues. It is up to the ECJ, when given the opportunity, to develop more precise principles as to the interpretation of the directive if the court finds it necessary.

Most Swedish trade mark lawyers probably consider the trade mark directive quite a modern piece of legislation. This is also true as far as at least most of the principles developed by the ECJ concerning the interpretation of the directive. This probably depends on the fact that the court seems to look at trade mark law as one part of the unfair competition legislation. This is a way of looking at trade mark legislation which is dominant in Swedish and other Nordic law.[82]

[80] Case C-259/02, *La Mer Technology v Laboratoires Goemar,* [2004] ECR I-1159.

[81] See the Swedish Supreme Court in NJA 2005 p 643.

[82] See eg K Wallberg, A Gunderssen and A Kylhammar in *NIR (Nordic Intellectual Property Law Review)* 2005 p 85 *et sec*, 106 *et sec*, and 120 *et sec* respectively.

9

Legal Consequences of Changed Rules on Companies' Capital

LARS HENRIKSSON*

1 INTRODUCTION

THE SECOND COMPANY Law Directive (the 2nd Directive)[1] was enacted in 1976 and establishes rules on the formation of public limited liability companies, minimum share capital requirements, distributions to shareholders and increases and reductions in capital. The aim of the Directive is to protect minority shareholders and third parties, eg investors, shareholders and creditors. Since its accession to the EU, Sweden has implemented the Directive in its national legislation.

In 1999 the Simpler Legislation for the Internal market (SLIM) group, and later in 2002 the Group of High Level Company Law Experts, identified some elements of the system provided by the 2nd directive that were deemed to be too inflexible and costly for companies. Based upon these analyses, the groups issued some recommendations for modifications.

In order to allow public limited liability companies to react more promptly, quickly and at less cost, to changes and developments in the markets relevant to these companies, the Commission has been working on a modernisation of the 2nd Directive.[2] The work resulted in a proposal for an amendment of the 2nd Directive, which has been agreed by the European Parliament.[3]

* Lars Henriksson is Associate Professor at Stockholm School of Economics, Department of Accounting and Business Law. I am indebted to Professor Erik Nerep for valuable comments on the manuscript to this article. Any remaining errors or shortcomings are naturally my own.

[1] Second Council Dir 77/81/EEC of 13 Dec 1976 on coordination of safeguards which, for the protection of the interests of members and others, are required by Member States of companies within the meaning of the second paragraph of the Treaty, in respect of the formation of public limited liability companies and the maintenance and alteration of their capital, with a view to making such safeguards equivalent, OJ L 26, 31/01/1977, pp 1–13.

[2] Proposal for a Directive of the European Parliament and of the Council amending Council Directive 77/91/EEC as regards the formation of public limited liability companies and the maintenance and alteration of their capital, COM(2004) 730—OJ C 24 of 29.01.2005.

[3] COD/2004/256.

Finally, in September 2006 Directive 2006/68/EC was passed amending the 2nd Directive (the Amending Directive)[4] The amendments will implement the recommendations and the changes will enable Member States, inter alia, to eliminate specific reporting requirements and to provide a harmonised legal procedure for creditors in the context of capital reduction.

This article will assess the simplification measures proposed regarding the formation, maintenance and alteration of companies' capital in relation to the recommendations submitted by SLIM and the Group of High Level Company Law Experts and as finally outlined in the Amending Directive. Furthermore, the main focal point of this chapter will be the impact of the Directive in relation to Swedish Company Law, especially the current Swedish Companies Act (SFS 2005:551).

2 MODERNISATION MEASURES

The 2nd Directive was passed in order to ensure minimum equivalent protection for both shareholders and creditors of public limited liability companies. In the preamble to the 2nd Directive, it was held that coordination of rules related to formation, maintenance, increase and reduction of the companies' capital was particularly important. Any stakeholder should have the possibility of acquainting himself with, inter alia, the composition of the company's capital, as the maintenance of the capital constitutes the creditors' security. Therefore, restrictions on the company's right to purchase own shares were also introduced in the Directive.

The European approach to Company law is much influenced by the stakeholder's view, which actually differs from the US approach, which favours the shareholder's view.[5] As Kübler points out, the overall purpose of European corporate law is not the maximisation of the shareholder's wealth or return on equity investments, but 'the accommodation and reconciliation of conflicting interests, primarily among shareholders, creditors and employees'.[6] This is the background to why most European countries have comprehensive rules on a regime of legal capital, which is, inter alia, viewed as a 'buffer' for creditors. US companies do not face an equivalent regime and this may cause competition conflicts between jurisdictions where the stakeholder's view may entail burdensome and inflexible rules for companies and create time-consuming processes when increasing or

[4] Dir 2006/68/EC of the European Parliament and of the Council amending Council Directive 77/91/EC as regards the formation of public limited liability companies and the maintenance of the their capital, OJ L 264, 25.9.2006, pp 32–6.

[5] See M Roe, *Political Determinants of Corporate Governance*, (Oxford, Oxford University Press, 2003) for an analysis of the differences between the European and the US system on company law.

[6] F Kübler, 'A Shifting Paradigm of European Company Law?', *11 Colum J Eur L* 219.

decreasing the capital of the company and thereby making the company react less quickly to market changes in comparison to US firms. In addition to this, few Europeans companies are free to choose the state of incorporation as a result of the 'real seat' theory, which causes both complicated and burdensome procedures when relocating the head office as well as adverse tax effects.[7] The European rules have been in force for a very long time and presumably as a result of the increase in internationalisation of business, multinational companies and convergences in accounting standards, the need to make the European system more efficient has become more apparent, although not to the extent that it should be abandoned in favour of the US regime.[8]

In 2003, the Commission reached the conclusion that a simplification and modernisation of the 2nd Directive would significantly contribute to the promotion of business efficiency and competitiveness, without reducing the protection for shareholders and creditors. The Commission does, however, recognise that the latter objective takes precedence over the simplification measures, but the measures finally decided upon do not necessarily stand in conflict with the superior objectives outlined in the original wording of the 2nd Directive.[9] On the contrary, a more efficient system may have benefits for all stakeholders in a company.

The responses to the Commission's communication was in general very much in keeping with proposals set out by the SLIM-group, and the Commission have also been investigating a completely new and alternative regime to the capital management regime, but that is still subject to further analysis.[10]

3 MINIMUM CAPITAL

As its point of departure, the 2nd Directive prescribes that the laws of the Member States shall require that companies, in order to be incorporated or to obtain business, must have a capital of no less than 25,000 Euros. In

[7] For an analysis of the problems of tackling the 'real seat' theory see M Nelson, *Aktiebolags etableringsrätt i EU—en studie utifrån målen Segers,* Daily Mail och Centros, *SvSkT,* p 635–656, 2002 and *The Seat Theory and the Incorporation Theory—an Analysis of the Meaning of the Freedom of Establishment*, IUR-Information, 2005(5) pp 3–13.

[8] For an in-depth analysis of the choice between different systems, see S Kiarie, 'At Crossroads: Shareholder value, Stakeholder Value and Enlightened Shareholder Value: Which Road Should the United Kingdom Take?' *ICCLR* 2006, 17(11), pp 329–43.

[9] See Commissions communication of 21 May 2003 to the Council and the European Parliament entitled 'Modernising Company Law and Enhancing Corporate Governance in the European Union—A plan to Move Forward'. See also p 6 in the preamble of the Amending Directive.

[10] See Synthesis of the responses to the Communication of the Commission to the Council and the European Parliament 'Modernising Company law and Enhancing Corporate Governance in the European Union—A Plan to Move Forward'—COM (2003) 284 final of 21 May 2003. A Working Document of DG Internal Market. 15.11.2003.

Sweden, public limited liability companies must have a minimum subscribed capital of SEK 500,000, which is more than double the minimum capital provided for by the 2nd Directive. Most of the issues discussed in this chapter are related to the reduction and change of the subscribed capital. The questions discussed below cover reporting procedures connected to contributions in kind, purchases of own shares, loans aimed at the acquisitions of a company's share by a third party, and finally protection of creditors' claims when reducing the subscribed capital.

4 CONTRIBUTION IN KIND

As it is a clear requirement that public limited liability companies must have a subscribed capital, it is important that in reality the capital has been paid to the company. When this is done in cash, normally no complex questions arise, as it is merely a question of proving that the money has actually been paid. However, if a shareholder contributes with considerations other than in cash, there is a need to make sure that the assets contributed are correctly valued etc. In addition to the rule on minimum capital, the 2nd Directive therefore sets out detailed rules on shares issued for a consideration other than in cash. The Directive requires that a report by one or more independent experts appointed or approved by an administrative or judicial authority shall be drawn up before the company is incorporated or authorised to commence business.[11] The report must be published according to the 1st Company Law Directive[12] and contain information as to each of the assets comprising the consideration, methods of valuation and a statement of whether the values resulting from this method are nominal, to the accountable par and to the premium on the shares to be issued for them.[13] Subject to certain conditions, the Directive allows Member States not to apply the rules on considerations in kind, where 90 per cent of the nominal value, or where there is no such value, of the accountable par, of all the shares are issued to one or more companies for a consideration other than in cash.[14] Also, where shares are issued for a consideration in kind a report must be drawn up by one or more independent experts before the increase in capital is made.[15]

[11] Art 10(1) of the 2nd Directive.

[12] First Council Directive 68/151/EEC of 9 Mar 1968 on co-ordination of safeguards which, for the protection of the interests of members and others, are required of companies by Member States within the meaning of the second paragraph of Art 58 of the Treaty, with a view to making such safeguards equivalent throughout the Community, OJ L 65, 14.3.1968, pp 8–12 (the 1st directive).

[13] Art 10(2) and 10(3) of the 2nd Directive.

[14] Art 10(4), subparas a–f.

[15] Art 27(2) of the 2nd Directive.

4.1 Relaxation of the EC Rules on Expert Opinions

The SLIM-group recommendations[16] involve a recommendation to relax the rules contained in Articles 10, 11 and 27 of the 2nd Directive and they propose that no expert opinion should be necessary in respect of the formation of the company or decisions to increase the capital, if the assets contributed have been valued by an independent expert, and the valuation report is sufficiently recent and reliable, and have been established in the same perspective of valuation and, finally, that there have occurred no major changes with respect to the assets contributed. Furthermore, an expert opinion should not be necessary if transferable securities are contributed and that these are valued at the price at which they are traded on a 'regulated market'.[17]

The amendment of the 2nd Directive involves first a new Article 10a, whereby it will be possible for Member States to set aside Articles 10(1)–10(3) in cases where a clear point of reference is available for the valuation of assets contributed in kind.[18] The Amending Directive explicitly refers to the MiFID regarding financial instruments or money-market instruments. No expert opinion shall be required where such securities or money-market instruments are valued at the weighted average price at which they have been trading on one or more regulated market(s)—as defined in the MiFID—for a sufficient period of time, to be determined by national law, preceding the effective date of contribution of the respective consideration in kind. However, if the price has been affected by 'exceptional circumstances' that would significantly change the value of the asset at the effective date of its contribution (including situations where the market for such transferable securities or money-market instruments has become illiquid), a revaluation subject to Articles 10(1), 10(2) and 10(3) must be carried out.

Regarding assets other than transferable securities and money-market instruments contributed in kind, no separate opinion is required if they have been subject to a *fair value opinion* by a recognised independent expert, provided that the value is not determined more than six months

[16] Recommendations by The Company Law Slim Working Group on the simplification of the First and Second Law Directives, p 4.

[17] The recommendation refers to Investment Services Dir (93/22/EEC), OJ L 141, 11.6.1993—repealed by the Markets in Financial Instruments Dir (2004/39/EC) (MiFID) OJ L 145, 30.4.2004, p 1–44. In Sweden, this would apply to securities traded on Stockholmsbörsen, the Nordic Growth Market (NGM), Aktietorget, which are designated and overseen by the Swedish Financial Supervisory Authority: see Notice from Member States on Annotated presentation of regulated markets and national provisions implementing relevant requirements of ISD (93/22/EEC), OJC 38/07, 2007.

[18] Art 1 of Directive 2006/68/EC of the European Parliament and of the Council amending Council Dir 77/91/EC as regards the formation of public limited liability companies and the maintenance of the their capital, OJ L 264, 25.9.2006, pp 32–6.

before the effective date of the asset contribution. Also, the valuation must have been performed in accordance with generally accepted valuation standards and principles in the Member State, provided that the standards chosen are applicable to the kind of assets to be contributed. Member States may also decide not to apply Articles 10(1)–10(3) when the value of these assets is derived from individual assets from the statutory accounts of the previous financial year.[19] Revaluation is, however, required if the fair value has changed owing to new qualifying circumstances. A protection of minority rights is also included in the Amending Directive as, in the absence of a revaluation, one or more shareholders holding an aggregate of at least five per cent of the company's subscribed capital on the day the decision on the increase in the capital is taken may demand a valuation by an independent expert, in which case Articles 10(1)–(3) shall apply. Such a demand may be submitted up until the effective date of the asset contribution under the condition that, at the date of the demand, the shareholder(s) in question still hold(s) an aggregate percentage of at least five per cent of the company's subscribed capital, as it was on the day the decision on the increase in the capital was taken.

4.2 Security Measures to Observe if a Member State Decides Not to Apply Articles 10(1)–10(3)

If consideration other than in cash as in Article 10a is allowed without an expert's report, the Amending Directive requires, under the new Article 10b(1), that a declaration must be published. This declaration shall contain a description of the contribution in kind at issue, its value, the source of the valuation and the method of valuation (where appropriate). Further, the declaration shall contain a statement of whether the value arrived at corresponds at least to the nominal value, or where there is no nominal value, the accountable par and, where appropriate, to the premium on the shares to be issued for such consideration. Lastly, the declaration shall include a statement that no new qualifying circumstances have occurred with regard to the original valuation. The declaration must be published within one month according to the 1st Company Law Directive.

Article 25 of the 2nd Directive regulates the situation where the statutes, or instrument of incorporation or the general meeting authorise a company body to decide on an increase in the subscribed capital. Under the new Article 10b(2), an announcement containing the date when the decision on the increase was made and the information accordingly listed in Article

[19] This possibility requires that the statutory accounts have been subject to an audit in accordance with Dir 2006/43/EC on statutory audits of annual accounts and consolidated accounts, OJ L 157, 9.6.2006, p 87.

10b(1) shall be published according to the 1st Company Law Directive, before the contribution of the asset as consideration other than in cash becomes effective. In such an event, the declaration shall be limited to the statement that no new qualifying circumstances have occurred since the aforementioned announcement was published.

Each Member State has an obligation under Article 10b(3) of the Amending Directive to provide adequate safeguards ensuring compliance with the procedure set out in Articles 10a and 10b in situations where a contribution for a consideration other than in cash is made.

Article 11 of the 2nd Directive is applicable to situations where the company acquires any assets belonging to a person or company or firm referred to in Article 3(i) (forming persons) for a consideration of not less than 10 per cent of the subscribed capital. In such a case, the Amending Directive stipulates that the acquisition shall be examined and details of it published in the manner provided for in Articles 10(1)–10(3) and that Articles 10a and 10b shall apply *mutatis mutandis*.

Finally, the Amending Directive also provides for a relaxation of the former requirement for independent expert opinions in cases where shares are issued for a consideration other than in cash in the course of an increase in the subscribed capital contained in Article 27(2) of the 2nd Directive. The Amending Directive now stipulates that in addition to Articles 10(2) and (3), Articles 10a and 10b shall also apply.

4.3 Expert Opinions in Swedish Company Law on Contribution in Kind

Rules on considerations other than in cash are contained in chapters 2 and 13 of the Swedish Companies Act (CA) (SFS 2005:551). Chapter 2 contains rules on formation and incorporation of the company, whereas chapter 13 deals with issuing of new shares.

Section 2:6 of the CA stipulates, regarding considerations other than in cash, only such property that is, or can be expected to be of use for the company's business can be accepted. This shall be judged in relation to what has been stated in the articles of association. Any kind of property can be used including reality and movable property.[20] Under section 2:7 of the CA the statute of incorporation shall contain a description of those circumstances which are of importance in relation to the usefulness of property contributed in kind, and for the valuation of such property. The description must contain information on how the value of the property has

[20] For a detailed analysis of what property can be accepted as consideration other than in cash, see E Nerep, *Aktiebolagsrättslig analys. Ett tvärsnitt av nyckelfrågor*, Stockholm: 2003, p 92. See also R Skog, under medverkan av Johan Danelius, *Rodhes Aktiebolagsrätt*, 21 edn, Stockholm: 2006; and S Andersson, S Johansson, R Skog, *Aktiebolagslagen. En kommentar. Del I*, p 2:11, Stockholm:2006.

been assessed and what legal and economic views have been taken into consideration when making the valuation.

According to section 2:19, considerations other than in cash must be accompanied by an auditor's opinion written and signed by an authorised public accountant (*auktoriserad revisor*), approved public accountant (*godkänd revisor*) or a registered public accounting firm (*registrerat revisionsbolag*). The opinion shall contain information on all property that is contributed, an assessment of whether the property is, or can be expected to be of use to the company's business and that the property in the statute of incorporation has been valued at more than the real value of the company. Furthermore, the auditor's opinion must also describe the method of valuation that has been used. In case there are difficulties in assessing the value of the property, this shall be noted in the opinion. Before the company can be registered, the auditor's opinion must be presented. Without such an opinion, the company cannot be registered.

Article 11 of the 2nd Directive has been implemented by section 2:29. of the Swedish Company Act. The statute applies only to public limited liability companies. According to section 2:29, the Board of Directors must refer to the general meeting any agreement within two years from the registration between the company and a founder of the company or a shareholder of such a company for a consideration of at least one-tenth of the subscribed capital (deferred non-cash consideration). This rule does not, however, apply to acquisitions made on a Swedish or foreign stock exchange, authorised market or any other regulated market located within or outside the EU.[21] In accordance with Article 11(2), the section of the law does not apply to acquisitions effected in the normal course of the company's business. Swedish legislation does not contain any counter-part to the provision that Article 11(1) does not apply to acquisitions effected at the instance or under the supervision of an administrative or judicial authority. These transactions are under section 2:30 subject to an auditor's opinion issued in accordance with section 2:19. It should be noted that the civil law consequences under section 2:9 b of the former Companies Act (SFS 1975:1383) implied that where the general meeting did not approve the transaction, it would be null and void. The legislator has not introduced any corresponding rule in the current Companies Act, and should the Board fail to submit the agreement to the general meeting in due time or without the auditor's opinion, the Board may be liable for damages according to chapter 29 of the Companies Act.[22]

Chapter 13 contains rules on the issuing of new shares. If new shares shall be paid in consideration other than cash, any proposal from the Board of

[21] By 'regulated market' the Swedish Act refers to MiFID-directive, See government bill, prop 2004/05:85, *Ny Aktiebolagslag*, p 536.

[22] See government Bill, prop 2004/05:85, *Ny Aktiebolagslag*, p 537.

directors should include information about this.[23] Any such proposal for the issuing of new shares, must under section 13:7, contain a statement of the circumstances that can be of importance for the assessment of the value of the property contributed in kind. In addition, an auditor's opinion is required and follows the same principles as those outlined for considerations other than in cash at the formation of the company. Therefore, under section 13:8, any property must be of use for the company's business and the value of any such property should not be greater than the real value of the company. Also, a description of the property and the method of valuation shall be presented as well as any difficulties in valuing the property in question. Qualified auditors are, as mentioned above, one or several authorised public accountant(s), approved public accountant(s) or a registered public accounting firm. If a special auditor has not been appointed, the company's auditor, which is appointed by the general meeting, shall issue the opinion.

A decision on issuing new shares cannot be registered prior to payment having been made in full, either in cash or by consideration other than cash. This entails also that an auditor's opinion has been presented in support of this fact.[24]

4.4 Analysis of Possible Changes to the Swedish Companies Act

In the government Bill leading to the Swedish Companies Act, it was recognised that there are several reasons why it is important that property contributed is assessed and valued correctly. Arbitrary valuation may result in the company, at the time of formation or when increasing the subscribed capital, not actually being provided with the necessary funds. A related issue is that any property considered shall not be subject to any third party claims. The former and current Swedish rules on an auditor's opinion have been considered to be simple and well functioning. In the preparatory work to the new Companies Act, the government did not receive any comments that these rules were viewed as overly cumbersome. The business community did not express a wish or need for changes to be made to the current rules.

It should be noted that regardless of whether the current Swedish rules remain unchanged or whether Sweden decides to implement Articles 10a and 10b, this will still entail costs for the companies as the rules on expert opinions cannot be abandoned altogether. The Ministry of Justice (the MOJ) forecasts that any change to the current Swedish system would involve new safeguards having to be introduced and these measures could be both extensive and complex.[25] This is based upon the mandatory rules

[23] Sections 13:5 and 2:6 of the Companies Act.
[24] Sections 2:13, 18 and 42 of the Companies Act.
[25] Memo from the Swedish Ministry of Justice of 23.1.2007, Promemoria, *Några frågor med anledning av ändringar i kapitaldirektivet.*

on 'point of time' for new valuations, minority protection rules, requirements on accounts and publication etc. Sweden has just finished a vast overview of the legislation relating to Swedish limited liability companies and any changes in this regard could potentially be more troublesome for companies. All in all, any changes in the direction provided for by the Amending Directive would in fact not create any actual relaxation of the administrative burden of the companies and it is doubtful if any such changes would improve efficiency either during the formation of the company or when increasing the subscribed capital by issuing new shares. It should also be borne in mind that in relation to the latter, that issuing of new shares is only one way of improving the company's equity and that other instruments are available as well.

The MOJ also believes that implementation of Articles 10a and 10b would lead to a less secure system from the creditors' point of view. Although this is not elaborated in the memo, the rationale behind this position appears to be that the real capital of the company may be less than was intended and registered, which in turn could lead to a false view of, inter alia, the company's creditworthiness. This position, however, presupposes that any opinion other than that of the auditor, would be less accurate and overly optimistic in terms of the real value of the assets. Notwithstanding the fears expressed in the memo, the Amending Directive still introduces demands on safeguards to counteract these potential adverse effects of a relaxation of the current rules. Again, the new rules are not intended to lessen the protection of the creditors, but to create a more efficient system for the companies to obtain capital by consideration other than in cash—especially in Member States where this process is complex and burdensome. Where an efficient system is already in place, subject to the demands on safeguards, the relaxation cannot be viewed as leading to a less secure system as this would imply disregarding the requirements on safeguards provided for in the amending directive.

Also, abandoning the auditor's opinion might, according the MOJ, lead to abuse and encourage the company to become involved in dubious transactions. Although that may be the case, I submit that this argument is highly speculative and weak in relation to the higher cost and increased complexity arguments along with the efficiency defence of the current system. It should be borne in mind that even the current system—albeit unlikely—may be abused by less serious auditors and it is also to be expected that the simplifications provided for in the Amending Directive can open the market to efficient independent experts, whose seriousness can be ensured by proper legislative safeguards. This neutralises the argument and brings the problem back to the need to introduce a more complex legislative measure that may be counter-productive; why fix something that is already functioning well?

The conclusions should not be viewed as a negative view in general of the Amending Directive as it can provide a legal basis for real simplification and enhancement of efficiencies in other Member States, but it is currently hard to see any advantages to introducing the relaxations in Swedish company law.

To summarise, it is therefore highly unlikely that Articles 10a and 10b will be implemented in Sweden.

5 PURCHASES OF OWN SHARES

In case a company should acquire shares in its own company (purchase of own shares), this would in reality imply that resources are transferred from the company to the shareholders without any business justification to support this transaction. Consequently, the purchase of own shares may erode the company's capital to the detriment of creditors. Purchases of own shares are therefore covered by the rules that are in place to safeguard the subscribed capital of the company. As a general rule, the purchase of own shares is not allowed, or should at least be very limited.

However there are both pros and cons to allowing the purchasing of own shares. The creditor's view set aside, it may lead to a more efficient use of the company's capital if the company were to have greater possibilities to acquire own shares.[26]

5.1 Current EC Regime on Purchases of Own Shares

Article 19 of the 2nd Directive presents the legal basis for allowing the purchasing of own shares. Where the laws of a Member State permit a company to acquire its own shares, either itself or through a person acting in his own name but on the company's behalf, such transactions shall be subject to a number of conditions, including the requirement of authorisation by the general meeting, in which the terms and conditions of such an acquisition shall be specified and the period of authorisation may not exceed 18 months. Furthermore, the nominal value or, in the absence thereof, the accountable par of the acquired shares, including shares previously acquired by the company and held by it, and shares acquired by a person acting in his own name but on the company's behalf, may not exceed 10 per cent of the subscribed capital. Until now, Member States have been free to introduce further restrictions on acquisition of own shares.

[26] Skog provides a very good analysis of the motives for purchases of own shares and provides a comprehensive overview of the literature in the field. Although this article does not intend to analyse the reasons why companies should be allowed to purchase own shares, it should be mentioned that companies sometime have excess liquidity that is better placed in own shares. Tax reasons, signals to shareholders and the stock market, increased profit per share and the ability of swiftly changing the capital structure of the Company are other examples. Purchases of own shares can be used as a tool to affect the market price of the shares, but can also be used as a 'poison pill' to avoid hostile take-overs etc. See R Skog, 'Aktiebolags förvärv av egna aktier—är det dags att ompröva förbudet?', JT Nr 3 1995/1996 s 749.

5.2 Changes of the Current EC Rules on Purchases of Own Shares

The Amending Directive introduces a replacement for the former Article 19(1) with completely new wording, introducing possibilities of relaxing national laws on purchases of own shares. The main change is that there is no longer an upper limit of 10 per cent. Secondly, the time of authorisation of purchasing of own share is extended from 18 months to five years. As previously, though, authorisation for acquisitions shall have been given by the general meeting, which shall determine the conditions of such acquisitions. The new working of Article 19(1) makes it possible for Member States to subject acquisitions to certain conditions. Firstly, the nominal value or, in the absence thereof, the accountable par of the acquired shares may not exceed a limit of less than 10 per cent of the subscribed capital.[27] Secondly, the power of the company to acquire its own shares, the maximum number of shares to be acquired, the duration of the period given and the maximum or minimum consideration shall be laid down in the statutes or in the instrument of incorporation of the company.[28] Thirdly, the company must comply with appropriate reporting and notification requirements.[29] Fourthly, certain companies may be required to cancel the acquired shares provided that an amount equal to the nominal value of the shares cancelled must be included in a reserve which cannot be distributed to the shareholders, except in the event of a reduction of the subscribed capital.[30] Lastly, the acquisition shall not prejudice the satisfaction of creditors' claims.[31] The list of permitted conditions is exhaustive. Hence, it is not possible for Member States to introduce further or other conditions.

5.3 Current Swedish Rules on Purchases of Own Shares

Since 1895, it has been prohibited for Swedish limited liability companies to purchase own shares. This prohibition has also been extended to cover their subsidiaries. Only in special circumstances is a company currently allowed to purchase own shares. However, even if a purchase is based upon an exceptional circumstance, the shares must be sold without delay and at the very latest within three years from the purchase. Otherwise, the shares in question are to be declared null and void.[32]

[27] Art 19(1) (a) (i), including shares previously acquired by a person acting in his own name but on the company's behalf. The exact limit may be determined by the Member States, although it cannot be less than 10%.

[28] Art 19(1) (a) (ii).

[29] Art 19(1) (a) (iii).

[30] Companies concerns may be determined by the Member State. The reserve may be used only for the purposes of increasing the subscribed capital by the capitalisation of reserves, Art 19(1) (a) (iv).

[31] Art 19(1) (a) (v).

[32] Sections 19:4–6 of the Companies Act.

Nonetheless, certain public limited liability companies enjoy limited freedom to acquire own shares. The companies must be 'listed' companies on the Swedish stock exchange, an authorised market or some other regulated market (as defined in the MiFID) and the methods of acquisition are also limited.[33] A company is not allowed to own more than 10 per cent of all shares in the company (including shares held in the company by subsidiaries).[34] Any shares acquired in violation of these conditions must be relinquished within six months of purchase, as the shares otherwise must be declared null and void.[35]

The rule contained in section 19:17 of the Companies Act is based upon Article 19(1) of the 2nd Directive.[36] According to that section, any decision on acquisitions of own shares must be taken by the general meeting, although the Board of Directors can be authorised by the general meeting to take this decision. Prior to the decision a proposal must be drafted, in which specified conditions must be fulfilled. The proposal must, inter alia, contain information on the number and type of shares and what compensation shall be paid for the shares, or the highest number of shares and the lowest and highest price that is to be paid for the shares.[37] The decision of the general meeting must contain this information in line with section 19:27 of the Companies Act. Where the acquisition of the shares is authorised to the Board of Directors, the Board of Directors must issue a proposal to the general meeting containing, inter alia, the method of acquisition, the highest number of shares to be purchased and lowest and highest price to be paid. Any authorisation to the Board of Directors is only valid until the next general meeting.

It must be concluded that the current Swedish legislation does not need to be amended as a result of the introduction of the new Article 19(1) (a) in the 2nd Directive. Neither does it appear to be necessary to introduce any change on account of Article 19(1) (b). According to the current Swedish Companies Act, purchases of own shares are explicitly regarded as a form of value transfer from the company and is therefore covered by the legal safeguards for the fixed capital. Any value transfer may not entail that full coverage of the fixed capital remains after the transfer in question.[38]

Article 19(1) (c) had its counterpart in the former section 7:8 of the 1975 Companies Act in Sweden. That section was, however, abolished in the current Companies Act, as it is no longer permitted to register newly issued shares prior to full payment having been effected. Hence, safeguards in line with the Directive requirements are already in place.[39]

[33] Sections 19:13, 14 of the Companies Act.
[34] Section 19:15 of the Companies Act.
[35] Section 19:15 of the Companies Act.
[36] The rule is equivalent to the former s 7:11 See also ch 16, s 10 in Swedish Government Official Reports SOU 2001:1 and government bill, prop 1999/2000:34 p 122.
[37] Sections 19:20–21 of the Companies Act.
[38] See section 17:1 p 2 and 17:3–4 of the Companies Act.
[39] See Government bill prop 2004/05:85 p 774 and s 13:28 para 1, p 2 of the Companies Act.

The Directive explicitly also states that national laws permitting purchasing of own shares do not violate the principle of equal treatment of all shareholders who are in the same position and do not stand in conflict with Directive 2003/6/EC on insider dealing and market manipulation (market abuse).[40]

The MOJ concludes that there is no need to change the current rules contained in the Companies Act as a result of the mandatory requirements in the new Article 19 of the 2nd directive.[41] I agree that the Amending Directive does not contain any new set rules that would *require* Sweden to change the current legislation. The question remaining is whether Sweden will take advantage of any relaxations provided for in the Amending Directive.

5.4 Relaxation of the Current Swedish Rules on Purchases of Own Shares

The MOJ has considered whether to use any of the discretionary relaxations provided for in the Amending Directive, after having concluded that there is no need to introduce any further mandatory rules.

5.4.1 Prolongation of the Authorisation Period of the Board of Directors

In relation to the current Swedish rule, the Amending Directive makes it possible to extend the current authorisation period by about four years. This would in fact increase flexibility for the companies, and the Board of Directors will have greater leeway in deciding when to execute the purchase in a manner that is most advantageous to the company. However, the MOJ maintains that the shareholders should have strong control and decisive influence over these kinds of decisions and that it is deemed important that the legislation promotes active ownership rather than makes shareholders more passive. During a five year period circumstances may change dramatically for purchases of own shares, both positively and negatively.

Without doubt, though, a longer authorisation period will introduce greater uncertainty in the decision of the shareholders at the general meeting. The MOJ also expresses the view that it should not be deemed overly troublesome for the general meeting to renew the issue at the next general meeting, should it be necessary. Hence, the MOJ does not see that the advantages of a longer authorisation period would outweigh the current rule.

[40] Dir 2003/6/EC of the European Parliament and of the Council on insider dealing and market manipulation (market abuse), OJ L 96, 12.4.2003, p 16.

[41] Memo from the Swedish Ministry of Justice of 23.1.2007, Promemoria, *Några frågor med anledning av ändringar i kapitaldirektivet*, p 15.

5.4.2 Abolishing The 10 Per Cent Limit and Ensuring Creditors' Claims

According to the Amending Directive it is possible, but not mandatory, to abolish the limit of purchases of own share to 10 per cent of the subscribed capital. It is therefore possible for Member States to decide whether to keep the former regulation or to introduce more relaxed rules. Undoubtedly, this would bring about greater flexibility for the companies. It can, in fact, be hard to activate the exact 10 per cent rule as the appropriate level as many benevolent and efficient purchases above the 10 per cent limit can be perceived. Furthermore, as the MOJ holds, there are other rules that are better suited to safeguarding the creditors' interests, like the general caution rule contained in section 17:3 on the Companies Act.[42] The MOJ recognises that there are both advantages and disadvantages in connection with the question of allowing a higher limit than 10 per cent and that it is hard to see any possible consequences of such a change, especially since the current rules have only been in place since 2000. The Governmental memo takes a 'wait-and-see' approach on the issue until the impact of the current rules has been thoroughly analysed. Therefore, pending the results of a public enquiry, no changes are to be expected to the current rules.

5.4.3 The Role of the Articles of Association

Article 19(1) (ii) makes it possible for Member States to require that the question of purchases of own shares shall be regulated in the articles of association. In Swedish law, there is no counterpart to this requirement. The MOJ expresses the view that it is hard to see whether the introduction of such a requirement would be of any value to either the company itself or to its shareholders. On the contrary, this would in fact imply a greater administrative burden. Hence, it is not recommended that any rule of kind should be introduced into Swedish Company Law.

5.4.4 New Reporting and Notification Requirements

Member States may, according to the Amending Directive, make purchases of own shares provided the company complies with appropriate reporting and notification requirements. Already there are several rules to this effect in Swedish law. Sections 19:19–29 of the Companies Act contain detailed rules on the matter. Also, according to section 6:1 of the Swedish Annual Report Act (SFS 1995:1554) the report of the Board of Directors in the annual report shall contain information on number and quota value of own shares that have been acquired during the fiscal year and the share of the subscribed capital that own shares amount to. Also, the Swedish

[42] For the same reasons, the Swedish Government does not recommend any further restrictions in line with Art19(1) (v).

Act, *lag om börs- och clearingverksamhet*, (SFS 1992:543) requires the Swedish Government or the Swedish Financial Supervisory Authority (*Finansinspektionen*) to regulate trading rules for a stock exchange in relation to a limited liability company's acquisition of own shares. Sweden has, therefore, already introduced such rules which can be used under Article 19(1) (iii). It is the opinion of the MOJ that any further reporting and information requirements are not required.[43]

5.4.5 Cancellation of Acquired Shares

Around the turn of the century a government Bill[44] considered whether companies should be allowed to sell/transfer own shares. It was concluded that this option should be available to certain companies and that this would contribute to a more efficient utilisation of the company's capital, and that it would possible for companies to have shares 'in stock' thereby increasing the financial readiness of the company. A rule of this kind could, however, have marginal effects on the stock markets where the company is listed, albeit these adverse effects could be minimised. Also, the right to sell off own shares could ease structural changes of the company. All in all, it was considered that the right to sell off own shares should be introduced in Swedish Company Law. This should now be contrasted to the possibility for Member States to introduce a requirement to cancel shares according Article 19(1) (iv). This would result in that an amount equal to the nominal value of the shares cancelled must be included in a reserve which cannot be distributed to the shareholders, except in the event of a reduction in the subscribed capital and that this reserve may only be used for the purposes of increasing the subscribed capital by the capitalisation of reserves. A requirement to cancel own shares would, according the Swedish Government, in principle be synonymous with redeeming the shares. This would be in conflict with the current rules. As a result, it is not recommended that any such rules are introduced in Swedish Company Law.

To conclude, it cannot presently be foreseen that Sweden will take advantage of any of the relaxations provided for in the amending directive. A public inquiry evaluating the effects of the current regime is likely to be appointed and until any report has been submitted it is hard to see any major changes taking place. It should be noted that the current rules are the result of a well-balanced analysis between risks and advantages of purchases of own shares and it is therefore hard to see at the present any clear necessity for further opening up of the system.[45]

[43] Memo from the Swedish Ministry of Justice of 23.1.2007, Promemoria, *Några frågor med anledning av ändringar i kapitaldirektivet*, p 16.

[44] Government Bill, prop 1999/2000:34 p 58.

[45] See also R Skog, above n 27, in a discussion of the reasons why purchases of own shares should be allowed in Sweden.

6 ACQUISITION LOANS

Since 1 January 2005, and based upon the former wording of Article 23 of the 2nd Directive, the former Swedish Companies Act contained a prohibition on a company advancing funds, making loans and providing security with a view to the acquisition of its shares by a third party. A similar prohibition is today found in section 21:5 of the current Companies Act.[46] The prohibition was motivated by the accession to the EU but also in order to ensure protection of creditors' claims.

The Amending Directive will change the wording of Article 23(1), whereby Member States shall have the possibility of permitting a company to, either directly or indirectly, advance funds or make loans or provide security, with a view to the acquisition of its shares by a third party. Should any Member State choose to implement such a permit in their national legislation this must be subject to a mandatory and exhaustive list of conditions set out in the Amending Directive by the introduction of the four subparagraphs.

Firstly, the transactions must take place under the responsibility of the administrative or management body at *fair market conditions*. Special regard must be given to interest received by the company and with regard to security provided to the company for the loans and advances. The creditworthiness of the third party—or each counterparty—must have been duly investigated.

Secondly, the transactions shall be submitted by the administrative or management body to the general meeting for prior approval, whereby two-thirds majority according to Article 40 is required. Previously, the administrative or management body must have submitted a written report to the general meeting, indicating the reasons for the transaction, the risks involved for the liquidity and solvency of the company and the price at which the third party is to acquire the share. The report must be published according the rules in Article 3 of the 1st Directive.

Thirdly, the aggregate financial assistance granted to third parties may at no time result in the reduction of the net assets below the subscribed capital, as specified in points (a) and (b) of Article 15(1). Also, among the liabilities in the balance sheet, the company must include a reserve, unavailable for distribution, of the amount of the aggregate financial assistance.

[46] The prohibition applies in every situation when a loan is granted in order to complete an acquisition of shares in the lending company in the sense that the acquirer, by executing final payment or on any other legal grounds, is entitled to take possession of the shares. This does not necessarily presuppose actual possession, but only that the acquirer has done what he is obliged to do under the acquisition contract in order to be able to insist on taking possession of the shares. See E Nerep, P Samuelsson, *Aktiebolagslagen- en kommentar. Kap11–22*, p 429.

Lastly, where a third party by means of financial assistance from a company that acquires that company's own shares or subscribes for shares issued in the course of an increase in the subscribed capital, such acquisition shall be made at a fair price.

Furthermore, the introduction of a new Article 23a in the 2nd Directive prescribes that in cases where individual members of the administrative or management body of the company—or parent undertaking[47]—being party to a transaction, or agents thereto, Member States shall ensure through adequate safeguards that such transactions does not conflict with the company's best interest.

6.1 Possible Changes in Swedish Company Law

It should be noted at the outset that the current rules have been enacted partly in order to comply with former rules in the 2nd Directive. The new rules provided in the Amending Directive do not require Member States to relax their legislation in this respect, but make it possible to do so. If, however, Sweden chose to relax the rules on these kinds of loans and financial aid, it would also be required to introduce the conditions presented above. The relevant question is, therefore, whether Sweden should use its discretionary power to relax the rules in this field.

On the one hand relaxing the rules would enhance the flexibility connected to changes in companies' ownership structure. It may very well be in the interest of a company to facilitate acquisitions of shares in the company. Furthermore, the funds that could be available are those that are distributable and it would seem natural that a company should have the possibility to have access to these funds to same extent as is possible for value transfers. Also the mandatory conditions demand that adequate safeguards must be in place to counteract any adverse effects.

On the other hand, this should be weighed against the interest of protecting minority shareholders' and creditors' claims in order to avoid disloyal transactions and other forms of abuse.

The MOJ recognises both sides of the problem, but emphasises that there has traditionally been a very negative view towards acquisition loans in Sweden. Also, no demands or wishes have been expressed—eg on grounds of competition with foreign companies—that the rules should be changed. Again the MOJ focuses on the fact that the current Swedish prohibition has an important role to play in the protection of a company's creditors and in order to avoid crime. Therefore, the risks involved in relaxing the current laws are too great to compensate for a relaxation of the rules.

[47] As defined in the Art 1 of Council Dir 83/349/EC on consolidated accounts, OJ L 193, 18.7.1983, p 1, last amended by directive 2006/43/EC.

Again, it must be noted that the MOJ paints a rather gloomy picture of the possible consequences of the relaxation of the rules. It is somewhat remarkable that the MOJ foresees market abuse and crime to an extent that will outweigh the flexibility provided to companies through this proposed relaxation of rules—especially in light of the safeguards provided for in the Amending Directive. It must therefore be questioned whether this negative view towards any change is really warranted. In any case, bearing in mind the current negative view on acquisition loans, any changes to Swedish company law in this field are not anticipated.

7 PROTECTION OF CREDITORS' CLAIMS WHEN REDUCING THE SUBSCRIBED CAPITAL

Traditionally, the rules connected to the protection of the company's capital have been regarded to be of utmost importance to the company's creditors. As a result, limitations on the possibility of reducing the capital have been in place ever since the 2nd Directive was introduced. In the event of a reduction of the subscribed capital, at least the creditors whose claims pre-date the publication of the decision to make the reduction shall, according to Article 32(1) of the 2nd Directive, be entitled at least to have the right to obtain *security for claims*, which have not fallen due by the date of that publication. That general rule will remain even in the new wording of Article 32(1). However, it is now required that Member States may not set aside such a right unless the creditor has adequate safeguards, or unless such safeguards are unnecessary with due regard to the assets of the company.

As before, it will remain open to the Member States to lay down the exact conditions for the exercise of the right provided for. However, in the new wording it is also required that Member States shall ensure that the creditors are authorised to apply to the appropriate administrative or judicial authority for adequate safeguards provided that they can credibly demonstrate that due to the reduction of the subscribed capital the satisfaction of their claim is at stake, and that no adequate safeguards have been obtained from the company.

The changes have been introduced in order to enhance standardised creditor protection in all Member States and to ensure that creditors should be able to resort, under certain conditions, to judicial and administrative proceedings where their claims are at stake as a consequence of a reduction in capital of a public limited liability company.[48] Hence, since the new wording is mostly concerned with requiring adequate administrative or judicial safeguards, the relevant question is whether the current Swedish system provides such adequate protection for creditors.

[48] See p 6 in the preamble of the Amending Directive.

7.1 Swedish Rules on Safeguards Regarding Reduction of Capital

If the reduction in the subscribed capital shall be allocated to freely distributable funds or as re-payment to shareholders the rules in sections 20:23–28 in the Swedish Companies Act must be considered.

Any such reduction may not be executed unless the Swedish Companies Registration Office, SCRO (*Bolagsverket*) gives its approval to the reduction. If there is a dispute in the subject matter, the court must give its approval. However, if the company undertakes measures that will ensure that neither the fixed capital, nor the subscribed capital will be reduced, no prior permission is required (section 20:23). If permission is required, all known creditors must be notified about the reduction. The notification must contain information on the creditors' right to oppose the company's decision to reduce the capital (section 20:24). The company must further apply for permission to execute the decision within two months from the registration of the decision to reduce the capital (section 20:25). Where the SCRO does not find any obstacles against the application to execute the decision, the authority shall notify the company's creditors. The notice shall include an order for those who wish to oppose the decision to do so by a certain date. The notice shall further include information that the creditor is otherwise considered to have approved the application. The notice shall be published as an official public notice in *Post-och Inrikes Tidningar* (PoIT) and a notice sent to the Swedish Enforcement Agency (section 20:26). Should any creditor oppose the reduction of capital, the SCRO shall hand the matter over to the competent district court, otherwise the execution of the reduction decision shall be approved (section 20:27). A decision to approve shall be registered in the register of associations, when it has entered into legal force (section 20:28). Special rules apply to banks and other credit institutions and always require the permit of the court. Also, a special statement from Swedish Financial Supervisory Authority is required.

In conclusion, in line with the opinion of the MOJ,[49] the current Swedish system is well aligned with the requirements set out in the amending directive. Hence, no further legislative measures should be necessary for Sweden to comply with the amended 2nd Directive in this field.

8 SUMMARY

The 2nd Directive maintains a balanced approach towards the stakeholders of public limited liability companies, even since the Amending Directive. The impact of the changes in the EC legislation must be regarded as very

[49] See memo from the Swedish Ministry of Justice of 23.1.2007, Promemoria, *Några frågor med anledning av ändringar i kapitaldirektivet*, p 16.

modest, as the MOJ does not see any need to change any of the current rules in Sweden. Nor does the MOJ see any advantages to introducing the relaxations provided for in the Amending Directive. Although one cannot rule out that relaxing the current rules may facilitate abuse and questionable transactions to the detriment of creditors and other stakeholders, the main reason to keep the current system is related to administrative issues. The current legislation on Swedish limited liability companies has just recently undergone a major update and during that process the issues now at hand were few. Thus, the significance of the issues appears to be quite small, despite the fact that relaxing the administrative load of companies would normally be considered to be positive from the companies' view. One most likely explanation for the limited impact of the changes is that the changes will only have marginally positive effects and that it is hard to see how those effects will outweigh any new legislation and thereto connected new burdens for Swedish companies.[50] Another reason as to why changes are unlikely is that the current system is the result of an existing careful balance between the different stakeholders' interests in the company.

This illustrates the problem of harmonising company law in the European Union and until a major change is discussed that could create a 'Delaware' effect it is unlikely that these measures will have great impact on Swedish national legislation.

BIBLIOGRAPHY

Andersson, S, Johansson, S, Skog, R, *Aktiebolagslagen. En kommentar. Del I*, Stockholm:2006.

Enriques, L, Gatti, M, 'The Uneasy Case for Top-Down Corporate Law Harmonization in the European Union', 27 *U Pa J Int'l Econ L* 939.

Kiarie, S, 'At Crossroads: Shareholder Value, Stakeholder Value and Enlightened Shareholder Value: Which Road Should the United Kingdom Take?' *ICCLR* (2006) 17(11), pp 329–43.

Kübler, F, 'A Shifting Paradigm of European Company Law?', 11 *Colum J Eur L* 219.

Nelson, M, Aktiebolags etableringsrätt i EU—en studie utifrån målen Segers, *Daily Mail och Centros*, SvSkT, pp 635–656, 2002.

——, 'The Seat Theory and the Incorporation Theory—an Analysis of the Meaning of the Freedom of Establishment', *IUR-Information*, 2005(5) pp 3–13.

Nerep, E, *Aktiebolagsrättslig analys. Ett tvärsnitt av nyckelfrågor*, Stockholm: 2003.

Nerep, E, Samuelsson, P, *Aktiebolagslagen- en kommentar. Kap11–22*, Stockholm: 2007.

[50] For a discussion of the drawbacks of harmonisation of company law within the EU, see L Enriques, M Gatti, 'The Uneasy Case for Top-Down Corporate Law Harmonization in the European Union', *27 U Pa J Int'l Econ L* p 939.

Roe, M, *Political Determinants of Corporate Governance*, Oxford, 2003.
Skog, R under medverkan av Danelius, J, *Rodhes Aktiebolagsrätt*, 21 edn, Stockholm: 2006.
Skog, R, *Aktiebolags förvärv av egna aktier—är det dags att ompröva förbudet?*, JT Nr 3 1995/1996 s 749.

Swedish Government Official Reports SOU 2001:1, *Ny aktiebolagslag*.
Memo from the Swedish Ministry of Justice of 23.1.2007, Promemoria, Några frågor med anledning av ändringar i kapitaldirektivet.
Government bill prop 2004/05:85.
Government bill, prop 1999/2000:34.
Government bill, prop 2004/05:85.

EU Documents

First Council Directive 68/151/EEC of 9 Mar 1968 on co-ordination of safeguards which, for the protection of the interests of members and others, are required by Member States of companies within the meaning of the second paragraph of Art 58 of the Treaty, with a view to making such safeguards equivalent throughout the Community, OJ L 65, 14.3.1968, pp 8–12 (the 1st directive).
Second Council Dir 77/81/EEC of 13 Dec 1976 on coordination of safeguards which, for the protection of the interests of members and others, are required by Member States of companies within the meaning of the second paragraph of the Treaty, in respect of the formation of public limited liability companies and the maintenance and alteration of their capital, with a view to making such safeguards equivalent, OJ L 26, 31/01/1977 (the 2nd directive).
Council Directive 93/22/EEC of 10 May 1993 on investment services in the securities field, OJ L 141, 11.6.1993, p. 27–46.
Directive 2004/39/EC of the European Parliament and of the Council of 21 April 2004 on markets in financial instruments amending Council Directives 85/611/EEC and 93/6/EEC and Directive 2000/12/EC of the European Parliament and of the Council and repealing Council Directive 93/22/EEC (MiFID), OJ L 145, 30.4.2004, p. 1–44.
Directive 2003/6/EC of the European Parliament and of the Council of 28 January 2003 on insider dealing and market manipulation (market abuse), OJ L 96, 12.4.2003, p. 16–25.
Directive 2006/43/EC of the European Parliament and of the Council of 17 May 2006 on statutory audits of annual accounts and consolidated accounts, amending Council Directives 78/660/EEC and 83/349/EEC and repealing Council Directive 84/253/EEC, OJ L 157, 9.6.2006, p. 87–107
Directive 2006/46/EC of the European Parliament and of the Council of 14 June 2006 amending Council Directives 78/660/EEC on the annual accounts of certain types of companies, 83/349/EEC on consolidated accounts, 86/635/EEC on the annual accounts and consolidated accounts of banks and other financial institutions and 91/674/EEC on the annual accounts and consolidated accounts of insurance undertakings, OJ L 224, 16.8.2006, p. 1–7.

Directive 2006/68/EC of the European Parliament and of the Council amending Council Directive 77/91/EC as regards the formation of public limited liability companies and the maintenance of the their capital, OJ L 264, 25.9.2006, pp 32–6.
Commission communication of 21 May 2003 to the Council and the European Parliament entitled 'Modernising Company Law and Enhancing Corporate Governance in the European Union—A plan to Move Forward'.
Synthesis of the responses to the Communication of the Commission to the Council and the European Parliament 'Modernising Company law and Enhancing Corporate Governance in the European Union—A Plan to Move Forward'—COM (2003) 284 final of 21 May 2003. A Working Document of DG Internal Market. 15.11.2003.
Proposal for a Directive of the European Parliament and of the Council amending Council Directive 77/91/EEC as regards the formation of public limited liability companies and the maintenance and alteration of their capital, COM(2004) 730—OJ C 24 of 29.01.2005.
Notice from Member States on Annotated presentation of regulated markets and national provisions implementing relevant requirements of ISD (93/22/EEC), OJC 38/07, 2007.

10

The EC Court of Justice and the Swedish Monopolies—An Analysis of the Case Law on State Monopolies

MARTIN JOHANSSON*

THE QUESTION OF the legality under Community law of State monopolies has long been the subject of debate and, at least with regard to certain aspects, still is today. In this debate two major lines of thought can be discerned, one that considers that, in principle, State monopolies are per se incompatible with Community law and one that considers that State monopolies are not as such forbidden, but must be adjusted so as to fulfil the requirements of Community law.[1]

The provisions of the EC Treaty that expressly deal with these questions are Article 31 (ex-Article 37 of the EC Treaty), relating to State monopolies of a commercial character, Article 86 (ex-Article 90 of the EC Treaty),

* Martin Johansson is Senior Counsel at the Brussels office of Advokatfirman Vinge. His former positions include Legal Officer at the EFTA Secretariat, during the negotiations of the EEA Agreement, and Legal Secretary at the EFTA Court, the EC Court of First Instance and the EC Court of Justice. He is inter alia co-author of 'EEA Law—A Commentary on the EEA Agreement' and has published a number of articles on Community and EEA law.

[1] See, inter alia, with regard to Art 31 EC (ex-Art 37 of the EC Treaty) and State monopolies of a commercial character, A Mattera, *Le marché unique européen. Ses règles, son fonctionnement,* 2ème édn, (Paris, Jupiter, 1990), pp 49–50. See also F Bluhm, 'De Sacchi à Franzén en passant par la Crespelle: jurisprudence récente de l'article 90', *Gazette du Palais* , 1999, p 1031, and 'The recent case law of the European Court of Justice on State monopolies and its implication for network industries', *Journal of Network Industries* 1, 2000, p 55; PJ Slot, Case note on 'Cases C-157/94, *Commission v Netherlands*; C-158/94, *Commission v Italy*; C-159/04, *Commission v France*; C-160/04, *Commission v Spain*; C-189/95, *Harry Franzén*; judgments of 23 Oct 1997, Full Court, [1997] ECR I-5699, I-5798, I-5815; I-5851, I-5909', 35 *CMLRev.* (1998), p 1183, as well as the Opinion of Advocate General Léger in Case C-438/02 *Criminal proceedings against Krister Hanner* [2005] ECR I-4551. For another article, containing an interesting comparison between the Swedish alcohol, medicinal preparations and gambling monopolies, inter alia examining and underlining the importance of the adaptation of the Swedish alcohol monopoly, carried out before the accession with a view to ensure the survival of the monopoly on the retail of alcoholic beverages, see J Hettne, 'EU, monopolen och försvaret av den rådande ordningen', *ERT* (*Europarättslig Tidskrift*) 2004, p 589.

dealing with public undertakings and undertakings to which Member States grant special or exclusive rights, and Article 295 EC (ex-Article 222 of the EC Treaty), according to which the Treaty shall not prejudice the rules in Member States governing the system of property ownership. However, as can be seen from the case law of the EC Court of Justice (the ECJ or the Court), the Treaty provisions on free movement of goods, freedom to provide services and freedom of establishment are also relevant.[2]

Until *Franzén*, which concerned the Swedish monopoly on the retail of alcoholic beverages,[3] the ECJ had held that while Article 31 EC does not require that State monopolies be abolished, they must be adjusted in such a way as to ensure that no discrimination exists and that the exclusive right to import manufactured products constitute discrimination prohibited by Article 31 EC in respect of Community exporters.[4] Import monopolies were thus per se considered illegal under Community law. This was also thought to apply to export monopolies,[5] but the case law was less clear with regard to other monopolies of a commercial character.

In *Franzén* the ECJ introduced a new element in the application of Article 31 EC, holding that that provision allows Member States to maintain certain monopolies of a commercial character as instruments for the pursuit of public interest aims, as well as 'restrictions on trade which are inherent in the existence of the monopolies in question'. This judgment was later confirmed in *Hanner*,[6] concerning the Swedish monopoly on the retail of medicinal preparations.

On 5 June 2007, the ECJ gave its judgment in *Rosengren*.[7] In this case a number of individuals had imported wine to Sweden via the internet. The question raised by the case was whether State measures such as the Swedish prohibition on private individuals directly importing alcoholic beverages, except while travelling abroad, fall to be examined under Article 31 EC or Article 28 EC and, if so, whether they are compatible with those provisions.

When it comes to State monopolies on the operation of lotteries and gambling, they are mainly analysed by the ECJ under the provisions on freedom to provide services, but also, at least with regard to certain aspects,

[2] In this article the present numbering of the Treaty provisions, introduced by the Treaty of Amsterdam, will be used, the former numbering only being indicated where necessary.

[3] Case C-189/95 *Criminal proceedings against Harry Franzén* [1997] ECR I-5909.

[4] See, inter alia, Case 59/75 *Pubblico Ministero v Manghera* [1976] ECR 91, paras 5 to 12.

[5] This was expressly confirmed in Case C-158/94 *Commission v Italy* [1997] ECR I-5789, para 24, and in Case C-159/94 *Commission v France* [1997] ECR I-5815, para 34, judgments delivered on the same day as *Franzén*.

[6] Case C-438/02 *Criminal proceedings against Krister Hanner* [2005] ECR I-4551.

[7] Case C-170/04 *Rosengren and Others v Riksåklagaren*, judgment of 5 Jun 2007, nyr (judgment given after the deadline for the present article). In parallel the Commission has brought an infringement action against Sweden, claiming that the Swedish rules on private imports of alcohol are contrary to Art 28 EC and cannot be justified under Art 30 EC, Case C-186/05 *Commission v Sweden*, pending.

under those on freedom of establishment. They are in principle considered to constitute restrictions on these two freedoms, but may, however, be permitted as exceptional measures expressly provided for in Articles 45 and 46 EC or justified by overriding reasons relating to the public interest. In this case they further have to be applicable without distinction, be suitable for achieving the objective which they pursue and not go beyond what is necessary in order to attain it.[8]

In *Wermdö Krog*,[9] Regeringsrätten, the Swedish Supreme Administrative Court, examined the compatibility of the Swedish monopoly on gambling and lotteries with Community law. However, basing itself on the case law of the ECJ in this field, Regeringsrätten regrettably decided that there was no need to make a reference for a preliminary ruling to the ECJ. Regeringsrätten's conclusion, that the Swedish gambling monopoly is compatible with the rules on freedom to provide services, is not uncontroversial.

Nevertheless, the Commission has started two infringement proceedings against Sweden, claiming that different aspects of the Swedish monopoly on gambling activities infringe Community law.[10] Furthermore, the Swedish government submitted written observations in the infringement case before the EFTA Court brought by the EFTA Surveillance Authority against Norway, in which ESA alleged that the Norwegian legislation giving exclusive rights to operate gaming machines to a State owned company, partly modelled on the corresponding Swedish legislation, infringes the provisions of the EEA Agreement relating to freedom of establishment and freedom to provide services (Articles 31 and 36 EEA are identical in substance to Articles 43 and 49 EC).[11] In addition, on 30 May 2007, the EFTA Court gave judgment in *Ladbrokes*, on a reference for an Advisory Opinion from Oslo Tingrett, requesting an interpretation of Articles 31 and 36 EEA in relation to the Norwegian betting and gambling monopoly in general,

[8] See, inter alia, Case C-124/97 *Markku Juhani Läärä and Others v Kihlakunnansyyttäjä (Jyväskylä) and Suomen valtio (Finnish State)* [1999] ECR I-6067, para 31, and Case C-243/01 *Criminal proceedings against Piergiorgio Gambelli and Others* [2003] ECR I-13031, paras 60, 64 and 65.

[9] Case n° 5819-01, RÅ 2004 ref. 95, judgment of 26 Oct 2004.

[10] The Commission sent a letter of formal notice to Sweden in Oct 2004, claiming that the Swedish legislation relating to different types of gaming machines is incompatible with Arts 28, 43 and 49 EC. In Dec 2006, the Commission sent a complementary letter of formal notice in this case, concentrating exclusively on those aspects that concern the free movement of gaming machines under Art 28 and 30 EC. In addition, in Apr 2006, the Commission sent letters of formal notice to Denmark, Finland, Germany, Hungary, Italy, the Netherlands and Sweden claiming that the restrictions in those Member States on the marketing and promotion of gambling and betting are contrary to Art 49 EC on the freedom to provide services. In addition, in Oct 2006, the Commission sent letters of formal notice to France, Austria and, again, Italy, relating to certain other aspects of the laws regulating gambling in these Member States. In March 2007, the Commission sent reasoned opinions to Denmark, Finland and Hungary and, in June 2007, to Sweden and France.

[11] Case E-1/06 *EFTA Surveillance Authority v Norway*, judgment of 14 Mar 2007, nyr.

raising a number of questions also raised by the Commission in its infringement proceedings against Sweden.[12]

It would thus seem that Swedish monopolies in one way or another, directly or indirectly, have contributed and are contributing to the development of the case law in this field. Even though, at present, there are no cases before the ECJ dealing with the Swedish betting and gambling monopolies, the cases that are presently pending before the ECJ and those that are in the pipe line would seem to provide an excellent occasion to have a look at the case law of the ECJ and the EFTA Court relating to State monopolies in general, using the above mentioned judgments dealing with the Swedish monopolies as illustrations.

The first part of this article contains a brief general introduction to the earlier case law on State monopolies. Thereafter the judgments of the ECJ in *Franzén* and in *Hanner,* as well as that of Regeringsrätten in *Wermdö Krog,* are presented and analysed inter alia in the light of other judgments of the ECJ. This is followed by a comparison between the case law on State monopolies of a commercial character and that on State measures in the gambling sector.

The article does not claim to deal exhaustively with all the aspects of the different cases analysed. It rather aims at making a few observations, on the basis of the present state of Community law, on some of the questions raised by these judgments and, in particular, on how the case law in these different fields may relate to each other.

1 INTRODUCTION TO THE CASE LAW OF THE ECJ ON STATE MONOPOLIES

1.1 State Monopolies of a Commercial Character—Article 31 EC

Article 31(1) EC provides that:

> Member States shall adjust any State monopolies of a commercial character so as to ensure that no discrimination regarding the conditions under which goods are procured and marketed exists between nationals of Member States.
>
> The provisions of this Article shall apply to any body through which a Member State, in law or in fact, either directly or indirectly supervises, determines or appreciably influences imports or exports between Member States. These provisions shall likewise apply to monopolies delegated by the State to others.

[12] Case E-3/06 *Ladbrokes Ltd. v the Government of Norway, Ministry of Culture and Church Affairs; and the Government of Norway, Ministry of Agriculture and Food*, judgment of 30 May 2007, nyr (judgment given after the deadline for the present article). Further, in Oct 2006, Verwaltungsgericht Köln, and in Dec 2006, Rechtbank van koophandel, Hasselt, referred references for a preliminary ruling to the ECJ concerning the question of whether the lottery and gambling monopolies in those States fulfil the suitability and proportionality criteria set out in the case law of the Court (Case C-409/06 *Winner Wetten GmbH v Mayor of Bergheim* and Case C-525/06 *NV De Nationale Loterij v BVBA Customer Service Agency*, respectively).

This provision only applies to trade in goods. Service monopolies are thus excluded from the scope of application[13] as are, in principle, production monopolies.[14]

In *Manghera*[15] the ECJ declared that Article 31(1) EC does not require that State monopolies are abolished, but that:

> they must be adjusted in such a way as to ensure that when the transitional period has ended such discrimination shall cease to exist.[16]

The Court held that the exclusive right to import manufactured products constitute, in respect of Community exporters, discrimination prohibited by Article 31(1) EC. It underlined that the obligation laid down in that provision:

> aims at ensuring compliance with the fundamental rule of free movement of goods throughout the common market, in particular by the abolition of quantitative restrictions and measures having equivalent effect in trade between Member States.

This objective would not be attained if:

> the free movement of goods from other Member States similar to those with which the national monopoly is concerned were not ensured.

Every national monopoly of a commercial character therefore had to be adjusted so as to eliminate the exclusive right to import from other Member States.[17]

Nevertheless, in *Hansen*[18] the ECJ stated that Article 31 EC:

> is intended to render the sales policy of a State monopoly subject to the requirements of the free movement of goods and of the equal opportunities which must be accorded to products imported from other Member States,

a statement that could be taken as already indicating that retail monopolies are not prohibited by Article 31 EC as long as there is no discrimination.[19]

The questions raised concern inter alia the suitability and the proportionality of the State betting and gaming monopolies, in particular with regard to their marketing policies.

[13] See Case 155/73 *Giuseppe Sacchi* [1974] ECR 409, para 10.

[14] But see Case C-378/88 *Commission v Greece* [1990] ECR I-4747 (paras 35 to 37), where the importation monopoly was indissociable from the production monopoly.

[15] Case 59/75 *Pubblico Ministero v Manghera* [1976] ECR 91.

[16] At para 5 of the judgment. In Case 91/78 *Hansen GmbH & Co v HZA Flensburg* [1979] ECR 935, para 8, the Court added that Art 31 EC remained applicable wherever, 'even after the adjustment prescribed in the Treaty, the exercise by a State monopoly of its exclusive rights entails a discrimination or restriction prohibited by that Article'.

[17] *Manghera*, paras 9, 10, 12 and 13.

[18] *Hansen*, para 13.

[19] Mattera considers that an exclusive right to import in fact constitutes a measure of equivalent effect, forbidden by Art 28 EC and that this means that, notwithstanding the legitimate existence of a retail sale monopoly in a Members State, any economic operator that fulfils the objective criteria of the national legislation, in conformity with Community law, has the right to import the products covered by the exclusive right of that monopoly (A Mattera, *Le marché unique européen. Ses règles, son fonctionnement*, 2ème édn, (Paris, Jupiter, 1990, pp 52–3).

Also *Commission v France*[20] could be interpreted as giving an indication in this direction. In this case, which concerned French legislation granting the monopoly on the retail of tobacco to the French revenue authorities (which administered it through retailers nominated as its agents), the ECJ found that the exercise of the power reserved to the government by the French legislation to fix the retail selling prices of manufactured tobacco, was contrary to Article 31 EC:

> inasmuch as the fixing of a price other than that determined by the manufacturer or importer [adversely affects] the marketing of imported tobacco under normal conditions of competition.[21]

Article 31 EC only relates to national provision which concern the exercise by a State monopoly of its specific function. In *Peureux I*,[22] the ECJ held that the rules contained in that provision:

> concern only activities intrinsically connected with the specific business of the monopoly and are irrelevant to national provisions which have no connexion with such specific business.

National legislation that does not concern the specific business thus falls outside the scope of application of Article 31 EC. Consequently, for example, national legislation regulating marketing, labelling or consumer information in general would not fall within the scope of application of Article 31 EC, but would have to be examined solely under Article 28 EC.[23] This is illustrated by the judgment in *Cassis de Dijon*,[24] where the ECJ held that Article 31 EC is:

> irrelevant with regard to national provisions which do not concern the exercise by a public monopoly of its specific function—namely, its exclusive right—but apply in a general manner to the production and marketing of alcoholic beverages, whether or not the latter are covered by the monopoly in question.

The effect on intra-Community trade of such provisions must be examined 'solely in relation to the requirements under Article [28 EC]'.[25]

As to the relationship between Article 31 EC and other provisions of the EC Treaty, it follows from the earlier case law that, in principle, the application of Article 31 EC does not exclude the application of other Articles

[20] Case 90/82 *Commission v France* [1983] ECR 2011.
[21] At paras 26 and 27 of the judgment.
[22] Case 86/78 *SA des grandes distilleries Peureux v directeur des Services fiscaux de la Haute Saône et du territoire de Belfort ('Peureux I')* [1979] ECR 897, para 35.
[23] Ex-Art 30 of the EC Treaty.
[24] Case 120/78 *Rewe-Zentral AG v Bundesmonopolverwaltung für Branntwein* ('*Cassis de Dijon*') [1979] ECR 649.
[25] At para 7 of the judgment.

of the Treaty. In *Peureux II*[26] the ECJ seemed to apply Articles 28 and 31 EC cumulatively. The Court held that:

> [a] national provision prohibiting the distillation, for the purpose of manufacturing products reserved to a national commercial monopoly, of raw materials coming from other Member States constitutes a measure having an effect equivalent to a quantitative restriction within the meaning of Article [28 EC] and a discrimination regarding the conditions under which goods are procured and marketed within the meaning of article [31(1) EC], where the prohibition does not apply to identical raw materials produced within the national territory.[27]

In *Hansen*,[28] the Court declared that a measure effected through the intermediary of a public monopoly, which may also be considered as an aid, is 'governed both by the provisions of Article [31 EC] and by those applicable to State aids'.[29] It then held that:

> Article [31 EC] constitutes in relation to Articles [87 and 88 EC] a *lex specialis* in the sense that State measures, inherent in the exercise by a State monopoly of a commercial character of its exclusive right must, even where they are linked to the grant of an aid to producers subject to the monopoly, be considered in the light of the requirements of Article [31 EC].[30]

1.2 State Monopolies in the Field of Services

In *Sacchi*,[31] the ECJ held that the existence of a monopoly in the provision of services is not as such incompatible with Community law, declaring that:

> [n]othing in the Treaty prevents Member States, for considerations of public interest, of a non-economic nature, from removing radio and television transmissions, including cable transmissions, from the field of competition by conferring on one or more establishments an exclusive right to conduct them.

The Court nevertheless pointed out that, for the performance of their tasks, these establishments remain subject to the prohibitions against discrimination and that, to the extent that this performance comprises activities of an economic nature, they are subject to the provisions referred to in Article 86 EC.[32]

[26] Case 119/78 *Grandes Distilleries Peureux v Directeur des Services Fiscaux* [1979] ECR 975.

[27] Para 32 of the judgment. See also Case 90/82 *Commission v France* [1983] ECR 2011, where the Court held that the measure concerned was contrary to both Art 28 and Art 31 of the EC Treaty.

[28] Case 91/78 *Hansen GmbH & Co v HZA Flensburg* [1979] ECR 935.

[29] At para 9 of the judgment.

[30] *Ibid*, para 10.

[31] Case 155/73 *Giuseppe Sacchi* [1974] ECR 409.

[32] At para 14 of the judgment.

In *ERT*,[33] the Court further underlined that it follows from Article 86(1) and (2) EC that the manner in which the monopoly is organised or exercised must not infringe the rules of the Treaty, in particular those relating to free movement of goods, freedom to provide services and the rules on competition.[34] The Court indicated that although the existence of a monopoly in the provision of services is not as such incompatible with Community law, the possibility cannot be excluded that the monopoly may be organised in such a way as to infringe the rules relating to freedom to provide services and that that would be the case, in particular, where the monopoly in question leads to discrimination between national television broadcasts and those originating in other Member States, to the detriment of the latter.[35]

National measures having such discriminatory effects are prohibited unless they fall within the derogation provided for in Article 45 EC, to which Article 55 EC refers, being justified on grounds of public policy, public security or public health.[36] If the restrictive national measures are not discriminatory, they may be justified by overriding reasons relating to the public interest (or imperative requirements),[37] such as professional rules intended to protect recipients of the service[38] and consumer protection.[39] However, they must be such as to guarantee the achievement of the intended aim and must not go beyond that which is necessary in order to achieve that objective.[40]

When it comes to gambling monopolies, the ECJ considers that, even if they involve no discrimination on grounds of nationality and apply without distinction to all operators who might be interested in the activity concerned, whether established in the Member State in question or in

[33] Case C-260/89 *Elliniki Radiophonia Tiléorassi AE and Panellinia Omospondia Syllogon Prossopikou v Dimotiki Etairia Pliroforissis and Sotirios Kouvelas and Nicolaos Avdellas and Others* [1991] ECR I-2925.

[34] At paras 11 and 12 of the judgment.

[35] *Ibid*, para 20.

[36] *Ibid*, para 24.

[37] The ECJ uses different expressions in its case law (imperative requirements in the general interest, overriding reasons relating to the public interest, reasons of overriding general interest, etc). It is, however, submitted that they all refer to the same thing and that no difference is intended. Hereinafter either overriding reasons relating to the public interest or imperative requirements will be used.

[38] See eg Joined Cases 110/78 and 111/78 *Van Wesemael* [1979] ECR 35, para 28.

[39] See eg Case 220/83 *Commission v France* [1986] ECR 3663, para 20; Case 252/83 *Commission v Denmark* [1986] ECR 3713, para 20; Case 205/84 *Commission v Germany* [1986] ECR 3755, para 30; Case 206/84 *Commission v Ireland* [1986] ECR 3817, para 20; Case 220/83 *Commission v France* [1986] ECR 3663, para 20; Case 252/83 *Commission v Denmark* [1986] ECR 3713, para 20; Case 205/84 *Commission v Germany* [1986] ECR 3755, para 30; Case 206/84 *Commission v Ireland* [1986] ECR 3817, para 20; and Case C-288/89 *Stichting Collectieve Antennevoorziening Gouda and others v Commissariaat voor de Media* [1991] ECR I-4007, para 14.

[40] See eg Case C-353/89 *Commission v Netherlands* [1991] ECR I-4049, paras 15 to 19; and Case C-288/89 *Stichting Collectieve Antennevoorziening Gouda and Others v Commissariaat voor de Media* [1991] ECR I-4007, para 15.

another Members State, the legislation regulating them constitutes an obstacle to the freedom to provide services in that it directly or indirectly prevents operators in other Member States from operating such an activity.[41]

Regarding the grounds of justification, the Court has taken note of the different aims of the national legislations concerned, inter alia preventing (or avoiding the risk) of crime and fraud, preventing gambling from being a source of private profit, ensuring fair play and that gamblers are treated correctly, avoiding the damaging individual and social consequences of the incitement to spend and authorising gambling only with a view to the collection of funds for charity or for other benevolent purposes.[42] According to the ECJ, those considerations, which must be taken together, concern such overriding reasons as consumer protection and the need to preserve public order.[43]

In this context the Court has pointed out that limited authorisation of gambling on the basis of special or exclusive rights granted or assigned to certain bodies, is acceptable only if it reflects a concern to bring about a genuine diminution in gambling opportunities and if the financing of social activities, through a levy on the proceeds of authorised games, constitutes only an incidental beneficial consequence and not the real justification for the restrictive policy adopted, adding that:

> even if it is not irrelevant that lotteries and other types of gambling may contribute significantly to the financing of benevolent or public-interest activities, that

[41] See, eg Case C-124/97 *Markku Juhani Läärä, Cotswold Microsystems Ltd and Oy Transatlantic Software Ltd v Kihlakunnansyyttäjä (Jyväskylä) and Suomen valtio (Finnish State)* [1999] ECR I-6067, paras 28 and 29, and Case C-67/98 *Questore di Verona v Diego Zenatti* [1999] ECR I-7289, paras 26 and 27.

[42] See Case C-275/92 *Her Majesty's Customs and Excise v Gerhart Schindler and Jörg Schindler* [1994] ECR I-1039, para 57, *Läärä*, para 32, *Zenatti*, para 30, Case C-6/01 *Associação Nacional de Operadores de Máquinas Recreativas (Anomar) and Others v Estado português* [2003] ECR I-8621, para 72, and Case C-243/01 *Criminal proceedings against Piergiorgio Gambelli and Others* [2003] ECR I-13031, para 67.

[43] See *Schindler*, para 58, *Läärä*, para 33, *Zenatti*, para 31, *Anomar*, para 73, and *Gambelli*, para 67. In Joined Cases C-338/04, C-359/04 and C-360/04 *Massimiliano Placanica and Others*, judgment of 6 Mar 2007, not yet reported, the ECJ made a distinction between, on the one hand, the objective of reducing gambling opportunities and, on the other hand, the objective of combating criminality by making the operators active in the sector subject to control and channelling the activities of betting and gaming into the systems thus controlled. However, in this case it was common ground that no justification for the Italian legislation was to be found in the objectives of limiting the propensity of consumers to gamble or of curtailing the availability of gambling (cf paras 52 to 54 of the judgment). Interestingly enough, in *Case E-3/06 Ladbrokes Ltd. v the Government of Norway, Ministry of Culture and Church Affairs; and the Government of Norway, Ministry of Agriculture and Food*, judgment of 30 May 2007, nyr, the EFTA Court, having recalled that 'justification grounds put forward by the State must be taken together and considered as a whole' (para 44), holds that '[t]o the extent the national court finds that the legislation at issue is based on more than one legitimate objective, it must assess the consistency of the gaming policy [...] in relation to each of these legitimate objectives' (para 52) and that '[a]s with regard to suitability, the necessity of the measure must, at the outset, be assessed in relation to each legitimate objective' (para 56).

> motive cannot in itself be regarded as an objective justification for restrictions on the freedom to provide services.[44]

The financing of social activities may thus not constitute the real justification for the restrictive policy adopted.[45]

The ECJ has recognized that, in this field, moral, religious and cultural factors, and the morally and financially harmful consequences for the individual and society associated with gambling and betting, justify that national authorities have the power to determine the extent of the protection to be afforded by a Member State on its territory. It is a matter for those authorities alone to define the objectives which they intend to protect, to determine the means which they consider most suited to achieve them and to consider whether, in the context of the aim pursued, it is necessary to prohibit activities of that kind, totally or partially, or only to restrict them and to lay down more or less rigorous procedures for controlling them.[46]

The Court has nonetheless emphasised that the restrictions concerned must be suitable for the objectives pursued and not go beyond what is necessary to attain them.[47]

With regard to the suitability, in *Gambelli* it held that the restriction must serve to limit betting and gambling activities in a consistent and systematic manner, adding that:

> [i]n so far as the authorities of a Member State incite and encourage consumers to participate in lotteries, games of chance and betting to the financial benefit of the public purse, the authorities of that State cannot invoke public order concerns relating to the need to reduce opportunities for betting in order to justify measures such as those at issue in the main proceedings.[48]

In the case concerned, the national court had pointed out that the Italian State was pursuing a policy of substantially expanding betting and gaming at national level with a view to obtaining funds.[49]

Concerning the assessment of the need for, and proportionality of, the measures adopted, the Court held in *Läärä* that the latter must be assessed solely by reference to the objectives pursued by the national authorities and the level of protection which they are intended to provide.[50] It declared that the question whether in order to achieve the objectives pursued:

> it would be preferable, rather than granting an exclusive operating right to the licensed public body, to adopt regulations imposing the necessary code of conduct

[44] See *Zenatti*, para 36. See also *Gambelli*, para 62.

[45] *Gambelli*, para 62.

[46] *Gambelli*, para 63, *Anomar*, paras 79 and 87, *Zenatti*, para 33, and *Läärä*, para 35. See also *Schindler*, paras 60 and 61.

[47] See eg *Läärä*, para 33, *Zenatti*, para 31, and *Gambelli*, para 65.

[48] *Gambelli*, paras 67 and 69.

[49] *Ibid*, para 68.

[50] *Läärä*, para 36. See also *Zenatti*, para 34, and *Anomar*, para 80.

> on the operators concerned is a matter to be assessed by the Member States, subject however to the proviso that the choice made in that regard must not be disproportionate to the aim pursued.[51]

The Court found that the measures concerned were 'certainly more efficient' in achieving the intended aim.[52] It concluded that in conferring exclusive rights on a single public body, the national legislation did not appear to be disproportionate to the objective pursued.[53]

However, in *Gambelli*, the ECJ emphasised that the national court had to consider whether:

> — the criminal penalty imposed on any person who from his home connects by internet to a bookmaker established in another Member State is not disproportionate, especially where involvement in betting is encouraged in the context of games organised by licensed national bodies;
> — the imposition of restrictions, accompanied by criminal penalties of up to a year's imprisonment, on intermediaries who facilitate the provision of services by a bookmaker in a Member State, other than that in which those services are offered, by making an internet connection to that bookmaker available to bettors at their premises, is a restriction that goes beyond what is necessary to combat fraud, especially where the supplier of the service is subject in his Member State of establishment to a regulation entailing controls and penalties and where the intermediaries are lawfully constituted; and
> — whether to prevent capital companies quoted on regulated markets of other Member States from obtaining licences to organise sporting bets, especially where there are other means of checking the accounts and activities of such companies, may be considered to be a measure which goes beyond what is necessary to check fraud.[54]

1.3 Article 86 EC

Article 86 EC provides:

> 1. In the case of public undertakings and undertakings to which Member States grant special or exclusive rights, Member States shall neither enact nor maintain in force any measure contrary to the rules contained in this Treaty, in particular to those rules provided for in Article 12 and Articles 81 to 89.

[51] *Ibid*, para 39.
[52] *Ibid*, para 41.
[53] *Ibid*, para 43.
[54] *Gambelli*, paras 72 to 74.

2. Undertakings entrusted with the operation of services of general economic interest or having the character of a revenue-producing monopoly shall be subject to the rules contained in this Treaty, in particular to the rules on competition, in so far as the application of such rules does not obstruct the performance, in law or in fact, of the particular tasks assigned to them. The development of trade must not be affected to such an extent as would be contrary to the interests of the Community.
3. The Commission shall ensure the application of the provisions of this Article and shall, where necessary, address appropriate directives or decisions to Member States.[55]

As mentioned above, the ECJ held in *Sacchi*[56] that Member States are allowed to grant special or exclusive rights to undertakings, but that for the performance of their tasks such undertakings remain subject to the prohibitions against discrimination and, to the extent the performance comprise activities of an economic nature, fall under the provisions referred to in Article 86 EC.[57]

However, in *Telecom I*[58] the ECJ narrowed down this rule, holding that, though Article 86 EC presupposes the existence of undertakings which have certain special or exclusive rights:

> it does not follow that all the special or exclusive rights are necessarily compatible with the Treaty. That depends on different rules, to which Article [86](1) refers.[59]

In this case, France had brought an action against the Commission for the annulment of a number of provisions of Commission Directive 88/301, on competition in the markets in telecommunications terminal equipment,[60] mainly on the ground of lack of powers of the Commission. Directive 88/301, which the Commission had adopted on the basis of Article 86(3) EC, inter alia required Member States having granted undertakings exclusive rights regarding the importation, marketing, connection, bringing into service of telecommunications terminal equipment and/or maintenance of such equipment to withdraw those rights.

[55] For a thorough analysis of Art 86 EC, see, eg, J Temple Lang, 'European Union Law Rules on State Measures Restricting Competition', *Kilpailuoikeudellinen vuosikirja/ Konkurrensrättslig årsbok (Finnish Competition Law Yearbook)*, 2, 2003, p 215.

[56] Case 155/73 *Sacchi* [1974] ECR 409, para 14.

[57] The reference in Art 86(1) EC to Arts 12 and 81 to 89 EC is not exhaustive, see, inter alia, Case 179/90 *Merci Convenzionali Porto di Genova* [1991] ECR I-5889, where the ECJ held that the measures concerned were contrary to Art 86(1) EC, not only in conjunction with Art 82 EC, but also in conjunction with Arts 28 and 39 EC.

[58] Case C-202/88 *France v Commission* [1991] ECR I-1223.

[59] At para 22 of the judgment.

[60] Commission Dir 88/301/EEC, of 16 May 1988, on competition in the markets in telecommunications terminal equipment (OJ 1988 L 131/73).

The ECJ held that the supervisory power conferred on the Commission by Article 86(3) EC includes the possibility of specifying, pursuant to that provision, obligations arising under the Treaty and that therefore the extent of that power depends on the scope of the rules with which compliance is to be ensured.[61] In a reasoning recalling *Manghera*,[62] the Court inter alia underlined that the existence of exclusive importing and marketing rights deprives traders of the opportunity of having their products purchased by consumers, and found that the Commission was right to consider exclusive importation and marketing rights in the telecommunications terminal sector incompatible with Article 28 EC.[63] Pointing to the need to take into account the competition aspects of Article 3(g) EC when interpreting Article 28 EC and to the link between, on the one hand, the exclusive marketing rights and, on the other, exclusive rights regarding the connection, bringing into service and maintenance of telecommunications terminal equipment, the ECJ found that the Commission had also been right to regard the latter as incompatible with Article 28 EC.[64]

It is interesting to note that the Court did not analyse the compatibility of the exclusive importing and marketing rights with Article 31 EC, although that provision was invoked by the French government. Nevertheless, it did analyse those two exclusive rights together, seemingly considering them as constituting one single monopoly or, at least, as being linked, and, as said above, its reasoning follows that of the *Manghera* case law.[65] As to the exclusive rights regarding the connection, bringing into service and maintenance of telecommunications terminal equipment, the Court also considered them as being linked to the marketing monopoly. If such a monopoly was no longer allowed, those exclusive rights could not be maintained either, since otherwise an economic operator would not be able to carry on his marketing activity in normal conditions of competition. These exclusive rights were therefore also incompatible with Article 28 EC.[66]

It might be that the ECJ did not consider Article 31 EC applicable to the monopolies concerned. In this regards it should be pointed out that with regard to possible justifications of the exclusive rights, the Court noted that in the Directive itself the Commission had specified the extent and the limits of the withdrawal of special and exclusive rights so as already to take into account requirements such as user safety, safety of employees

[61] *France v Commission*, para 21.
[62] Case 59/75 *Pubblico Ministero v Manghera* [1976] ECR 91.
[63] *France v Commission*, paras 34 and 39.
[64] *Ibid*, paras 41 to 43.
[65] *Ibid*, paras 34 and 35.
[66] *Ibid*, paras 40 to 43.

of public telecommunications network operators, protection of public telecommunications networks from harm and interworking of terminal equipment in justified cases.[67]

In *Telecom II*,[68] the Court, making several references to *Telecom I*, likewise upheld Commission Directive 90/388 on competition in the markets for telecommunications services,[69] also adopted on the basis of Article 86(3) EC, in so far as it required the Member States to withdraw all exclusive rights for the supply of telecommunications services other than voice telephony. The ECJ inter alia pointed out that since Article 49 EC,[70] like Article 28 EC, is a directly applicable provision, the Commission was empowered, with a view to promoting the effective exercise of the freedom to provide services, to specify the obligations arising from that Article without the need for any prior legislative action on the part of the Council.[71]

In *Gas and Electricity*,[72] the ECJ expressly established that Article 86(2) EC may be relied upon:

> to justify the grant by a Member State, to an undertaking entrusted with the operation of services of general economic interest, of exclusive rights which are contrary to, in particular, Article [31 EC], to the extent to which performance of the particular tasks assigned to it can be achieved only through the grant of such rights and provided that the development of trade is not affected to such an extent as would be contrary to the interests of the Community.[73]

In those cases the Court, having recalled that in allowing derogations to be made from the general rules of the Treaty in certain circumstances, Article 86(2) EC seeks to reconcile the Member States' interest in using certain undertakings, in particular in the public sector, as an instrument of economic or fiscal policy with the Community's interest in ensuring

[67] *Ibid,* para 37. It is also worth noting that, when delivering its judgment, the Court was surely aware that there was a parallel case pending before it, in which an action for annulment had been brought against the Telecommunication *services* Directive (see below, n 68 and 69) and it would probably have been difficult to motivate different outcomes in the two cases.

[68] Joined Cases C-271/90, C-281/90 and C-289/90 *Spain, Belgium and Italy v Commission* [1992] ECR I-5833.

[69] Commission Dir 90/388/EEC, of 28 Jun 1990, on competition in the markets for telecommunications services (OJ 1990 L 192/10).

[70] Ex-Art 59 of the EC Treaty.

[71] *Spain, Belgium and Italy v Commission*, para 21.

[72] Case C-157/94 *Commission v Netherlands* [1997] ECR I-5699, Case C-158/94 *Commission v Italy* [1997] ECR I-5789, and C-159/94 *Commission v France* [1997] ECR I-5815 (collectively *'Gas and Electricity'*), judgments delivered on the same day as Case C-189/85 *Criminal proceedings against Harry Franzén* [1997] ECR I-5909 (see, below, S 2.1). There was a fourth judgment, in Case C-160/94 *Commission v Spain* [1997] ECR I-5851, but in this case the application of the Commission was dismissed as it had not demonstrated the existence of any Spanish legislative provisions granting the claimed exclusive rights to the State undertaking Redesa.

[73] At paras 32, 43 and 49 of the respective judgment.

compliance with the rules on competition and the preservation of the unity of the common market,[74] held that Member States:

> cannot be precluded, when defining the services of general economic interest which they entrust to certain undertakings, from taking account of objectives pertaining to their national policy or from endeavouring to attain them by means of obligations and constraints which they impose on such undertakings.[75]

It further made clear that the transfer of the exclusive rights must be proportionate, in that it may not go further than what is necessary to enable the undertaking concerned to perform, under economically acceptable conditions, the tasks of general economic interest assigned to it.[76] The Court declared that, in order for the Treaty rules not to be applicable to an undertaking entrusted with a service of general economic interest under Article 86(2) EC, it is sufficient that the application of those rules obstructs the performance, in law or in fact, of the special obligations incumbent upon that undertaking or, in other words, that in the absence of the rights at issue, it would not be possible for the undertaking to perform the particular tasks entrusted to it, defined by reference to its public-service obligations.[77]

2 THE 'SWEDISH' CASE LAW

2.1 Franzén

2.1.1 The Judgment

Franzén[78] concerned the Swedish monopoly on the retail of alcoholic beverages, 'Systembolaget'. On 1 January 1995, the day of Sweden's accession to the EU, Harry Franzén, the owner of a food store, sold wine in his shop. Some of the wine he had purchased from Systembolaget and some he had imported from Denmark. He was prosecuted for unlawfully selling and keeping alcoholic beverages.

Landskrona Tingsrätt (Landskrona District Court) made a reference for a preliminary ruling to the ECJ relating to the interpretation of Articles 28 and 31 EC.

[74] The Court referred to Case C-202/88 *France v Commission* [1991] ECR I-1223, para 12.

[75] *Commission v Netherlands*, paras 39 and 40, and *Commission v France*, paras 55 and 56.

[76] *Commission v Netherlands*, paras 3 and 64, *Commission v Italy*, para 60, and *Commission v France*, paras 54 and 107.

[77] *Commission v Netherlands*, paras 43 and 52, and *Commission v France*, paras 59 and 95.

[78] Case C-189/85 *Criminal proceedings against Harry Franzén* [1997] ECR I-5909.

The Court, referring to *Miritz*,[79] *Cassis de Dijon*,[80] *Peureux I*[81] and *Hansen*,[82] first made a distinction between domestic provisions relating to the existence and operation of the monopoly and those which, although not governing the operation of the monopoly, nevertheless have a direct bearing upon it, such as the rules relating to production and wholesale licences. The former provisions have to be examined with reference to Article 31 EC, which is specifically applicable to the exercise by a domestic commercial monopoly of its exclusive rights. The effect on intra-Community trade of the latter provisions, which are separable from the operation of the monopoly although they have a bearing upon it, must be examined with reference to Article 28 EC.[83]

With regard to Article 31 EC, the Court recalled its constant case law according to which that provision does not require national monopolies having a commercial character to be abolished, but requires them to be adjusted in such a way as to ensure that no discrimination regarding the conditions under which goods are procured and marketed exists between nationals of Member States.[84]

The ECJ, however, developed this case law further, holding, at paragraph 39 of the judgment, that:

> The purpose of [Article 31 EC] is to reconcile the possibility for Member States to maintain certain monopolies of a commercial character as instruments for the pursuit of public interest aims with the requirements of the establishment and functioning of the common market. It aims at the elimination of obstacles to the free movement of goods, save, however, for restrictions on trade which are inherent in the existence of the monopolies in question.

It then underlined that Article 31 EC consequently:

> requires that the organization and operation of the monopoly be arranged so as to exclude any discrimination between nationals of Member States as regards conditions of supply and outlets, so that trade in goods from other Member States is not put at a disadvantage, in law or in fact, in relation to that in domestic goods and that competition between the economies of the Member States is not distorted.[85]

[79] Case 91/75 *HZA Göttingen and Bundesfinanzminister v Wolfgang Miritz GmbH & Co* [1976] ECR 217.

[80] Case 120/78 *Rewe-Zentral AG v Bundesmonopolverwaltung für Branntwein ('Cassis de Dijon')* [1979] ECR 649.

[81] Case 86/78 *SA des grandes distilleries Peureux v directeur des Services fiscaux de la Haute-Saône et du territoire de Belfort* [1979] ECR 897.

[82] Case 91/78 *Hansen GmbH & Co v HZA Flensburg* [1979] ECR 935.

[83] *Franzén*, paras 34 to 36 of the judgment.

[84] *Ibid*, para 38. The Court here inter alia referred to Case 59/75 *Pubblico Ministero v Manghera* [1976] ECR 91, para 5, Case 91/78 *Hansen GmbH & Co v HZA Flensburg* [1979] ECR 935, para 8, and Case 78/82 *Commission v Italy* [1983] ECR 1955, para 11.

[85] *Franzén*, para 40. The Court here referred to Case 78/82 *Commission v Italy* [1983] ECR 1955, para 11.

In the case at hand, the public interest aim was the protection of public health against the harm caused by alcohol.[86]

In order to determine whether a retail monopoly like Systembolaget was arranged in a way that met the conditions for being compatible with Article 31 EC, set out in paragraphs 39 and 40 of the judgment, the ECJ analysed the product selection system, the monopoly's sales network and the promotion of alcoholic beverages and came to the conclusion that those conditions were met.

With regard to the product selection system, the ECJ pointed out that it was based on criteria independent of the origin of the products. The monopoly's purchase plan was based on foreseeable changes in consumer demand, the calls for offers concerned all production or wholesale licence-holders and all types of beverages, irrespective of their origin, the offers were selected on the basis of purely commercial or qualitative criteria, there were other ways for traders to have their products marketed by the monopoly and traders were entitled to be told the reasons for decisions taken by the monopoly regarding the selection of beverages, and could challenge such decisions before a board offering every guarantee of independence.[87]

As to the sales network, the Court noted that, while it was true that the monopoly only had a limited number of 'shops', it did not appear that the number of sales outlets were limited to the point of compromising consumers' procurement of supplies of domestic or imported alcoholic beverages and, anyway, this did not adversely affect the sale of alcoholic beverages from other Member States more than the sale of alcoholic beverages produced in Sweden.[88]

Regarding the promotion of alcoholic beverages, the ECJ first observed that the restriction of the possibilities for promoting alcoholic beverages to the public was inherent in a situation where there is only one operator on the market for their retail. It added that the monopoly rules did not prohibit producers or importers from promoting their products to the monopoly, that the promotion of alcoholic beverages to the public was subject to a general restriction, which had not been called into question by the applicant, and that the monopoly was required to adopt marketing and advertising measures which were impartial and independent of the origin of the products and to endeavour to make known new beverages to consumers whilst taking account of the restrictions in the Law on Alcohol.[89] Finally, the promotion used by the monopoly applied independently of products' origin and was not in itself apt to put at a disadvantage, in fact or in law,

[86] *Franzén*, para 41.
[87] *Ibid*, paras 43 to 52.
[88] *Ibid*, paras 53 to 57.
[89] Alkohollag (1994:1738).

beverages imported from other Member States in relation to those produced on national territory.[90]

With regard to the provisions of the domestic legislation which, although not, strictly speaking, governing the operation of the monopoly, nevertheless had a direct bearing upon it, the Court held that a licensing system for the importation of alcoholic beverages such as the Swedish one:

> imposes additional costs on such beverages, such as intermediary costs, payment of charges and fees for the grant of a licence and costs arising from the obligation to maintain storage capacity in Sweden and that domestic legislation of that kind is contrary to Article 28 EC.[91]

As to the possible justification of the legislation concerned under Article 30 EC,[92] the ECJ held that, although the protection of human health against the harmful effects of alcohol was indeed a ground of justification, the Swedish government had not established:

> that the system set up by the Law on Alcohol, in particular as regards the conditions relating to storage capacity and the high fees and charges which licence-holders are required to pay, was proportionate to the public health aim pursued or that this aim could not have been attained by measures less restrictive of intra-Community trade.[93]

2.1.2 Analysis

What is new in *Franzén* is first of all that the ECJ further develops the definition of the aim of Article 31 EC, for the first time declaring that the purpose of that provision is to:

> reconcile the possibility for Member States to maintain certain monopolies of a commercial character *as instruments for the pursuit of public interest aims* with the requirements of the establishment and functioning of the common market. It aims at the elimination of obstacles to the free movement of goods, *save, however, for restrictions on trade which are inherent in the existence of the monopolies in question* (emphasis added).[94]

The Court introduces an element that is very close to the possibility of justifying measures contrary to Article 28 EC on the basis of Article 30 EC or, on the basis of the case law, as measures aimed at fulfilling mandatory requirements. The formulation 'instruments for the pursuit of public interests aims' recalls the corresponding formulations used inter alia in the field of the freedom to provide services, such as 'overriding reasons relating to

[90] *Franzén*, paras 58 to 66.
[91] *Ibid*, paras 71 and 73.
[92] Ex-Art 36 of the EC Treaty.
[93] *Franzén*, para 76.
[94] *Ibid*, para 39.

the public interest'.[95] By the introduction of this element, the Court makes it clear that, under certain conditions, it is still possible to maintain State monopolies, something that was not altogether apparent from the earlier case law.

It should be noted here that it is of course not the first time the Court introduces a new element into the application of a provision of the EC Treaty, the explicit traces of which may not at first glance emerge from the text of the provision itself. Suffice it here to mention the theory of mandatory requirements under Article 28 EC and that, parallel, of overriding reasons relating to the public interest under Article 49 EC, referred to above.

In addition, the Court examined the domestic provisions relating to the existence and operation of the State monopoly with reference to Article 31 EC, while it examined those domestic provisions which, although not, strictly speaking, regulating the functioning of the monopoly, and thus being separable from its operation, nevertheless had a direct bearing upon it, with reference to Article 28 EC. It is submitted that this is in line with the earlier case law holding that Article 31 EC only relates to national provision which concern the exercise by a State monopoly of its specific function and this also seems to be confirmed by the reference to that case law.[96]

Moreover, given that the ECJ analysed the measures relating to the existence and operation of the State monopoly exclusively under Article 31 EC and did not proceed with an analysis also under Article 28 EC of those measures, it seems to be clear from *Franzén* that if the measures under scrutiny are compatible with Article 31 EC, Article 28 EC is not applicable. Furthermore, on the same day as it delivered its judgment in *Franzén*, the ECJ also delivered judgment in *Gas and Electricity*.[97] In these cases the ECJ held that since the exclusive import rights concerned were contrary to Article 31 EC, it was unnecessary to consider whether they were contrary to Article 28 EC or, consequently, whether they might possibly be justified under Article 30 EC.[98] It would thus appear that Articles 28 and 31 EC are in principle not cumulatively applicable: if a measure is compatible with Article 31 EC, the application of Article 28 EC is excluded, and if the measure is in contrary to Article 31 EC, there is no need to apply Article 28 EC.

[95] See, eg, Case C-288/89 *Stichting Collectieve Antennevoorziening Gouda and Others v Commissariaat voor de Media* [1991] ECR I-4007, para 13.

[96] Eg Case 120/78 *Rewe-Zentral AG v Bundesmonopolverwaltung für Branntwein ('Cassis de Dijon')* [1979] ECR 649; Case 86/78 *SA des grandes distilleries Peureux v directeur des Services fiscaux de la Haute-Saône et du territoire de Belfort ('Peureux I')* [1979] ECR 897; and Case 91/78 *Hansen GmbH & Co v HZA Flensburg* [1979] ECR 935, see S 1.1, above.

[97] Case C-157/94 *Commission v Netherlands* [1997] ECR I-5699, Case C-158/94 *Commission v Italy* [1997] ECR I-5789, and C-159/94 *Commission v France* [1997] ECR I-5815 (*'Gas and Electricity'*).

[98] At paras 24, 33 and 41 of the respective judgment.

It would also seem to be clear from *Franzén* and *Gas and Electricity* that measures contrary to Article 31 EC may not be justified under Article 30 EC.

The ECJ recently gave judgment in a second case concerning the Swedish alcohol monopoly: *Rosengren*.[99] In this case, Högsta domstolen (the Swedish Supreme Court) asked the Court to pronounce itself on the question of whether a national rule in a Member State, prohibiting private imports of products the retail sale of which is subject to a monopoly in that Member State, should be examined under Article 31 EC or under Article 28 EC and, if so, whether such a rule is compatible with the applicable provision.

Under Swedish law there is no general right to import alcoholic beverages privately, even though persons over the age of twenty may import alcohol purchased while travelling abroad. In the case at hand, Mr Rosengren and a number of other individuals ordered Spanish wine advertised on a Danish website, some of it by mail-order and some directly from the producer. The wine, which was imported into Sweden by a private carrier without being declared at customs, was confiscated at the border.

In his Opinion of 30 March 2006, Advocate General Tizzano recalled that the case law preceding *Franzén* holds that Article 31 EC concerns not national provisions related to the monopoly's exclusive right, but rather those which are 'intrinsically connected with the specific business' of the monopoly.[100] He observed that *Franzén* too could be read in accordance with this interpretation,[101] referring to the fact that at paragraph 49 in *Franzén* the Court considered under Article 31 EC, not only the provisions concerning Systembolaget's sales network and promotion, but also all the rules concerning the system by which products are selected, including the rule which reserves to the monopoly the task of importing at customers' request alcoholic drinks not in the assortments on offer. The Advocate General came to the conclusion that the provision prohibiting private imports of alcohol must be deemed to be a provision relating to the operation of the Swedish monopoly and hence fall to be considered under Article 31 EC.[102] He pointed to the fact that that prohibition too is calculated

[99] Case C-170/04 *Rosengren and Others v Riksåklagaren*, judgment of 5 Jun 2007, nyr. For a comment on this case and the legality of the Swedish rules on private imports of alcohol, see M Bergström, 'Lagenligheten av de svenska alkoholinförselreglerna', *ERT (Europarättslig Tidskrift)* 2004, p 589. As mentioned above, n 7, in parallel the Commission has brought an infringement action against Sweden, claiming that the Swedish rules are contrary to Art 28 EC.

[100] *Rosengren*, Opinion of Advocate General Tizzano, of 30 Mar 2006, para 38. The Advocate General referred inter alia to *Peureux I*, para 35, underlining that what matters is not the exclusive right per se but the monopoly function with a view to which the exclusive right is accorded.

[101] Paras 40 and 42 of the Opinion.

[102] *Ibid*, paras 40 and 43.

to ensure that private persons wishing to purchase alcoholic beverages in Sweden have access to these only through Systembolaget's shops and sales outlets.[103] As to the question of whether the ban on private imports of alcoholic beverages is compatible with Article 31 EC, Advocate General Tizzano considered that the import ban does not in itself place goods from other Member States at a disadvantage since, just as home-produced goods, they may be purchased by private individuals only in the sales outlets of Systembolaget and, if they are not available in the assortment on offer there, they both have to be ordered through Systembolaget.[104, 105]

The Court, however, came to the conclusion that the import ban should be assessed under Article 28 EC and not under Article 31 EC.

It construed its previous case law on Article 31 very narrowly, declaring that the specific function of Systembolaget is the exclusive right of retail sales of alcoholic beverages to consumers in Sweden, a right that does not cover the importation of those beverages. The prohibition on private individuals directly importing alcoholic beverages thus did not govern the monopoly's exclusive right. Consequently, that measure did not concern the monopoly's exercise of its specific function and therefore did not relate to the very existence of the monopoly.[106]

With regard to the operation of the monopoly, the Court held that the import ban 'does not truly regulate' that operation, 'since it does not relate to the methods of retail sale of alcoholic beverages on Swedish territory'. The Court seemed to consider that only provisions relating to the methods of retail sale can constitute rules relating to the operation of a retail sale monopoly.[107]

In *Rosengren*, the ECJ thus uses wording that is much more narrow than 'relating to the existence and operation of the monopoly' as set out in *Franzén*. The ECJ appears to be going back on its previous case law, seemingly considering Article 31 EC almost as a derogation from the rule set out in Article 28 EC—and not just a limitation of it—which, as an exception to a fundamental rule, must be given a strict interpretation.

[103] *Ibid*, para 44.
[104] *Ibid*, para 56.
[105] By Order of 14 Jun 2006, not published in the ECR (but, in Swedish and in French, on the home page of the ECJ: www.curia.europa.eu), the Court re-opened the oral procedure, inviting the parties to concentrate their pleadings on the question whether or not rules such as the Swedish import ban are to be considered as separable from rules relating to the operation of the monopoly on the retail of alcohol. The hearing having taken place on 19 Sep 2006, Advocate General Mengozzi (formerly Judge at the Court of First Instance of the EC) delivered his Opinion on 30 Nov. He came to the same conclusions as Advocate General Tizzano (who, in the meantime, had been appointed Judge at the ECJ), on the above mentioned points.
[106] *Rosengren*, paras 20 to 22.
[107] *Ibid*, para 24.

As to the application of Article 28 EC, the ECJ considered the import ban to amount to a quantitative restriction on imports, within the meaning of that provision, which cannot be justified under Article 30 EC on grounds of protection of public health, since it is neither suitable for attaining the objective of limiting alcohol consumption generally, nor proportionate for attaining that of protecting young persons against the harmful effects of such consumption.[108]

2.2 Hanner

2.2.1 The Judgment

In *Hanner*[109] the ECJ was confronted with the Swedish national monopoly on the retail of medicinal preparations, 'Apoteket'. Between 30 May and 27 July 2001, Bringwell International AB, had marketed, in breach of the Swedish rules reserving retail sales of medicinal preparations to Apoteket, 12 packages of Nicorette patches and of Nicorette chewing gum, products which under the Swedish legislation are regarded as non-prescription medicinal preparations. The Swedish authorities brought criminal proceedings against Mr Hanner in his capacity of general manager of the company.

Just as in *Franzén*,[110] the Court first recalled that, although it does not require total abolition of State monopolies of a commercial character, Article 31(1) EC requires them to be adjusted in such a way as to ensure that no discrimination regarding the conditions under which goods are procured and marketed exists between nationals of Member States.[111]

It then referred to paragraphs 39 and 40 of *Franzén*, quoting the former word by word. The Court concluded that it is necessary to examine whether the way in which the State monopoly in question is organised and operates is liable to place medicinal preparations from other Member States at a disadvantage or whether that monopoly does in practice place such medicinal preparations at a disadvantage.[112]

In order to examine the first of these conditions, the ECJ recalled the three aspects of Systembolaget that it analysed in *Franzén* in order to determine whether that monopoly was arranged in a way that met the conditions for being compatible with Article 31 EC, formulating them in a way that

[108] *Ibid*, paras 36 and 58. For a comment on this judgment, see M Johansson, '*Rosengren*—A '*Franzén* light'?', *ERT* (*Europarättslig Tidskrift*) 2007, p 608.

[109] Case C-438/02 *Criminal proceedings against Krister Hanner* [2005] ECR I-4551.

[110] Case C-189/85 *Criminal proceedings against Harry Franzén* [1997] ECR I-5909.

[111] *Hanner*, para 34.

[112] *Ibid*, paras 35, 36 and 38. On this point the ECJ slightly developed the case law, as it considered that the first of these two conditions follows from para 40 of *Franzén* while adding the latter in the case at hand.

makes them generally applicable. Thus confirming the application of these criteria, it held that:

— the selection system of a sales monopoly must be based on criteria that are independent from the origin of the products and must be transparent by providing both for an obligation to state reasons for decisions and for an independent monitoring procedure,
— the retail network of such a monopoly must be organised in such a way that the number of sales outlets is not limited to the point of compromising consumers' procurement of supplies, and
— such a monopoly's marketing and advertising measures must be impartial and independent of the origin of the products and must endeavour to make known new products to consumers.[113]

The Court then observed that in the case at hand there was no provision for a purchasing plan or for a system of 'calls for tenders' within the framework of which producers whose products were not selected would be entitled to be apprised of the reasons for the selection decision. Nor was it possible to contest such decisions before an independent supervisory authority. On the contrary, Apoteket appeared, in principle, to be entirely free to select a product range of its choice.[114]

Having found that the selection system of Apoteket did not ensure that all discrimination was ruled out and that it was liable to place trade in medicinal preparations from other Member States at a disadvantage as compared with trade in Swedish medicinal preparations, the Court did not go any further in its analysis. It held that the State monopoly was not arranged in such a way as to exclude any discrimination against medicinal preparations from other Member States and that it therefore infringed Article 31(1) EC.[115]

The Swedish government having contended that the sales regime could nonetheless be justified, the ECJ recognized that:

> Article 86(2) EC may be relied upon to justify the grant by a Member State, to an undertaking entrusted with the operation of services of general economic interest, of exclusive rights which are contrary to Article 31(1) EC, to the extent to which performance of the particular tasks assigned to it can be achieved only through the grant of such rights and provided that the development of trade is not affected to such an extent as would be contrary to the interests of the Community.[116]

Nevertheless, a sales regime such as the Swedish one could not be justified under Article 86(2) EC 'in the absence of a selection system that

[113] *Hanner*, paras 39 to 41.
[114] *Ibid*, para 42.
[115] *Ibid*, paras 43 and 44.
[116] *Ibid*, para 47.

excludes any discrimination against medicinal preparations from other Member States'.[117]

2.2.2 Analysis[118]

In this case, the ECJ in principle confirmed *Franzén*.[119] It is interesting to note that the Court did so in spite of the Advocate General's sharp criticism of that judgment. In fact, Advocate General Léger invited the Court not to apply the *Franzén* judgment in *Hanner*, being of the view that the solution identified by that judgment was not a correct interpretation of the provisions of the Treaty.[120]

Hanner nevertheless leaves a number of questions open and, perhaps, most importantly, that of whether Apoteket could be considered an instrument for the pursuit of a public interest aim also with regard to the sale of non-prescription preparations, and whether the resulting restrictions on trade could be considered inherent in the existence of the monopoly (and yet the question was expressly raised by the referring court).

The Court thus stopped short of touching on the question of whether a distinction should be made between prescription and non-prescription medicinal preparations. It would have been interesting to see whether the ECJ would have been inspired by its judgment in *DocMorris*,[121] where it held that Article 30 EC may be relied on to justify a national prohibition on the sale by mail order of medicinal products, the sale of which is restricted to pharmacies in the Member State concerned, in so far as the prohibition covers prescription medicines, but not with regard to non-prescription medicines. It is not to be excluded that, following a comparable reasoning, the monopoly conferred on Apoteket would not have been considered as pursuing a public interest aim in relation to non-prescription medicinal preparations.[122]

These questions thus having been left open, it did at the time seem rather probable that there would be a new case before the Swedish courts and another reference for a preliminary ruling to the ECJ, concentrating, in

[117] *Ibid*, para 48.

[118] For further analyses of the judgment in *Hanner* and its effects on the Swedish legislation, see J Hettne, 'Apoteksdomen—Monopolet på fallrepet?' *ERT (Europarättslig Tidskrift)* 2005, p 562, and P Lindfelt & L Hiljemark, 'Apoteksdomen—det rättsliga och politiska efterspelet', *ERT* 2005, p 697 (P Lindfelt and L Hiljemark were two of the lawyers representing Mr Hanner before the ECJ).

[119] Case 189/95 *Criminal proceedings against Harry Franzén* [1997] ECR I-5909.

[120] *Hanner*, Opinion of Advocate General Léger, paras 45 and 81.

[121] Case C-322/01 *Deutscher Apothekerverband eV v 0800 DocMorris NV and Jacques Waterval* [2003] ECR I-14887.

[122] On this point see also J Hettne, 'Apoteksdomen—Monopolet på fallrepet?', *ERT (Europarättslig Tidskrift)* 2005, p 562, at pp 568–9, who comes to the same conclusion looking at the question from a proportionality perspective.

particular, on the non-prescription preparations.[123] However, the recently elected centre right government in Sweden having announced that it will abolish the exclusive rights of Apoteket, it no longer seems very likely that such a case will be brought.[124]

With regard to the application of Article 86 EC, the ECJ confirmed its case law established in *Gas and Electricity*,[125] according to which Article 86(2) EC may be relied upon to justify the grant of exclusive rights which are contrary to Article 31 EC.[126]

In addition, it seems to follow from *Hanner* that in order to be justified under Article 86(2) EC, the measures through which the undertaking concerned is granted exclusive rights must not have the effect of discriminating against products or services from other Member States.

2.3 Wermdö Krog

2.3.1 The Judgment

Wermdö Krog[127] concerned the rules regulating gambling in Sweden and, more specifically, the prohibition in Article 38 of the Swedish Lotteries Act[128] which prohibits the promotion, as a commercial activity or otherwise for the purposes of making money, of not permitted domestic lotteries and of foreign lotteries.[129]

Lotteriinspektionen (the Swedish Gaming Board) had ordered Wermdö Krog, a Swedish restaurant, under penalty of a fine of some 9,000 EUR, to cease acting as intermediary for SSP Overseas Betting Limited, a company with its seat in London, inter alia offering bets on the games of the English and Scottish football leagues. Wermdö Krog appealed against this decision.

Regeringsrätten held from the outset that the ban on the promotion of lotteries organised abroad—as well as the Swedish lottery legislation in general—was contrary to the provisions of the EC Treaty on freedom to

[123] See also Hettne, *ibid*, p 569.

[124] See eg, *Global Competition Review*, 7 Dec 2006, 'Sweden targets drugs monopoly' (www.globalcompetitionreview.com).

[125] Case C-157/94 *Commission v Netherlands* [1997] ECR I-5699, Case C-158/94 *Commission v Italy* [1997] ECR I-5789, and C-159/94 *Commission v France* [1997] ECR I-5815.

[126] At paras 32, 43 and 49 of the respective judgment.

[127] Judgment of Regeringsrätten of 26 Oct 2004, Case no 5819-01 *Wermdö Krog*, RÅ 2004 ref 95. On the same day Regeringsrätten delivered judgment in a second case concerning the Swedish gambling legislation, Case no 7119-01, *AB*, RÅ 2004 ref 96. However, in this judgment Regeringsrätten in principle only referred to its judgment in *Wermdö Krog*.

[128] Lotterilag 1994:1000.

[129] For an analysis of Art 38 of the Swedish Lotteries Act and the 'promotion ban', see S Eriksson, 'Är förbudet att främja deltagande i utländska spel och lotterier förenligt med EG-rätten?', *ERT (Europarättslig Tidskrift)* 2006, p 45.

provide services and freedom of establishment. It was consequently necessary to examine whether the promotion ban could be justified.

In this regard Regeringsrätten carried out a rather thorough analysis of the case law of the ECJ in the field of gambling, in particular *Schindler*,[130] *Läärä*,[131] *Zenatti*[132] and *Gambelli*.[133] It underlined that the ECJ had expressly referred to the 'peculiar nature' of lotteries, which justified restrictions which would not have been accepted with regard to other kinds of economic activity.[134] It recalled that according to the ECJ it was not possible to disregard the moral, religious or cultural aspects of lotteries, and other types of gambling, in all the Member States. The Member States had a tendency to restrict, even prohibit, the practice of gambling and to prevent it from being a source of private profit. The ECJ had also emphasised that lotteries involve a high risk of crime or fraud and that they are an incitement to spend, which may have damaging individual and social consequences. Further, it was not without relevance that lotteries could make a significant contribution to the financing of benevolent or public interest activities such as social works, charitable works, sport or culture.[135]

Regeringsrätten then pointed out that according to the ECJ those particular factors justify national authorities having a sufficient degree of latitude to determine what is required to protect the players and to maintain order in society as regards the manner in which lotteries are operated, the size of the stakes and the allocation of the profits they yield.[136]

Regeringsrätten furthermore stated that the ECJ in principle even accepts such drastic measures as the total prohibition of this kind of activity and the establishment of a monopoly.

Nevertheless, Regeringsrätten recalled that the national measures concerned must not be discriminatory and, in particular, they have to be suitable for achieving the objective they pursue as well as necessary and proportional.

Regeringsrätten emphasised the importance of establishing the real objective of the legislation under scrutiny and recalled that the Court had held that it is not irrelevant that lotteries and other types of gambling may contribute significantly to the financing of benevolent or public-interest

[130] Case C-275/92 *Her Majesty's Customs and Excise v Gerhart Schindler and Jörg Schindler* [1994] ECR I-1039.

[131] Case C-124/97 *Markku Juhani Läärä, Cotswold Microsystems Ltd and Oy Transatlantic Software Ltd v Kihlakunnansyyttäjä (Jyväskylä) and Suomen valtio (Finnish State)* [1999] ECR I-6067.

[132] Case C-67/98 *Questore di Verona v Diego Zenatti* [1999] ECR I-7289.

[133] Case C-243/01 *Criminal proceedings against Piergiorgio Gambelli and Others* [2003] ECR I-13031.

[134] Regeringsrätten referred to *Schindler*, para 59.

[135] Regeringsrätten referred to *Schindler*, para 60, *Läärä*, para 13, and *Zenatti*, para 14.

[136] Regeringsrätten referred to *Schindler*, para 61, *Läärä*, paras 14 and 35, *Zenatti*, paras 15 and 33, and *Gambelli*, para 63.

activities, but that such a motive cannot in itself justify a restriction of the freedoms set out in the Treaty, but must only constitute an incidental beneficial consequence.[137] The national measures must be suitable for reducing gambling opportunities and contribute to limiting the activity in a consistent and systematic manner and Member State authorities may not encourage increased gambling for the benefit of the public purse.[138]

As to the proportionality criteria, Regeringsrätten stated that, in the light of the statement of the ECJ regarding the freedom of the Member States to choose the level and method of protection of the objectives recognized as legitimate by the Court, it seemed to play a less salient role. The measures concerned must be assessed solely by reference to the objectives pursued and the level of protection which they were intended to provide.[139] If there were alternative solutions, the choice of solution fell within the Member States' margin of appreciation, provided that the alternative chosen did not 'seem to be' or 'appear' disproportionate to the intended aim.[140]

With regard to the Swedish regime and, in particular, the 'promotion ban', Regeringsrätten held that it was non discriminatory and that its objectives were in conformity with the overriding reasons relating to the public interest laid down by the case law of the ECJ. It was also compatible with Community law to apply a system with a general authorisation requirement, in practice reserving market access to only a limited number of actors.

Regeringsrätten thereafter examined the application of the proportionality criteria. It noted that the marketing in the field of gambling was both intensive and quantitatively important. It could well be said that the gambling companies authorised by the Swedish State, with the expression used in *Gambelli*, 'incite and encourage consumers to participate in lotteries, games of chance and betting',[141] but in order for the Swedish system to be disqualified under Community law, the measures concerned furthermore had to be adopted 'to the benefit of the public purse'.

In this regard, Regeringsrätten considered that, even if it would be naive to assume that the considerable economic contribution of the lotteries was purely of subsidiary importance for the authorities, it would also be wrong to assume that the income aspect would be the only, or the completely dominant, reason for taking a tolerant view on the marketing measures of the gambling companies. In fact, in practice the Swedish gambling market was subject to competition, since residents, via the internet or otherwise, were free to participate in lotteries organised abroad. In order to channel

[137] Regeringsrätten referred to *Schindler*, para 60, *Zenatti*, para 36 and *Gambelli*, para 62.
[138] Regeringsrätten referred to *Zenatti*, para 36, and *Gambelli*, paras 67 to 69.
[139] Regeringsrätten referred to *Läärä*, para 36, and *Zenatti*, para 34.
[140] Regeringsrätten referred to *Läärä*, para 39, and *Gambelli*, para 75.
[141] *Gambelli*, para 69.

the desire to gamble to activities considered to provide better consumer protection and less risk of irregularities, it would not be reasonable to refuse those undertakings that are authorised to carry out such activities to actively promote their products and present them in a way that attracts those that are interested in gambling, and induces them to prefer the forms of gambling that are State controlled to other variants. Even if the relaxed view of the authorities as to the periodically rather aggressive marketing of the gambling companies could cast doubts on the real objective, Regeringsrätten was of the view that this circumstance was not enough to conclude that the principal objective of the Swedish lottery legislation was to enrich the State and State-aided activities.

Regeringsrätten recognised that there were lacks in the State supervision of the gambling sector. The gambling companies authorised and controlled by the State appeared primarily to be working on a commercial basis and their agents did not appear to be subject to any direct surveillance by Lotteriinspektionen. Nevertheless, Regeringsrätten was of the view that the fact that the supervision in certain respects was less effective did not mean that it was without importance for the possibility to achieve the objectives. The lacks did not demonstrate that the objective of the Swedish gambling regime was not the one indicated.

Regeringsrätten was furthermore of the view that, when granting the gambling authorisations, the Government had not solely paid regard to the State finances.

As concluding remarks, Regeringsrätten pointed out that precisely in the field of gambling the ECJ had been very tolerant with regard to the considerable restrictions to the freedom to provide services and to the freedom of establishment frequently occurring in the Member States. The Swedish lottery legislation and its application did on different points certainly raise questions of compatibility with the conditions set up by the ECJ, but on the whole the Swedish system did nevertheless have to be considered to fulfil the requirements.

2.3.2 Analysis[142]

Regeringsrätten did not make a reference for a preliminary ruling to the ECJ, as it considered that the latter had made clear that there was no need for further precisions of Community law in a case like this, but that it was

[142] For a comment on Case C-275/92 *Her Majesty's Customs and Excise v Gerhart Schindler and Jörg Schindler* [1994] ECR I-1039, Case C-124/97 *Markku Juhani Läärä, Cotswold Microsystems Ltd and Oy Transatlantic Software Ltd v Kihlakunnansyyttäjä (Jyväskylä) and Suomen valtio (Finnish State)* [1999] ECR I-6067, *Zenatti* and *Gambelli* and an analysis of the compatibility of the Swedish betting and gaming monopoly with Community law in the light of those judgments, see U Bernitz, 'Nationella spelmonopol i ljuset av Gambellimålet', *ERT (Europarättslig Tidskrift)* 2004, p 451. For critical analysis of *Wermdö Krog*, including the question of whether the objective of the Swedish legislation is to limit

up to the national courts, basing themselves on the criteria already set out in the case law, to decide whether a national lottery regime could be accepted. It might well be that, in general, Regeringsrätten was not wrong on this point. However, given its analysis and application of the suitability and proportionality criteria, it could well be argued that it ought to have made a reference to the ECJ and, since it is a court of last instance, even that it was under an obligation to do so.

One candidate for such a reference could have been a question on the application of the grounds of justification. It is, in fact, a bit surprising that Regeringsrätten seems to emphasise that nothing indicates that the *principal objective* of the Swedish lottery legislation is to enrich the State and State-aided activities, given that the ECJ has held that the restrictions concerned must:

> reflect a concern to bring about a genuine diminution of gambling opportunities, and the financing of social activities through a levy on the proceeds of authorised games *must constitute only an incidental beneficial consequence* and not the real justification for the restrictive policy adopted (emphasis added).[143]

It is submitted that the interpretation of the ECJ is a bit more restrictive than that of Regeringsrätten. On this point, the EFTA Court in *ESA v Norway* came to the conclusion that:

> limiting the reduction in revenues for humanitarian and socially beneficial causes from machine gaming was not the real justification [of the contested legislation], within the meaning of *Zenatti*, for the restrictive policy adopted but a beneficial consequence which is incidental in the meaning that it is accessory.[144]

The EFTA Court based this conclusion on the fact that:

> the contested legislation is based on the assumption that the introduction of an exclusive right would provide an opportunity to fight gambling addiction, *inter*

gambling and whether at all that legislation could be justified on moral, religious and cultural grounds, see also N Wahl, 'Vad är oddsen för att det svenska spelmonopolet är förenligt med EG-rätten?—Regeringsrättens dom i Wermdö Krog', *ERT* 2005, p 119, and O Wiklund & H Bergman, 'Europeiseringstendenser och domstolskritik i svensk rätt—Regeringsrättens domar i spelmålen', *ERT* 2005, p 713.

[143] Case C-67/98 *Questore di Verona v Diego Zenatti* [1999] ECR I-7289, para 36, and Case C-243/03 *Criminal proceedings against Piergiorgio Gambelli and Others* [2003] ECR I-13031, para 62. The ECJ confirmed its case law on his point in Joined Cases C-338/04, C-359/04 and C-360/04 *Criminal proceedings against Massimiliano Placanica and Others*, judgment of 6 Mar 2007, nyr, para 53. On this point, see also O Wiklund & H Bergman, 'Europeiseringstendenser och domstolskritik i svensk rätt—Regeringsrättens domar i spelmålen', *ERT (Europarättslig Tidskrift)* 2005, p 713, at pp 721–2.

[144] *ESA v Norway*, para 39. In Case E-3/06 *Ladbrokes Ltd. v the Government of Norway, Ministry of Culture and Church Affairs; and the Government of Norway, Ministry of Agriculture and Food*, judgment of 30 May 2007, nyr, para 46, the EFTA Court held that: '[t]he motive of financing benevolent or public-interest activities cannot in itself be regarded as an objective justification for restrictions on free movement. Such financing may not constitute the real justification for the restrictive policy adopted, but only a beneficial consequence which is incidental in the meaning that it is accessory'.

> *alia* through limiting gaming opportunities while at the same time limiting the reduction in revenues through the lowering of operational costs and the elimination of the profit of private operators.[145]

A second candidate for a reference for a preliminary ruling would have been the question of the interpretation to be given to the proportionality criterion applied by the ECJ.[146] On the one hand, especially *Schindler*,[147] *Läärä*,[148] *Zennatti* and *Anomar*[149] could be taken to indicate that, as noted by Regeringsrätten, this criterion plays a less salient role in the field of gambling regulation:

> [D]etermination of the scope of the protection which a Member State intends providing in its territory in relation to lotteries and other forms of gambling falls within the margin of appreciation which the Court, in paragraph 61 of *Schindler*, recognised as being enjoyed by the national authorities. It is for those authorities to consider whether, in the context of the aims pursued, it is necessary to prohibit activities of that kind, totally or partially, or only to restrict them and to lay down more or less rigorous procedures for controlling them.
>
> In those circumstances, the mere fact that a Member State has chosen a system of protection different from that adopted by another Member State cannot affect the appraisal as to the need for and proportionality of the provisions adopted. They must be assessed solely in the light of the objectives pursued by the national authorities of the Member State concerned and of the level of protection which they seek to ensure.[150]

Moreover, in *Läärä* the Court declared that the national measure concerned was 'certainly more effective' in achieving the intended aim[151] and both in

[145] *ESA v Norway*, para 37. It is in this context interesting to note that in *Ladbrokes*, para 48, the EFTA Court, referring to *Schindler*, paras 57 to 61, and *Zenatti*, paras 30 and 31, pointed out that: '[i]t follows from the case law of the ECJ that the aim of preventing gambling from being a source of private profit may in principle justify restrictions on the right of establishment and free movement of services'. However, '[a]s an aim in itself, it would seem that this aim must be based on a resentment of games of chance for reasons of morality, in particular if it relates to non-addictive games. Thus, the aim of preventing gambling from being a source of private profit can serve as justification only if the restrictive measures reflect that moral concern. If a State-owned monopoly is allowed to offer a range of gambling opportunities, the measure cannot be said to genuinely pursue this aim.'

[146] Also Wahl seems to question whether Regeringsrätten should not have referred a preliminary question to the ECJ on this point, N Wahl, 'Vad är oddsen för att det svenska spelmonopolet är förenligt med EG-rätten?—Regeringsrättens dom i Wermdö Krog', *ERT (Europarättslig Tidskrift)* 2005, pp 119, at p 127.

[147] Case C-275/92 *Her Majesty's Customs and Excise v Gerhart Schindler and Jörg Schindler* [1994] ECR I-1039.

[148] Case C-124/97 *Markku Juhani Läärä, Cotswold Microsystems Ltd and Oy Transatlantic Software Ltd v Kihlakunnansyyttäjä (Jyväskylä) and Suomen valtio (Finnish State)* [1999] ECR I-6067.

[149] Case C-6/01 *Associação Nacional de Operadores de Máquinas Recreativas (Anomar) and Others v Estado português* [2003] ECR I-8621.

[150] *Zenatti*, paras 33 and 34. See also *Schindler*, para 61, *Läärä*, paras 35 and 36, *Anomar*, paras 79 and 80, and *Gambelli*, para 63.

[151] *Läärä*, para 41.

Läärä and in *Zenatti*, the Court seems to be satisfied that the criterion is fulfilled if the national measures concerned 'do not appear to be disproportionate' to the objectives they pursue.[152] This also appears to be the reading of Regeringsrätten.

On the other hand, in *Läärä*, in *Zenatti* as well as in *Anomar*, the ECJ recalled that the national measures concerned had to gurantee the intended aims and not go beyond what is necessary in order to achieve them[153] and in *Gambelli* the ECJ, after having recalled the existence on the part of the national authorities of a margin of appreciation sufficient to enable them to determine what consumer protection and the preservation of public order require, held that:

> [i]n any event, in order to be justified the restrictions on freedom of establishment and on freedom to provide services must satisfy the conditions laid down in the case-law of the Court,[154]

referring to its judgments in *Kraus*[155] and *Gebhard*.[156] Enumerating the four conditions set out in those judgments, the Court inter alia observed that the restrictions may not go beyond what is necessary in order to attain the objective which they pursue.[157]

It might be that the case law should be interpreted as meaning that with regard to the choice of level of protection to be afforded, or, as expressed in *Anomar*, of the objectives to be protected and the means most suited to achieve them,[158]—ie whether lotteries and other forms of gambling should be prohibited or not, totally or partially, or whether they should be restricted, through the granting of exclusive or special rights or, for example, through the adoption of a regulatory framework—where the Member States have a margin of appreciation, the measures adopted should be assessed:

> solely in the light of the objectives pursued by the national authorities of the Member State concerned and of the level of protection which they seek to ensure.[159]

Läärä seems to suggest that, compared to alternative measures, the adopted measures should be more effective in achieving the objectives they pursue.[160]

In this regard, it is interesting to note that the ECJ has already used a formulation that is close to the one used in *Schindler*, *Läärä*, *Zenatti*, *Anomar*

152 *Läräa*, para 42, and *Zenatti*, para 37.
153 *Läräa*, paras 31 and 33, *Zenatti*, paras 29 and 31, and *Anomar*, para 86.
154 *Gambelli*, paras 63 and 64.
155 Case C-19/92 *Dieter Kraus v Land Baden-Württemberg* [1993] ECR I-1663.
156 Case C-55/94 *Reinhard Gebhard v Consiglio dell'Ordine degli Avvocati e Procuratori di Milano* [1995] ECR I-4165.
157 *Gambelli*, para 65.
158 *Anomar*, para 87.
159 *Anomar*, para 80, and Zenatti, para 34. See also *Läärä*, para 36.
160 See *Läärä*, paras 41 and 42.

and *Gambelli* in other cases in the field of freedom to provide services, in relation to the protection of public health. Having first recalled the absence of Community harmonisation measures, the Court has held that:

> it is for the Member States to decide on the degree of protection which they wish to afford to public health and on the way in which that protection is to be achieved. They may do so, however, only within the limits set by the Treaty and must, in particular, comply with the principle of proportionality.[161]

In *Commission v France*[162] and *Bacardi*,[163] the Court added that this:

> requires that the measures adopted be appropriate to secure the attainment of the objective which they pursue and not go beyond what is necessary in order to attain it.[164]

Also in these cases, the application of the proportionality criteria seems possibly less strict than normally. In *Aragonesa*,[165] for example, the ECJ held that the criterion concerned 'does not appear to be manifestly unreasonable' and that the measure at issue 'cannot in any event be criticized for being disproportionate to its stated objective'.[166]

According to Advocate General Tizzano:

> what must be ascertained is not which measures would be feasible and more effective in abstract terms but whether the actual measures adopted by [the Member State concerned] are appropriate for achieving the degree of protection of public health pursued by that State and do not go beyond what is necessary for that purpose.[167]

In the case in point, he held that, in his view, without the measure at issue, '*[the] very objective*' pursued by the national legislature could not be pursued 'with the *same degree of effectiveness*' (emphasis added).[168]

[161] Joined Cases C-1/90 and C-176/90 *Aragonesa de Publicidad Exterior SA and Publivía SAE v Departamento de Sanidad y Seguridad Social de la Generalitat de Cataluña* [1991] ECR I-4151, para 16. See also C-262/02 *Commission v France* [2004] ECR I-6569, para 24, and C-429/02 *Bacardi France SAS, formerly Bacardi-Martini SAS v Télévision française 1 SA (TF1), Groupe Jean-Claude Darmon SA and Girosport SARL* [2004] ECR I-6613, para 33.

[162] Case C-262/02 *Commission v France* [2004] ECR I-6569.

[163] Case C-429/02 *Bacardi France SAS, formerly Bacardi-Martini SAS v Télévision française 1 SA (TF1), Groupe Jean-Claude Darmon SA and Girosport SARL* [2004] ECR I-6613.

[164] *Commission v France*, para 24, and *Bacardi*, para 33.

[165] Joined Cases C-1/90 and C-176/90 *Aragonesa de Publicidad Exterior SA and Publivía SAE v Departamento de Sanidad y Seguridad Social de la Generalitat de Cataluña* [1991] ECR I-4151.

[166] At paras 17 and 18, respectively, of the judgment.

[167] Case C-170/04 *Klas Rosengren and Others v Riksåklagaren*, judgment of 5 Jun 2007, nyr, Opinion of Advocate General Tizzano, delivered on 30 Mar 2006, para 78. This application of the proportionality criterion seems to be confirmed by the ECJ in its analysis in paras 48 to 57 of the judgment.

[168] *Ibid*, para 81. The Court, however, came to the opposite conclusion, see S 2.1.2.

This interpretation also seems to be in line with the judgment in *ESA v Norway*,[169] in which the EFTA Court held that:

> In the case at issue, the Norwegian legislature has not opted for a total ban. Instead it has chosen a monopoly system with a view to reduce the risk of gambling addiction to a level which it deems acceptable and to reduce crime and malpractice. In such a situation, the necessity test consists in an assessment of whether the monopoly option is functionally needed in order to reduce the problems to the level opted for, or whether this reduction could equally well be obtained through other, less restrictive means such as admitting private operators under a stricter licensing regime. The necessity of the contested legislation thus requires that the introduction of a monopoly leads to a more effective achievement of the aims set than other less restrictive measures (see *Läärä*, at paragraphs 41 and 42).[170]

The EFTA Court then pointed out that:

> In the Court's view, it is reasonable to assume that a monopoly operator in the field of gaming machines subject to effective control by the competent public authorities will tend to accommodate legitimate concerns of fighting gambling addiction better than a commercial operator or organisations whose humanitarian or socially beneficial activities partly rely on revenues from gaming machines. Furthermore, it is plausible to assume that in principle the State can more easily control and direct a wholly State-owned operator than private operators. Through its ownership role, the State has additional ways of influencing the behaviour of the operator besides public law regulations and surveillance. In fact, the effectiveness of public control and enforcement of a genuinely restrictive approach to machine gaming are the focal point of the proportionality assessment in this case. In a situation where the reform of the gaming machine regulation in Norway has not yet taken effect, the Court cannot base itself on the general assumption that public control and policy enforcement will not satisfy these requirements.[171]

The EFTA Court concluded that the Defendant had sufficiently demonstrated that the exclusive right system opted for by Norway:

> is likely to be more effective in order to achieve the objectives of the legislation, considered as a whole, than the other means proposed by the Applicant.[172]

[169] Case E-1/06 *ESA v Norway*, judgment of 14 Mar 2007, nyr.

[170] At para 49 of the judgment.

[171] *Ibid,* para 51. However, in *Ladbrokes*, para 62, the EFTA Court seems to strengthen the language somewhat, holding that the national court 'will have to examine, in particular, whether Norsk Tipping has less economic incentives to breach the rules regulating the sector of games of chance or less of an interest in an aggressive marketing strategy than a commercial operator under a licensing system. Furthermore, the national court will have to evaluate whether effective control may be exercised and is actually being exercised by the State on Norsk Tipping and whether private service providers operating under a licensing system cannot be subjected to the same kind of control.'

[172] *Ibid,* para 52.

It is submitted that *Placanica*[173] does not add very much on this point. The ECJ held that:

> although the Member States are free to set the objectives of their policy on betting and gaming and, where appropriate, to define in detail the level of protection sought, the restrictive measures that they impose must nevertheless satisfy the conditions laid down in the case law of the Court as regards their proportionality.[174]

Apart from the 'where appropriate', the exact meaning of which is not quite clear, this does in principle seem to be no more than a summary of the existing case law.[175] As to the actual application of the proportionality criterion, the Court indicated that, in the case in point, it should be examined in relation to the objective of preventing the exploitation of activities in the betting and gaming sector for criminal or fraudulent purposes and it seems to suggest that in that context the national court should examine whether the limitation set by the Italian government of the total number of licenses is proportionate to the aim pursued.[176]

On the other hand, the EFTA Court in *Ladbrokes* made an interesting addition to its reasoning in *ESA v Norway*, defining the limits to the discretion of the national authorities in setting the level of protection in the field of gambling.[177]

The EFTA Court declared that:

> where other, less restrictive measures would have the effect of fully achieving the objectives at the level of protection chosen, an exclusive rights system could not be considered necessary simply because it might offer an even higher level of protection (emphasis added).[178]

It pointed to the fact that if the national authorities have opted for a rather low level of protection, it is less probable that a monopoly is the only way of achieving the level of protection sought and more likely that less restrictive means, such as a licensing system, could suffice.[179] It also emphasised that the restrictions placed on the monopoly provider must be taken into account when identifying the level of protection actually sought by the

[173] Joined Cases C-338/04, C-359/04 and C-360/04 *Criminal proceedings against Massimiliano Placanica and Others*, judgment of 6 Mar 2007, nyr.

[174] At para 48 of the judgment.

[175] The EFTA Court seems to have reached the same conclusion in *ESA v Norway*, where after having quoted, at para 29, *Placanica*, paras 47 and 48, it applies the proportionality criterion in accordance with what would seem to be the existing case law of the ECJ (see above, n 170 and 171).

[176] *Placanica*, paras 57 and 58.

[177] Replying to an argument by the Norwegian Government, the EFTA Court also made abundantly clear that, although the national authorities do have such a discretion, "this does not mean that the measures are sheltered from judicial review as to their necessity" (para 55 of the judgment).

[178] *Ibid*, para 58.

[179] *Ibid*, para 59.

authorities under the exclusive rights system. In this regard, it pointed to a number of factors which would have to be taken into account, such as the number of gaming opportunities and the level of gaming activity tolerated as well as the extent and effect of marketing and development of games of chance.[180]

In this context, it is also worth noting that *Gambelli*, in which the Court seemed to indicate that the national court should make a 'standard' application of the proportionality criterion, did not concern the choice of level of protection to be afforded (or of the objectives to be protected and the means most suited to achieve them),[181] but (i) the conditions for submitting invitations to tender for licences to organise bets on sporting events, (ii) the prohibition, enforced by criminal sanctions, on participating in betting games organised in Member States other than the country where the bettor is established and (iii) the prohibition, also enforced by criminal sanctions, for intermediaries on facilitating the provision of betting services on sporting events organised by a supplier established in a Member State other than that in which the intermediaries pursue their activity.

A third candidate for a preliminary reference to the ECJ would have been the different aspects of the suitability criteria.

In this regard, the interpretation of Regeringsrätten of paragraph 69 of *Gambelli*[182] is questionable. It does not seem to follow from the ECJ's statement that, in order for the restrictions concerned not to be considered suitable for achieving the objective of preserving public order, and thus for the authorities not be able to invoke such concerns relating to the need to reduce opportunities for gambling in order to justify the measures concerned, the financial aspect (the 'income aspect') must be the *only* or the *completely dominant* reason for taking a tolerant position on the marketing measures of the gambling companies. It would rather seem enough that those marketing measures are adopted to the financial benefit of the public purse (without that having to be the only or the completely dominant reason) in order for the Member State action not to be considered as consistent with the objective of reducing gambling opportunities.[183]

[180] *Ibid*, paras 60 and 61.

[181] On this point, in *Placanica* the ECJ seems to have applied the proportionality criterion to the choice of level of protection (see paras 56 and 57), but it did not indicate whether a different application than the one that follows from the existing case law was intended.

[182] 'In so far as the authorities of a Member State incite and encourage consumers to participate in lotteries, games of chance and betting to the financial benefit of the public purse, the authorities of that State cannot invoke public order concerns relating to the need to reduce opportunities for betting in order to justify measures such as those at issue in the main proceedings.'

[183] In *Placanica*, it was considered common ground, 'according to the case-law of the Corte suprema di cassazione, that the Italian legislature is pursuing a policy of expanding activity in the betting and gaming sector, with the aim of increasing tax revenue, and that no justification for the Italian legislation is to be found in the objectives of limiting the propensity of consumers to gamble or of curtailing the availability of gambling' (see para 54 of the judgment).

In addition, the channelling argument made by Regeringsrätten,[184] according to which those operators that are authorised to carry out gambling activities must be allowed to actively promote their products and present them in a way that attracts the persons that are interested in gambling and that makes them prefer the forms of gambling that are State controlled to other variants organised abroad, is not very convincing, especially not after the judgment in *Lindman*.[185] In this case, which concerned national legislation under which winnings from games of chance organised in other Member States were treated as income chargeable to income tax, whereas winnings from games of chance conducted in the Member State in question were not taxable, the ECJ held:

> the file transmitted to the Court by the referring court discloses no statistical or other evidence which enables any conclusion as to the gravity of the risks connected to playing games of chance or, *a fortiori, the existence of a particular causal relationship between such risks and participation by nationals of the Member State concerned in lotteries organised in other Member States* (emphasis added).[186]

The ECJ did, however, admit the channelling argument in *Placanica*, holding that:

> it is possible that a policy of controlled expansion in the betting and gaming sector may be entirely consistent with the objective of drawing players away from clandestine betting and gaming—and, as such, activities which are prohibited—to activities which are authorised and regulated;

that:

> in order to achieve that objective, authorised operators must represent a reliable, but at the same time attractive, alternative to a prohibited activity;

and that:

> [t]his may as such necessitate the offer of an extensive range of games, advertising on a certain scale and the use of new distribution techniques.[187]

It should nevertheless be recalled that this was done against the background of the rather special situation in Italy. The Court observed inter alia that

[184] With regard to the channeling argument and the promotion by the Swedish gambling monopoly of its activities, see also N Wahl, 'Vad är oddsen för att det svenska spelmonopolet är förenligt med EG-rätten?—Regeringsrättens dom i Wermdö Krog', *ERT (Europarättslig Tidskrift)* 2005, p 119, at pp 125–6, and O Wiklund & H Bergman, 'Europeiseringstendenser och domstolskritik i svensk rätt—Regeringsrättens domar i spelmålen', *ERT* 2005, p 713, at pp 722–4.

[185] Case C-42/02 *Diana Elisabeth Lindman* [2003] ECR I-13519.

[186] Para 27 of the judgment.

[187] *Placanica*, para 55.

an investigation by the Finance and Treasury Committee of the Italian Senate:

> led to the conclusion that the activities of clandestine betting and gaming, prohibited as such, are a considerable problem in Italy, which it may be possible to solve through the expansion of authorized and regulated activities. Thus, according to that investigation, half the total turnover figure for the betting and gaming sector in Italy is generated by illegal activities.[188]

In Ladbrokes the EFTA Court made a somewhat extensive interpretation of paragraph 55 of Placanica, holding that it followed from that paragraph:

> that in order to persuade people who might otherwise engage in games which pose crimerelated problems, to turn instead to authorised games, controlled expansion in the gaming sector, including the offer of an extensive range of games, advertising on a certain scale and the use of new distribution techniques may be necessary (emphasis added).[189]

The EFTA Court concluded that:

> [s]imilar channelling measures may be envisaged for the purpose of drawing players away from highly addictive games offered via the Internet or other channels which are hard to suppress. It is for the State to demonstrate that such channelling measures, including, if relevant, the development of new games, may reasonably be assumed to serve their purpose.[190]

It is however doubtful whether this is a correct interpretation of *Placanica*. As stated above, the situation in Italy was rather special and the ECJ referred to 'clandestine betting and gaming', not games 'which pose crimerelated problems', a definition which is not very clear. In any case, allowing the monopoly provider to develop and market addictive games, as a means of fighting gaming addiction by drawing players away from highly addictive games offered via the Internet as suggested by the EFTA Court, seems questionable, at least from a moral point of view.

A fourth candidate for a reference for a preliminary ruling could have been the question of whether lacks in the State supervision of the gambling activity, inter alia allowing gambling operators, authorised and controlled by the State, primarily to be working on a commercial basis, has any effect on the application of the suitability criterion.

As the EFTA Court underlined in *ESA v Norway*,

> a consistent and systematic approach to fighting gambling addiction must also encompass an effective control of the exclusive right holder's activities.[191]

[188] *Ibid*, para 56.
[189] *Ladbrokes*, para 54.
[190] *Ibid.*
[191] *ESA v Norway*, para 46.

In *Ladbrokes*, it held that the national court had to examine whether effective control may be exercised and is actually being exercised by the State on the monopoly provider.[192]

3 THE CASE LAW ON STATE MONOPOLIES OF A COMMERCIAL CHARACTER AND THAT ON STATE MEASURES IN THE GAMBLING SECTOR—A COMPARISON

State monopolies of a commercial character are allowed under Community law if they constitute instruments for the pursuit of public interest aims. An exception is made to the elimination of obstacles to the free movement of goods for restrictions on trade which are inherent in the existence of these monopolies.[193]

The organisation and operation of the monopoly must be arranged so as to exclude any discrimination; trade in goods from other Member States must not be put at a disadvantage, in law or in fact, in relation to that in domestic goods.[194]

It is submitted that the organisation and operation of the monopoly must also be suitable for the achievement of the public interest aim pursued, as this would seem to be inherent in the Court's reasoning. If State monopolies are allowed to be maintained as instruments for the pursuit of public interest aims, it seems evident that they have to be suitable for achieving those aims.

Regarding the proportionality criterion, the situation is less clear. In *Franzén* the ECJ did not examine, at least not explicitly, the proportionality of the measure chosen to achieve the public interest aim concerned, ie the choice of a retail sale monopoly. This would seem to indicate that it is for the Member States to decide whether a State monopoly of a commercial character is the means best suited to achieve the public interest aim pursued. This limitation in the application of the proportionality criterion seems to be confirmed by paragraph 39 in *Franzén,* where the Court held that restrictions on trade which are inherent in the existence of a monopoly are allowed, without questioning the existence in itself.[195]

Two observations must, however, be made in this regard.

First, Article 31 EC is only applicable to provisions 'relating to the existence and operation of the monopoly', it is 'specifically applicable to the

[192] *Ladbrokes*, para 62

[193] Case C-189/85 *Criminal proceedings against Harry Franzén* [1997] ECR I-5909, para 39, and Case C-438/02 *Criminal proceedings against Krister Hanner* [2005] ECR I-4551, para 35.

[194] *Franzén*, para 40, *Hanner*, paras 36 to 38.

[195] See also H Ragnemalm and M Melin, 'Svenska affärer', Förvaltningsrättslig tidskrift 1998, p 29, at p 37, who are of the view that monopolies that are justified by a public interest aim may restrict trade but only to the extent that this follows from the monopoly construction itself.

exercise, by a domestic commercial monopoly, of its exclusive rights'.[196] Other provisions, 'which are separable from the operation of the monopoly although they have a bearing upon it', have to be examined under Articles 28 and 30 EC,[197] implying the application of the normal criteria for the justification of restrictions on the free movement of goods, including the proportionality criterion.

Secondly, it is submitted that some sort of proportionality test, albeit possibly a less strict one, will have to be applied also to the provisions falling within the scope of application of Article 31 EC, if for no other reason, given that the proportionality principle is a general principle of Community law and as such of general application.[198] Although in *Franzén* the ECJ did not explicitly examine whether the measures concerned were proportionate, it could be argued that it partly did so implicitly in its examination of the different elements of the monopoly. In fact, Advocate General Léger considers that when holding in *Franzén* that Article 31 EC does not prohibit restrictions on the free movement of goods which are inherent in the existence of that monopoly, the Court meant restrictions which do not go beyond what is necessary in order to attain the aim pursued.[199] Indeed, it could be argued that it is inherent in the Court's statement according to which Member States may 'maintain certain monopolies of a commercial character as instruments for the pursuit of public interest aims', that the establishment of such a monopoly must not, in itself, be disproportionate to the public interest aim pursued, since otherwise it would not be an instrument for the pursuit of the aim concerned.

For this purpose, the appropriate test would seem to be the one suggested by Advocate General Tizzano in *Rosengren*, slightly adapted for the purposes of Article 31 EC: it is not which measures would be feasible and more effective in abstract terms that need to be ascertained, but whether the actually adopted rules relating to the existence and operation of the monopoly are appropriate for achieving the public interest aim pursued and do not go beyond what is necessary for that purpose.[200]

[196] See *Franzén*, para 35, and the case law referred to (Case 91/75 *Hauptzollamt Göttingen v Miritz* [1976] ECR 217, para 5; Case 120/78 *REWE-Zentral AG v Bundesmonopolverwaltung für Branntwein ('Cassis de Dijon')* [1979] ECR 649, para 7; and Case 91/78 *Hansen v Hauptzollamt Flensburg* [1979] ECR 935, paras 9 and 10).

[197] See *Franzén*, para 36, and the case law referred to (*Miritz*, para 5, *Cassis de Dijon*, para 7, and Case 86/78 *Peureux v Services Fiscaux de la Haute-Saône et du Territoire de Belfort ('Peureux I')* [1979] ECR 897, para 35).

[198] Hettne is of a similar view, J Hettne, 'Apoteksdomen—Monopolet på fallrepet?', *ERT (Europarättslig Tidskrift)* 2004 p 562, at p 569.

[199] Case C-438/02 *Criminal proceedings against Krister Hanner* [2005] ECR I-4551, Opinion of Advocate General Léger, para 76.

[200] Case C-170/04 *Klas Rosengren and Others v Riksåklagaren*, judgment of 5 Jun 2007, nyr, Opinion of Advocate General Tizzano, delivered on 30 Mar 2006, para 78. See also S 2.3.2, above.

With regard to State measures in the gambling sector, a key element of the case law of the ECJ seems to be what the Court considers to be the special nature of gambling,[201] relating to moral, religious and cultural factors and to the morally and financially harmful consequences for the individual and society associated with gaming and betting.[202]

Nevertheless, the Court considers that also in this sector, in order to be justified, the restrictions on freedom of establishment and on freedom to provide services must satisfy the conditions laid down in its case law, ie they have to be justified by overriding reasons relating to the public interest, be applied without discrimination, be suitable for achieving the objective which they pursue and not go beyond what is necessary in order to attain it.[203]

As to the application of the suitability criteria, the ECJ in *Gambelli* stressed that, in order to be suitable for achieving the above mentioned public interest objectives, the restrictions 'must serve to limit betting activities in a consistent and systematic manner'. It added that:

> [i]n so far as the authorities of a Member State incite and encourage consumers to participate in lotteries, games of chance and betting to the financial benefit of the public purse, the authorities of that State cannot invoke public order concerns relating to the need to reduce opportunities for betting in order to justify measures such as those at issue in the main proceedings.[204]

Member State action must thus be consistent with the public order objective invoked.

Finally, with regard to the application of the proportionality criterion, it is submitted that the ECJ makes a distinction between, on the one hand, the choice of level of protection to be afforded, or of the objectives to be protected and the means most suited to achieve them, and, on the other, the other measures relating to the system opted for,[205] comparable to the distinction made in the application of Article 31 EC between the measures relating to the existence and operation of the monopoly and those which are separable form the operation of the monopoly although having a bearing upon it.[206]

[201] In Case C-275/92 *Her Majesty's Customs and Excise v Gerhart Schindler and Jörg Schindler* [1994] ECR I-1039, para 59, the Court referred to 'the peculiar nature of lotteries'.

[202] See eg Case C-243/01 *Criminal proceedings against Piergiorgio Gambelli and Others* [2003] ECR I-13031, para 62, and Joined Cases C-338/04, C-359/04, C-360/04 *Criminal proceedings against Massimiliano Placanica and Others*, judgment of 6 Mar 2007, nyr, para 47.

[203] See eg Case C-124/97 *Markku Juhani Läärä, Cotswold Microsystems Ltd and Oy Transatlantic Software Ltd v Kihlakunnansyyttäjä (Jyväskylä) and Suomen valtio (Finnish State)* [1999] ECR I-6067, paras 28 to 31, Case C-67/98 *Questore di Verona v Diego Zenatti* [1999] ECR I-7289, paras 26 to 29, and *Gambelli*, paras 60, 64 and 65.

[204] *Gambelli*, paras 67 and 69. See also *Placanica*, paras 53 and 54.

[205] See eg, on the one hand, *Läärä*, paras 35 to 42, *Zenatti*, paras 33 to 35, and, on the other, *Gambelli*, paras 72 to 74. See also *Anomar*, para 87.

[206] See *Franzén*, paras 35 and 36.

As to the choice of level of protection, or of the objectives to be protected and the means most suited to achieve them, it would seem that also here the appropriate test is the one indicated by Advocate General Tizzano in *Rosengren* in relation to the protection of public health under Article 28 EC, ie that it is not which measures would be feasible and more effective in abstract terms that must be ascertained, but whether the actual measures adopted by the Member State are appropriate for achieving the degree of protection of the overriding reason relating to the public interest pursued by that State and do not go beyond what is necessary for that purpose.[207] This would seem to correspond to the formulation used by the Court in *Läärä*, *Zenatti* and *Anomar*, according to which the need for, and proportionality of, the provisions adopted:

> must be assessed solely in the light of the objectives pursued by the national authorities of the Member State concerned and of the level of protection which they seek to ensure.[208]

It would further seem that this was the test applied by the ECJ in *Läärä*, when it came to the conclusion that the monopoly regime concerned was more efficient in achieving the objectives pursued than a system of special rights,[209] as well as by the EFTA Court in *ESA v Norway*, where, referring to *Läärä*, it held that the necessity of the contested legislation requires that 'the introduction of a monopoly leads to a more effective achievement of the aims set than other less restrictive measures'.[210]

This also seems to be in line with *Ladbrokes*, where the EFTA Court went further and specified that:

> where other, less restrictive measures would have the effect of fully achieving the objectives at the level of protection chosen, an exclusive rights system could not be considered necessary simply because it might offer an even higher level of protection.[211]

The other measures relating to the system of protection opted for should be examined with reference to the 'standard' application of the proportionality criteria, as it has been set out in the cases such as *Gebhard* and

[207] Case C-170/04 *Klas Rosengren and Others v Riksåklagaren*, judgment of 5 June 2007, nyr, Opinion of Advocate General Tizzano, delivered on 30 Mar 2006, para 78. In *Zenatti*, para 37, the ECJ held that the national court has to verify whether the restrictions imposed by the national legislation in question 'do not appear disproportionate' in the light of the objectives pursued.

[208] See *Anomar*, para 80, *Läärä*, para 36, and *Zenatti*, para 34.

[209] *Läärä*, para 41. See also Joined Case C-1/90 and C-176/90 *Aragonesa de Publicidad Exterior SA and Publivía SAE v Departamento de Sanidad y Seguridad Social de la Generalitat de Cataluña* [1991] ECR I-4151, para 24, and Case C-170/04 *Klas Rosengren and Others v Riksåklagaren*, pending, Opinion of Advocate General Tizzano, delivered on 30 Mar 2006, para 81.

[210] Case E-1/06 *ESA v Norway*, judgment of 14 Mar 2007, nyr, para 49.

[211] Case E-3/06 *Ladbrokes Ltd. v the Government of Norway, Ministry of Culture and Church Affairs; and the Government of Norway, Ministry of Agriculture and Food*, judgment of 30 May 2007, nyr, para 58.

Kraus.[212] This interpretation would seem to be confirmed by *Gambelli*, which did not concern the choice of level of protection, or the means to achieve the objectives pursued, but rather the rules for the operation of the gambling activity, and in which the ECJ indicated that the national court should apply the proportionality criterion in the habitual 'strict' way.[213]

Even if in *Placanica* the ECJ might be understood to suggest that there should be no difference in the application of the proportionality criterion,[214] it is difficult to draw any final conclusion from this judgment, since the Court itself does not give much indication as to the application of the criterion, but in principle only refers the national court to the existing case law.

Consequently, an analysis of the case law on State monopolies of a commercial character and of that on State measures in the gambling sector does seem to show a rather far-reaching similarity between the two.

4 CONCLUSION

It would thus seem possible to conclude, firstly, that it follows from the case law as it stands today that State monopolies are not as such forbidden, but they must be adjusted so as to fulfil the requirements of Community law.

Secondly, with regard to that adjustment, and if the above analysis is correct, there would seem to be an ongoing gradual rapprochement between the ECJ's case law on State monopolies of a commercial character and that on gambling monopolies, which in its turn probably indicates a general rapprochement between the Court's view on State monopolies in trade in goods and that on State monopolies in the service sector.

In this regard, with *Franzén*[215] the Court introduced a new element in the interpretation and application of Article 31 EC, holding that the purpose of that provision is to reconcile the possibility for Member States to maintain certain monopolies of a commercial character as instruments for the pursuit of *public interest aims* with the requirement of the establishment and functioning of the common market and that restrictions on trade which are inherent in the existence of such monopolies are allowed.

This new element very much resembles the case law of the Court concerning State measures in the gambling sector, recalling that obstacles to freedom to provide services and to freedom of establishment may be justified

[212] Case C-19/92 *Dieter Kraus v Land Baden-Württemberg* [1993] ECR I-1663 and Case C-55/94 *Reinhard Gebhard v Consiglio dell'Ordine degli Avvocati e Procuratori di Milano* [1995] ECR I-4165.

[213] *Gambelli*, paras 72 to 74. In *Anomar*, para 87, the ECJ indicated that the rules for the operation and playing of games must 'have been deemed compatible with the Treaty'.

[214] *Placanica*, para 48.

[215] Case C-189/95 *Criminal proceedings against Harry Franzén* [1997] ECR I-5909.

by overriding reasons relating to the *public interest*. In *Franzén* the public interest aim pursued was the protection of public health, which is also considered an overriding reason relating to the public interest in the fields of free movement of services and freedom of establishment.

Furthermore, in both cases the restrictions must be applied *without discrimination* and it seems self evident that the *suitability criterion*—the measures concerned have to be such as to guarantee the achievement of the objective they pursue—is applicable also with regard to State monopolies of a commercial character, since it would not make sense to permit such a monopoly if it was not suitable to fulfil the public interest aim pursued by the Member State concerned.

Moreover, with regard to the *proportionality criterion*, there is probably less of a difference than first meets the eye.

First of all, Article 31 EC only applies to the provisions relating to the existence and operation of the monopoly. Other provisions of the domestic legislation which are separable from the operation of the monopoly although they have a bearing upon it must be examined with reference to Articles 28 and 30 EC, implying that, in order to be justified, they inter alia have to fulfil the proportionality criterion.

The case law on State measures in the gambling sector seems to make a comparable distinction between, on the one hand, the provisions determining the level of protection to be afforded by the Member State, or the objectives to be protected and the means most suited to achieve them, and, on the other, other domestic provisions relating to the system of protection opted for, for which the Court seems to make the habitual strict application of the proportionality criterion.

It is submitted that, as the provisions determining the level of protection to be afforded in the field of gambling, also the provisions relating to the existence and operation of a State monopoly of a commercial character will have to be subject to some kind of proportionality test, if for no other reasons, since the proportionality principle is a general principle of Community law.

Secondly, it is submitted that the appropriate test to be applied to both is the one suggested by Advocate General Tizzano in *Rosengren*[216] in relation to the protection of public health under Article 28 EC, ie that it is not which measures would be feasible and more effective in abstract terms that must be ascertained, but whether the actual measures adopted by the Member State are appropriate for achieving the public interest aim/level of protection intended by that State and do not go beyond what is necessary for that purpose.

[216] Case C-170/04 *Klas Rosengren and Others v Riksåklagaren*, judgment of 5 June 2007, nyr, Opinion of Advocate General Tizzano, delivered on 30 Mar 2006.

Thirdly, it is clear inter alia from *Hanner*[217] that in case a State monopoly should be considered incompatible with the rules on free movement of goods, freedom to provide services and freedom of establishment, Article 86 EC may be invoked.

That Article may be relied upon by a Member State to justify the grant to an undertaking of exclusive rights which are contrary to other provisions of the Treaty. However, in such a case, the undertaking concerned must either have been entrusted with the operation of *services of general economic interest*, a notion which does not in all parts coincide with that of a 'public interest aim' or of an 'overriding reason relating to the public interest', or be a revenue producing monopoly.[218]

Further, also here it would seem evident that the measures concerned must be suitable, having to be such as to guarantee the provisions of the service with which the undertaking has been entrusted. In addition, the measures can only be justified to the extent to which performance of the particular tasks assigned to the undertaking can be achieved only through the grant of an exclusive right and will thus have to be proportionate. Finally, it would seem to follow from *Hanner* that the measures may not be discriminatory.

BIBLIOGRAPHY

Bergström, M, 'Lagenligheten av de svenska alkoholinförselreglerna', *ERT* (*Europarättslig Tidskrift*) 2004, p 589.

Bernitz, U, 'Nationella spelmonopol i ljuset av Gambellimålet', *ERT* (*Europarättslig Tidskrift*) 2004, p 451.

Bluhm, F, 'De Sacchi à Franzén en passant par la Crespelle: jurisprudence récente de l'article 90', *Gazette du Palais*, 1999, p 1031.

——, 'The recent case law of the European Court of Justice on State monopolies and its implication for network industries', *Journal of Network Industries* 1, 2000, p 55.

Eriksson, S, 'Är förbudet att främja deltagande i utländska spel och lotterier förenligt med EG-rätten?' *ERT* (*Europarättslig Tidskrift*) 2006, p 45.

Global Competition Review, 7 December 2006, 'Sweden targets drugs monopoly', www.globalcompetitionreview.com.

Hettne, J, 'EU, monopolen och försvaret av den rådande ordningen', *ERT* (*Europarättslig Tidskrift*) 2004, p 589.

——, 'Apoteksdomen—Monopolet på fallrepet?', *ERT* (*Europarättslig Tidskrift*) 2005, p 562.

[217] Case C-438/02 *Criminal proceedings against Krister Hanner* [2005] ECR I-4551.

[218] It is questionable whether gambling monopolies and the Swedish monopoly on the retail of alcohol could be considered as being entrusted with a service of general economic interest. However, it is not excluded that at least the gambling monopolies could be considered to be revenue producing monopolies, see Opinion of Advocate General La Pergola, para 30, in Case C-124/97 *Markku Juhani Läärä, Cotswold Microsystems Ltd and Oy Transatlantic Software Ltd v Kihlakunnansyyttäjä (Jyväskylä) and Suomen valtio* (*Finnish State*) [1999] ECR I-6067.

Johansson, M, '*Rosengren*—A '*Franzén* light'?', *ERT* (*Europarättslig Tidskrift*) 2007, p 608.

Lindfelt, P, and Hiljemark, L, 'Apoteksdomen—det rättsliga och politiska efterspelet', *ERT* (*Europarättslig Tidskrift*) 2005, p 697.

Mattera, A, *Le marché unique européen. Ses règles, son fonctionnement,* 2ème éd, (Paris, Jupiter, 1990).

Ragnemalm, H, and Melin, M, 'Svenska affärer', *Förvaltningsrättslig tidskrift* 1998, p 29.

Slot, P J, Case note on 'Cases C-157/94, *Commission v Netherlands*; C-158/94, *Commission v Italy*; C-159/04, *Commission v France*; C-160/04, *Commission v Spain*; C-189/95, *Harry Franzén*; judgments of 23 October 1997, Full Court, [1997] ECR I-5699, I-5798, I-5815, I-5851, I-5909', 35 *Common Market Law Review* (1998), p 1183.

Temple Lang, J, 'European Union Law Rules on State Measures Restricting Competition', *Kilpailuoikeudellinen vuosikirja/Konkurrensrättslig årsbok* (Finnish Competition law Yearbook) 2, 2003, p 215.

Wahl, N, 'Vad är oddsen för att det svenska spelmonopolet är förenligt med EG-rätten?—Regeringsrättens dom i Wermdö Krog', *ERT (Europarättslig Tidskrift)* 2005, p 119.

Wiklund, O, and Bergman, H, 'Europeiseringstendenser och domstolskritik i svensk rätt—Regeringsrättens domar i spelmålen', *ERT (Europarättslig Tidskrift)* 2005, p 713.

Index